AF556043

Export and Import Procedures, Documentation and Logistics

Export and Import Procedures, Documentation and Logistics

Abir Lal Mukherjee

RANDOM PUBLICATIONS
NEW DELHI (INDIA)

Export and Import Procedures, Documentation and Logistics

ISBN 978-93-5111-448-2

Published in 2014 in India by

RANDOM PUBLICATIONS

4376-A/4B, Gali Murari Lal, Ansari Road
New Delhi-110 002
Phone : +91-11-43580356, +91-11-23289044
e-mail: randomexports@gmail.com, sales@randompublications.com, info@randompublications.com

Reprinted 2023

Type Setting by : Keystoneprintads, Delhi-110051
Printed at : Replika Press Pvt. Ltd.

Preface

The term export means shipping the goods and services out of the port of a country. The seller of such goods and services is referred to as an "exporter" who is based in the country of export whereas the overseas based buyer is referred to as an "importer". In International Trade, "exports" refers to selling goods and services produced in the home country to other markets.

Export of commercial quantities of goods normally requires involvement of the customs authorities in both the country of export and the country of import. Nonetheless, these small exports are still subject to legal restrictions applied by the country of export. An export's counterpart is an import.

The theory of international trade and commercial policy is one of the oldest branches of economic thought. Exporting is a major component of international trade, and the macroeconomic risks and benefits of exporting are regularly discussed and disputed by economists and others. Two views concerning international trade present different perspectives. The first recognizes the benefits of international trade. The second concerns itself with the possibly that certain domestic industries (or laborers, or culture) could be harmed by foreign competition.

Methods of export include a product or good or information being mailed, hand-delivered, shipped by air, shipped by vessel, uploaded to an internet site, or downloaded from an internet site. Exports also include the distribution of information that can be sent in the form of an email, an email attachment, a fax or can be shared during a telephone conversation.

Trade barriers are generally defined as government laws, regulations, policy, or practices that either protect domestic products from foreign competition or artificially stimulate exports of particular domestic products. While restrictive business practices sometimes have a similar effect, they are not usually regarded as trade barriers. The most common foreign trade barriers are government-imposed measures and policies that restrict, prevent, or impede the international exchange of goods and services.

Exporting to foreign countries poses challenges not found in domestic sales. With domestic sales, manufacturers typically sell to wholesalers or direct to retailer or even direct to consumers. When exporting, manufacturers may have to sell to importers who then in turn sell to wholesalers. Extra layer(s) in the chain of distribution squeezes margins and manufacturers may need to offer lower prices to importers than to domestic wholesalers.

I thank all members of my team who have helped in the preparation of the book. My special thanks go to "Random Publications" who have published the book.

– Abir Lal Mukherjee

Contents

1

Introduction

GENERAL PROVISIONS

Goods are imported in India or exported from India through sea, air or land. Goods can come through post parcel or as baggage with passengers. Procedures naturally vary depending on mode of import or export. Procedures discussed in this Chapter are applicable for imports by sea, air or land, but not as baggage or postal dispatch.

COMPUTERISATION OF CUSTOMS WORK

Work of customs at Delhi airport has been computerized. Work at Mumbai port is also computerized. Whenever the work is computerized, documents like IGM and Bill of Entry have to be filed electronically. Procedure in computerized environment has been specified in CC, New Delhi PN 22/98 dated 8.5.1998. Guidelines for preparing data file for Bill of Entry and shipping bills for Mumbai Customs House has been prescribed vide PN 108/99 dated 30-9-1999 and PN 10/2001 dated 30.1.2001.

ENTRY

'Entry' in relation to goods means an entry made in a Bill of Entry, Shipping Bill or Bill of Export. It includes:

- Label or declaration accompanying the goods which contains description, quantity and value of the goods, in case of postal articles u/s 82
- Entry to be made in case of goods to be exported
- Entry in respect of goods imported which are not accompanied by label or declaration made as per provisions of section 84.

AMENDMENT TO DOCUMENTS

Importer, exporter or 'Person In charge' have to submit various documents to customs authorities like Bill of Entry, Import Manifest, Export

Manifest etc. Some times, it may become necessary to amend the document due to various reasons like change in classification, clerical mistake in document, change in unloading / loading plan of vessel etc. In such case, permission to amend these documents have to be obtained from customs authorities. [section 149]. Such permission can be given if there are no fraudulent intentions. In case of bill of entry, shipping bill or bill of export, it can be amended after clearance only on the basis of documentary evidence which was in existence at the time the goods were cleared, warehoused or exported, and not on basis of any subsequent document.

Customs Station

Imported goods are permitted to be unloaded only at specified places. Similarly, goods can be exported only from specified area. In view of this, a definition of 'Customs Station' is important. Customs area means all area of Customs Station and includes any area where imported goods or export goods are ordinarily kept pending clearance by Customs authorities. Thus, 'Customs Area' could include some area even outside the 'Customs Station'. Customs Station means:

- Customs port
- Inland container depot
- Customs airport and
- Land customs station.

Section 7 of Customs Act empowers CBEC (Board) to appoint:

- Customs ports
- Customs airports
- Places for inland container depots
- Coastal ports.

These are appointed by issuing a notification. Section 8 authorises Commissioner of Customs to approve proper places in any customs port, customs airport or costal port for unloading and loading of goods or for any class of goods and specify the limits of customs area. Thus, the place (city / town / village etc.) is approved by CBEC, while exact location within that city / town / village is approved by Commissioner of Customs.

IMPORT PROCEDURES

Procedures have to be followed by 'person-in-charge of conveyance' as well as the importer.

WHO IS 'PERSON IN CHARGE'

As per section 2(31), 'person in charge' means:

- In case of vessel - its master

- In case of aircraft - its commander or pilot-in-charge
- In case of train - its conductor or guard and
- In case of vehicle or other conveyance - its driver or other person in charge.

The significance of this definition is –

- He is responsible for submitting Import Manifest and Export Manifest
- He is responsible to ensure that the conveyance comes through approved route and lands at approved place only.
- He has to ensure that goods are unloaded after written order, at proper place. Loading also has to be only after permission.
- He has to ensure that conveyance does not leave without written order of Customs authorities.
- He can be penalised for
  - Giving false declaration and statement
  - shortages or non-accounting of goods in conveyance

Procedure to be followed by the Carrier

The 'person in charge of conveyance' (carrier of goods) has to follow prescribed procedure.

Arrival at customs port/airport only

Section 29 provides that person-in-charge of a vessel or an aircraft entering India shall call or land at customs port or customs airport *only*. It can land at other place only if compelled by accident, stress of weather or other unavoidable cause.

In such case, he should report to nearest police station or Customs Officer. While arriving by land route, the vehicle should come by approved route to 'land customs station' only.

Import Manifest / Report

Person-in-charge of vessel, aircraft or vehicle has to submit Import Manifest / Report. [also termed as IGM - Import General Manifest]. The import manifest in case of vessel or aircraft is required to be submitted *prior* to arrival of a vessel or aircraft. Import report (in case of vehicle) has to be submitted within 12 hours of arrival at the customs station.

If the report / manifest could not be submitted within prescribed time, person-in-charge or any person specified as responsible by a notification is liable to penalty upto Rs 50,000. Such penalty will not be imposed if the excise officer is satisfied that there was sufficient cause for the delay. [section 30(1)]. IGM can be submitted electronically through floppy where EDI facility is available.

IMPORT MANIFEST IS REQUIRED TO BE SUBMITTED BEFORE ARRIVAL OF AIRCRAFT OR VESSEL

Section 30(1) of Customs Act provides that Import Manifest should be filed before arrival of ship or aircraft. Normally, the Agents submit the Import Manifest before arrival, so that maximum possible formalities are completed before vessel or aircraft arrives. This also enables importers to file 'Bill of Entry' in advance.

Grant of Entry Inwards by Customs Officer

Unloading of cargo can start only after Customs Officer grant 'Entry Inwards'. Such entry inwards can be granted only when berthing accommodation is granted to a vessel. If there is heavy congestion at port, shipping berth may not be available and in such case, 'Entry Inwards' cannot be granted. This date is highly relevant for determining rate of customs duty applicable.

Carrier responsible for shortages during unloading

If the goods are short landed, the carrier is liable to pay penalty upto twice the amount of duty payable on such short landed goods. It has been held that tally sheet prepared by Port Trust authorities on unloading of goods is a statutory document and should be accepted in preference to steamer survey - *Scindia Steam Navigation* v. *CC* - 1988 (33) ELT (CEGAT) followed in *re India Steamship Co. Ltd.* - 1992 (57) ELT 510 (GOI).

Procedure by Importer

The importer importing the goods has to follow prescribed procedures for import by ship/air/road. (There is separate procedure for goods imported as a baggage or by post.)

Bill of Entry

This is a very vital and important document which every importer has to submit under section 46. The Bill of Entry should be in prescribed form. The standard size of Bill of Entry is 16" × 13". However, for computerisation purposes, 15" × 12" size is permitted. (Mumbai Customs Public Notice No. 142/93 dated 3-11- 93). Bill of Entry should be submitted in quadruplicate – original and duplicate for customs, triplicate for the importer and fourth copy is meant for bank for making remittances. Under EDI system, Bill of Entry is actually printed on computer in triplicate only after 'out of charge' order is given. Duplicate copy is given to importer.

Types of Bill of Entry

Bills of Entry should be of one of three types. Out of these, two types are for clearance from customs while third is for clearance from warehouse.

BILL OF ENTRY FOR HOME CONSUMPTION

This form, called 'Bill of Entry for Home Consumption', is used when the imported goods are to be cleared on payment of full duty. *Home consumption means use within India*. It is white coloured and hence often called 'white bill of entry'.

BILL OF ENTRY FOR WAREHOUSING

If the imported goods are not required immediately, importer may like to store the goods in a warehouse without payment of duty under a bond and then clear from warehouse when required on payment of duty. This will enable him to defer payment of customs duty till goods are actually required by him. This Bill of Entry is printed on yellow paper and often called 'Yellow Bill of Entry'. It is also called 'Into Bond Bill of Entry' as bond is executed for transfer of goods in warehouse without payment of duty.

BILL OF ENTRY FOR EX-BOND CLEARANCE

The third type is for Ex-Bond clearance. This is used for clearance from the warehouse on payment of duty and is printed on green paper. The goods are classified and value is assessed at the time of clearance from customs port. Thus, value and classification is not required to be determined in this bill of entry. The columns in this bill of entry are similar to other bills of entry. However, declaration by importer is not required as the goods are already assessed.

RATE OF DUTY FOR CLEARANCE FROM WAREHOUSE

It may be noted that rate of duty applicable is as prevalent on date of removal *from warehouse*. Thus, if rate has changed after goods are cleared from customs port, customs duty as assessed on yellow bill of entry and as paid on green bill of entry will not be same.

- *Mention of BIN on Bill of Entry* – A BIN (Business Identification Number) is allotted to each importer and exporter w.e.f. 1.4.2001. It is a 15 digit code based on PAN of Income Tax (PAN is a 10 digit code). [Earlier an EC (Import Export code) number issued by DGFT was required to be mentioned on Bill of Entry].
- *Filing of Bill of Entry* - Normally, Bill of Entry is filed by CHA on behalf of the importer. Customs work at some ports has been computerised. In that case, the Bill of Entry has to be filed electronically, *i.e.* through Customs EDI system through computerisation of work. Procedure for the same has been prescribed vide Bill of Entry (Electronic Declaration) Regulations, 1995.
- *Documents to be submitted by Importer* - Documents required by customs authorities are required to be submitted to enable them to (*a*) check the goods (*b*) decide value and classification of goods and

(*c*) to ensure that the import is legally permitted. *The documents that are essentially required are* : (i) Invoice (ii) Packing List (iii) Bill of Lading / Delivery Order (iv) GATT declaration form duly filled in (v) Importers / CHAs declaration duly signed (vi) Import Licence or attested photocopy when clearance is under licence (vii) Letter of Credit / Bank Draft wherever necessary (vii) Insurance memo or insurance policy (viii) Industrial License if required (ix) Certificate of country of origin, if preferential rate is claimed. (x) Technical literature. (xi) Test report in case of chemicals (xii) Advance License / DEPB in original, where applicable (xiii) Split up of value of spares, components and machinery (xiv) No commission declaration. – A declaration in prescribed form about correctness of information should be submitted. – *Chapter 3 Para 6 and 7 of CBE&C's Customs Manual, 2001.* The Noting is now done electronically in large ports, while it is done manually in small ports. Thoka Number (Serial Number) is given while noting the Bill of Entry.

- *Electronic submission under EDI system* – Where EDI system is implemented, formal submission of Bill of Entry is not required, as it is generated in computer system. Importer should submit declaration in electronic format to 'Service Centre'. A signed paper copy of declaration for non-repudiability should be submitted. Bill of Entry number is generated by system which is endorsed on printed check list. Original documents are to be submitted only at the stage of examination.

ASSESSMENT OF DUTY AND CLEARANCE

The documents submitted by importer are checked and assessed by Customs authorities and then goods are cleared. Section 2(2) defines 'assessment' as follows – 'Assessment' includes provisional assessment, reassessment and any order of assessment in which the duty assessed is Nil. Thus, 'assessment' includes 'Nil' assessment.

NOTING OF BILL OF ENTRY

Bill of Entry submitted by importer or Customs House Agent is cross-checked with 'Import Manifest' submitted by person in charge of vessel / carrier. It is noted if the description tallies. 'Noting' really means taking on record by customs officer. This date is relevant for determining rate of customs duty. Thoka number (serial number) is given in the import section. Otherwise, it is returned for clarifications. In case of EDI system, noting is done by the system itself which also generates bill of entry number. Date of presentation of bill of entry is highly relevant and the rate of duty as applicable on this date will be considered for calculating the duty payable. Bill of Entry is accepted only after proper scrutiny *vis-a-vis* import manifest and various declarations given in bill of entry and attached documents like invoice, bill of lading etc. If such documents are not attached, the authorities can refuse to accept the Bill of Entry, and hence submission of such incomplete Bill of Entry cannot be taken as date of presentation of Bill of Entry - *Simla Agencies* v. CC - 1993 (63) ELT 248 (CEGAT).

Prior Entry of Bill of Entry

After the goods are unloaded, these have to be cleared within stipulated time - usually three working days. If these are not so removed, demurrage is charged by port trust/airport authorities, which is very high. Hence, importer wants to complete as many formalities as possible before ship arrives. Proviso to Section 46(3) of Customs Act allows importer to present bill of entry upto 30 days before *expected date of arrival* of vessel. In such case, duty will be payable at the rate applicable on the date on which 'Entry Inward' is granted to vessel and not the date of presentation of Bill of Entry, *but rate of exchange will be as prevalent on date of submission of bill of entry.* - confirmed in CC, New Delhi circular No 64/96 dated 10.12.1996 and CBE&C circular No 22/97-Cus dated 4.7.1997.

ASSESSMENT OF CUSTOMS DUTY

Section 17 provides that assessment of goods will be made after Bill of Entry is filed. Date stamp of receipt is put on the 'Bill of Entry' and then it is sent to appraising department either manually or electronically There are various Appraising groups for different Chapter headings. Each group is under an Assistant/Deputy Commissioner. Group consists of 'Examiners' and 'Appraisers'.

APPRAISING THE GOODS

Appraiser has to:

- correctly classify the goods
- decide the Value for purpose of Customs duty
- find out rate of duty applicable as per any exemption notification and
- verify that goods are not imported in violation of any law.

He can call for any further documents that may be required for assessment. If he is of the opinion that goods have to be examined for appraisal, he will issue an examination order, usually on the reverse of Bill of Entry. If such order is issued, the Bill of Entry is presented to appraising staff at docks / air cargo complexes, where the goods are examined in presence of importer's representative. Assessment is finalised after getting the report of examination. – *Chapter 3 Para 11 and 12 of CBE&C's Customs Manual, 2001.*

VALUATION OF GOODS

As per rule 10 of Customs Valuation Rules, the importer has to file declaration about full 'value' of goods. If the assessing officer has doubts about the truth and accuracy of 'value' as declared, he can ask importer to submit further information, details and documents. If the doubt persists, the assessing officer can reject the value declared by importer. [rule 10A(1) of Customs Valuation Rules].

If the importer requests, the assessing officer has to give reasons for doubting the value declared by importer. [rule 10A(2)]. If the value declared by importer is rejected, the assessing officer can value imported goods on other basis *e.g.* value of identical goods, value of similar goods etc. as provided in Customs Valuation Rules. [This amendment has been made w.e.f. 19.2.98, as per WTO agreement. However, it has been held that burden of proof of under valuation is on department]. - - Assessing Officer should not arbitrarily reject the declared value and increase the assessable value. He should follow due process of law and issue appealable order. – MF(DR) circular No. 16/2003-Cus dated 17-3-2003.

APPROVAL OF ASSESSMENT

The assessment has to be approved by Assistant Commissioner, if the value is more than Rs one lakh. (in cases covered under 'fast track clearance for imports', appraiser is also authorised to approve valuation). After the approval, duty payable is typed by a "pin-point typewriter" so that it cannot be tampered with. As per CBE&C circular No. 10/98-Cus dated 11-2-1998, Assessing Officer should sign in full in Bill of Entry followed by his name, preferably by rubber stamp.

EDI ASSESSMENT

In the EDI system, the cargo declaration is transferred to assessing officer in the groups electronically. Processing is done on the screen itself. All calculations are done by the system itself. If assessing officer needs clarification, he can raise a query. The query is printed at service centre and importer replies through service centre. Facility of tele-enquiry about status of documents is provided in major customs stations. Under EDI, normally, documents are inspected only after assessment. After assessment, copy of Bill of Entry is printed at service centre. Final Bill of Entry is printed only after 'Out of Charge' order is given by customs officer. – *Chapter 3 Para 18 to 22 of CBE&C's Customs Manual, 2001.*

PAYMENT OF CUSTOMS DUTY

After assessment of duty, necessary duty is paid. Regular importers and Custom House Agents keep current account with Customs department. The duty can be debited to such current account, or it can be paid in cash/DD through TR-6 challan in designated banks. After payment of duty, if goods were already examined, delivery of goods can be taken from custodians (port trust) after paying their dues. If goods were not examined before assessment, these have to be submitted for examination in import shed to the examining staff. After shed appraiser gives 'out of charge' order, delivery of goods can be taken from custodian.

First and second system of assessment

There are two systems of assessment. Section 17(2) provides for assessment after examination of goods and section 17(4) provides for assessment on basis of documents, followed by inspection and testing of goods.

"First appraisement system" or *'first check procedure'* is followed if the appraiser is not able to make assessment on the basis of documents submitted and deems that inspection is necessary. Goods are examined first and then these are assessed. This method is followed only if assessment is not possible on basis of documents. - - The importer himself may also request 'first check procedure', if he cannot give all required details regarding description / value of goods. He has to make request for first check examination at the time of filing of Bill of Entry or at data entry stage in case of EDI. He has to give reason for seeking first appraisement.

The examination order is recorded on Bill of Entry and then returned to importer / CHA. It is then presented to import shed for examination. The shed appraiser / Dock examiner examines the goods as per examination order and records his findings. If samples are required, they are taken out. In case of EDI system, the report of examination is given in the computer itself. The goods are then assessed to duty by appraiser. - *Chapter 3 Para 23 of CBE&C's Customs Manual, 2001.*

In *"Second Appraisement System"* or *'second check procedure'*, which is normally followed, assessment is done on basis of documents and then goods are examined. Such examination is not mandatory. It is done on selective basis on the basis of 'risk assessment' or specific intelligence report. Section 17(4) of Customs Act specifically provides that if initially assessment is done on basis of documents, re-assessment can be done after examination or testing of goods or otherwise, if it is found subsequent to examination or testing or otherwise, that any statement made on Bill of Entry or any information supplied is not true in respect of matter relevant to assessment of duty.

First appraisement is generally carried out in following cases - * If complete documents are not submitted * Goods are to be tested for correct classification * Goods are re-imported * Goods are damaged or deteriorated and abatement is claimed * Goods are abandoned and remission of duty is applied for * When goods are provisionally assessed * When importer himself requests for examination of goods before payment of duty.

EXAMINATION OF GOODS

Examiners carry out physical examination and quantitative checking like weighing, measuring etc. Selected packages are opened and examined on sample basis in 'Customs Examination Yard'. Examination report is prepared by the examiner.

Accelerated Clearance of Imports and Exports Scheme (ACS)

Finance Minister, in his budget speech on 28-2- 2003, had announced a 'self assessment scheme' for importers and exporters. As per the scheme, importer will himself determine classification of goods including claim for exemption benefits. Computer System will calculate the duty based on his declaration. Physical inspection of imported goods will be done by riskassessment and management techniques on a computer based system and not on the orders of customs examining staff. Audit of import documents will not be by existing system of concurrent audit but will be done by post-clearance audit, as prevalent in developed countries.

Subsequently, a Accelerated Clearance of Import and Export Scheme (ACS) has been announced vide MF(DR) circular No. 30/2003-Cus dated 4-4-2003. The scheme is announced through administrative instructions, without making any change in statutory provisions. Hence, the scheme is not same as 'self removal' under Central Excise. Presently, the scheme is introduced on trial basis at Air Customs, Sahar (Mumbai), ICD, New Delhi and Chennai Sea Customs. In case of imports, the scheme will be open to all status holders under EXIM policy, Central and State Government PSUs and other importers who have been importing for at least two years and have filed at least 25 Bills of Entry in preceding year.

In case of exports, the scheme will be open to all status holders under EXIM policy, EOU/STP/EHTP units whose goods have been sealed in presence of customs/excise officers, Central and State Government PSUs, manufacturer-exporters who have been exporting for at least two years and have filed at least 25 Shipping Bills in preceding year and bulk exporters. - - Certain sensitive items have been excluded from the provisions. Importer/exporter intending to avail this facility has to make application to Commissioner. The clearances will be subject to post clearance audit.

Provisional Assessment -

Section 18 of Customs Act, 1962 provide that provisional assessment can be done in following cases:

- When Customs Officer is satisfied that importer or exporter is unable to produce document or furnish information required for assessment
- It is deemed necessary to carry out chemical or other tests of goods
- When importer/exporter has produced all documents, but Customs Officer still deems it necessary to make further enquiry.

In such cases, assessment is done on provisional basis. The importer/ exporter has to furnish guarantee/security as required by Customs Officer for payment of difference if any.

Goods can be cleared after payment of duty provisionally assessed and after providing the security. After final assessment, difference is paid by importer or refunded to him as the case may be. If the imported goods were warehoused after provisional assessment, the Customs Officer may require importer to execute a bond for twice the difference in duty, if duty finally assessed is higher [section 18(2)(*a*)]. The bond is called as 'P D Bond' (Provisional Duty Bond). The bond is with security or surety. Bank guarantee can also be given as a security.

Checking of duty drawback / license documents

Documents in respect of Duty Entitlement Pass Book (DEPB), advance license, duty drawback etc. will be checked.

Execution of bond and payment of duty

Once the duty is assessed, the bill of entry is returned to importer. The Bill of Entry should be presented to comptist for calculation and pinpointing of the duty.

If bond has to be executed, it will be taken in bond section.

- *Payment of duty* - If goods are to be removed to a warehouse, duty payment is not required. The goods can be taken to a warehouse under bond, without payment of duty. However, if goods are to be removed for home consumption, payment of customs duty is required. CHA or the importer can take it for payment of customs duty. Large importers and CHA have P.D. accounts with customs. Duty can be paid either in cash or through P.D. account. P. D. account means provisional duty account. This is a current account, similar to PLA in central excise. The importer or CHA pays lump sum amount in the account and gets credit on the amount paid. He can pay customs duty by debiting the amount in P.D. (Provisional Duty) account. If the importer does not have an account, he can pay duty by cash using TR-6 challan. Of course, payment through PD account is very convenient and quick. The duty should be paid within five working days (*i.e.* within five days excluding holidays) after the 'Bill of Entry' is returned to the importer for payment of duty. [section 47(2)]. (Till 11-5-2002, the period allowed was only 2 days).
- *Interest for late payment* - If duty is not paid within 5 working days as aforesaid, interest is payable. Such interest can be between 10% to 36% as may be notified by Central Government. [Section 47(2) of Customs Act, 1962.]. Interest rate is 15% w.e.f. 13-5-2002.

[Notification No. 28/2002-Cus(NT) dated 13-5-2002] Earlier, interest rate was 24% p.a, w.e.f. 1-3-2000, as per notification No. 34/2000-Cus(NT)].

- *Disposal if goods are not cleared within 30 days* - As per section 48 of Customs Act, goods must be cleared within 30 days after unloading. Customs Officer can grant extension. Otherwise, goods can be sold after giving notice to importer. However, animals, perishable goods and hazardous goods can be sold any time - even before 30 days. Arms & ammunition can be sold only with permission of Central Government.

Out of Customs Charge Order

After goods are examined, it is verified that import is not prohibited and after customs duty is paid, Customs Officer will issue 'Out of Customs Charge' order under section 47. Goods can be cleared from customs area only on receipt of such order. This is an 'adjudicating order' within the meaning of Customs Act, even if it is passed by Appraiser and not by Assistant Commissioner.

Demurrage if goods not cleared

Heavy demurrage is payable if goods are not cleared from port within three days.

Import of software through data communication

Import of software through data communication / telecommunication is permitted. Since such imports are not available for physical verification, proper accountal in books should be maintained. Unit intending to import software through datalink is required to inform estimated annual requirement to Development Commissioner of EOU / Director of STP. This should be approved by him. [what for ?]. After import of software through internet, written information should be submitted to Director of STP / Development Commissioner of EOU and importer shall get a certificate. This certificate should be submitted to Assistant / Dy Commissioner of Customs within 48 hours, along with Bill of Entry and certificate from Development Commissioner of EOU / Director of STP. He will issue 'out of charge' order. The documents such as invoice etc. will be routed through bank. - MF(DR) circular No. 58/2000-Cus dated 10-7-2000.

Relevant Date for Rate and Valuation of Customs Duty

Section 15 of Customs Act prescribes that rate of duty and tariff valuation applicable to imported goods shall be the rate and valuation in force at one of the following dates.

- If the goods are entered for home consumption, the date on which bill of entry is presented

- In case of warehoused goods, when Bill of Entry for home consumption is presented u/s 68 for clearance from warehouse and
- In other cases, date of payment of duty.

CONCEPT OF TERRITORIAL WATERS NOT RELEVANT

It may be noted that concept of ' date of entering into territorial waters' is not relevant for purposes of determination of rate of customs duty.

EXPORT PROCEDURES

Procedures have to be followed by:

- 'Person-in-charge of conveyance' and
- The exporter

The procedures are similar to procedures for import, of course, in reverse direction.

NO STOPPAGE OF EXPORT CONSIGNMENT

Exports are vital for our economy. Any stoppage in export consignment means loss of export orders to the exporter and loss of foreign exchange to the country. Hence, it has been provided that movement of export consignment will not be interrupted and no export consignment shall be withheld for any reason whatsoever. In case of any doubt, customs authorities may ask for an undertaking that the export is on sole responsibility of the exporter. [Highlights of EXIM policy 1997-2002 as amended on 13.4.1998].

Procedures by person in charge of conveyance

Any new airline, shipping line, steamer agent should be registered in Customs Systems for electronic processing of shipping bills etc. The 'person in charge of conveyance' has to follow prescribed procedures.

Entry Outward

The vessel should be granted 'Entry Outward'. Loading can start only after entry outward is granted. (section 39 of Customs Act). Steamer Agents can file 'application for entry outwards' 14 days in advance so that intending exporters can start submitting 'Shipping Bills'. This ensures that formalities are completed as quickly as possible and loading in ship starts quickly.

LOADING WITH PERMISSION

Export goods can be loaded only after Shipping Bill or Bill of Export, duly passed by Customs Officer is handed over by Exporter to the person-in-charge of conveyance. In case of baggage and mail bags, shipping bill is not necessary, but permission of Customs Officer is required (section 40).

Export Manifest

As per section 41, an Export Manifest/Export Report in prescribed form should be submitted before departure. [The report is popularly called as 'Export General Manifest' - EGM]. The details required are similar to import manifest.

Such manifest/report can be amended or supplemented with permission, if there was no fraudulent intention. Such report should be declared as true by the person-in-charge signing the export manifest. This report is not required if the conveyance is carrying only luggage of occupants.

Procedures to be followed by Exporter

Export procedures have been summarized in Chapter 3 Part II of CBE&C's Customs Manual, 2001. Every exporter should take following initial steps -- Obtain BIN (Business Identification Number) from DGFT.

It is a PAN based number Open current account with designated bank for credit of duty drawback claims Register licenses / advance license / DEPB etc. at the customs station, if exports are under Export Promotion Schemes Exporter has to submit 'shipping bill' for export by sea or air and 'bill of export' for export by road.

Goods have to be assessed for duty, even if no duty is payable for most of exports, as 'Nil Duty' assessment is also an assessment.

Shipping Bill to be submitted by Exporter

Shipping Bill and Bill of Export Regulations prescribe form of shipping bills. It should be submitted in quadruplicate. If drawback claim is to be made, one additional copy should be submitted. There are five forms :

- Shipping Bill for export of goods under claim for duty drawback - these should be in Green colour
- Shipping Bill for export of dutiable goods - this should be yellow colour
- shipping bill for export of duty free goods - it should be white colour
- shipping bill for export of duty free goods ex-bond - *i.e.* from bonded store room - it should be pink colour
- Shipping Bill for export under DEPB scheme - Blue colour.

The shipping bill form requires details like name of exporter, consignee, Invoice Number, details of packing, description of goods, quantity, FOB Value etc. Appropriate form of shipping bill should be used. Relevant documents *i.e.* copies of packing list, invoices, export contract, letter of credit etc. are also to be submitted. In case of excisable goods, from ARE-1 prepared at the time of clearance from factory should also be submitted. Customs authorities give serial number (called *'Thoka Number'*) to shipping bill, when it is presented.

Excise formalities at the time of Export

If the goods are cleared by manufacturer for export, the goods are accompanied by ARE-1 (earlier AR-4). This form should be submitted to customs authorities. The Customs Officer certifies that the goods under this form have indeed been exported. This form has then to be submitted to Maritime Commissioner for obtaining 'proof of export'. The bond executed by Manufacturer-exporter with excise authorities is released only when 'proof of export' is accepted by Maritime Commissioner or Assistant Commissioner, where bond was executed.

Duty drawback formalities

If the exporter intends to claim duty drawback on his exports, he has to follow prescribed procedures and submit necessary papers. The procedures are discussed in the chapter on 'Export Incentives'. He has to make endorsement of shipping bill that claim for duty drawback is being made. If he fails to do so due to genuine reasons, Commissioner of Customs can grant exemption from this provision. [proviso to rule 12(1)(a) of Duty Drawback Rules].

G R / SDF / SOFTEX Form under FEMA

Reserve Bank of India has prescribed GR / SDF form under FEMA. "G R" stands for 'Guaranteed Receipt' form, while SDF stands for 'Statutory Declaration Form'). SDF form is to be used where shipping bills are processed electronically in customs house, while GR form is used when shipping bills are processed manually in customs house.

Other documents required for export

Exporter also has to prepare other documents like:

- Four copies of Commercial Invoice
- Four copies of Packing List
- Certificate of Origin or pre-shipment inspectison where required
- Insurance policy.
- Letter of Credit
- Declaration of Value
- Excise ARE-1/ARE-2 form as applicable
- GR / SDF form prescribed by RBI in duplicate
- Letter showing BIN Number.

RCMC certificate from Export Promotion Council

Various Export Promotion Councils have been set up to promote and develop exports. (*e.g.* Engineering Export Promotion Council, Apparel Export

Promotion Council, etc.) Exporter has to become member of the concerned Export Promotion Council and obtain RCMC - Registration cum membership Certificate.

Check in customs

Document submitted is processed by customs authorities, and following are checked - *Chapter 3 Para 39 of CBE&C's Customs Manual, 2001.* –

- Value and classification of goods under drawback schedule in case of drawback shipping bills
- Export duty / cess if applicable
- Advance License shipping bills are checked to ensure that description in invoice and final product specified in Advance License matches. If necessary, samples may be drawn and assessment may be done after visual inspection or testing
- Exportability of goods under EXIM policy and other laws - Some exports are totally prohibited under various Acts *e.g.* items restricted or prohibited under Foreign Trade (Regulation) Act; antiques; art treasures; Arms; narcotics etc. Some items like tea, coffee and coir products can be exported only against authorisation/licence under respective Acts.

Examination of goods before export

After shipping bill is passed by export department, the goods are presented to shed appraiser (exports) in dock for examination. Goods will be examined by examiner. This inspection is necessary:

- To ensure that prohibited goods are not exported
- Goods tally with description and invoice
- Duty drawback, where applicable, is correctly claimed.

Let Export Order by Customs Authorities

Customs Officer will verify the contents and after he is satisfied that goods are not prohibited for exports and that export duty, if applicable is paid, will permit clearance. (section 51) by giving 'let ship' or 'let export' order. GR-1, ARE-1, octroi papers, quota certification for export etc. are also signed. Exporter's copy of shipping Bill, GR-1, ARE-1 etc. duly certified are handed over to exporter or CHA. Drawback claims papers are also processed. - *Chapter 3 Para 43 and 60 of CBE&C's Customs Manual, 2001.*

Processing under EDI system

Under EDI system, declarations in prescribed form are to be filed through 'Service Centre' of customs. After verification, shipping bill number is generated by the system, which is endorsed on printed checklist generated for verification of data. Goods are inspected at docks on the basis of printed check list. All documents are submitted to Customs Officer along with checklist. If goods and documents are found in order, 'let export' order is issued. Then two copies of Shipping Bill are generated – one customs and other exporter's copy.

Exporter's copy is generated only after EGM (Export General Manifest) is submitted by shipping agent. These are signed by CHA and customs officer and then by Appraiser. SDF, ARE- 1, octroi papers, quota certification for export etc. are also signed. Exporter's copy of Shipping Bill, SDF, ARE- 1 etc. duly signed are handed over to exporter or CHA. - *Chapter 3 Paras 42 to 60 of CBE&C's Customs Manual, 2001.*

Conveyance to leave on written order

The vessel or aircraft which has brought imported goods or which carry export goods cannot leave that customs station unless a written order is given by Customs Officer. Such order is given only after:

- Export manifest is submitted
- Shipping bills or bills of export, bills of transhipment etc. are submitted
- Duties on stores consumed are paid or payment of the same is secured
- No penalty is leviable
- Export duty, if applicable, is paid.

Such permission is not required if the conveyance is carrying only luggage of occupants.

OTHER CUSTOMS PROCEDURES

Besides the aforesaid procedures, various other procedures have been prescribed. These are mainly to be followed by the person in charge of conveyance.

- *Boat Notes* - If the vessel has to unload only a small cargo, it may not spend time in having berth in the port. If the small cargo is to be sent to shore, it may be loaded in a small boat and sent to shore. As per section 35, such small boat must be accompanied by a 'Boat Note'. Boat Notes Regulations provide that such Boat Notes will be issued by Customs Officer. It will be maintained in duplicate and should be serially numbered. Boat Note should be in prescribed form. In case of export, if small export cargo is to be loaded in ship through small boat, no Boat Note is required if the cargo is accompanied by the 'Shipping Bill', otherwise, Boat Note is required. Boat Note is also required for transhipment of cargo, *i.e.* transfer from one ship to another or for re-shipment.

- *Transit Goods* - Section 53 provide that any goods imported in any conveyance will be allowed to remain on the conveyance and to be transited without payment of customs duty, to any place out of India or any customs station. However, all these goods must be mentioned in import manifest or import report submitted by person in charge of conveyance. Such goods should not be 'prohibited goods' under section 11 of Customs Act. [The conveyance may be vehicle, ship or aircraft]. After transit, the goods may go to another customs station. On arrival at customs station, the goods will be liable to customs duty as if it is first importation in India. - section 55.
- *Transhipment of Goods* - Goods imported in any customs station can be transhipped without payment of duty, u/s 54 of Customs Act. Transhipment means transfer from one conveyance to another. [The conveyance may be vehicle, ship or aircraft]. Such transhipment may be to any major port or airport in India. The goods can be transhipped to any other customs station in India if customs officer is satisfied that the goods are *bonafide* intended for transhipment to any customs station. The facility is available at all customs ports and Inland Container Depots (ICDs). [*Notification No. 50/95-Cus(NT) dated 6-9-95*]. Goods to be transhipped must be specified in Import Manifest or Import report and a 'Bill of Transhipment' should be submitted to Customs Officer. In case of goods being transhipped under an international treaty or bilateral agreement between Government of India and Government of a foreign country, a Declaration of Transhipment shall be submitted instead of Bill of Transhipment. [section 54(1)]. [India has such bilateral agreement with Nepal]. Such goods should not be 'prohibited goods' under section 11 of Customs Act. The goods should be sealed during transhipment by customs officer. A bond has to be executed for the purpose. After execution of bond, a certificate from customs officer has to be submitted within one month that goods have been properly transferred. [Goods Imported (Conditions of Transhipment) Regulations, 1995]. On arrival at customs station, they will be liable to customs duty as if it is first importation in India. - section 55.

TRANSIT AND TRANSHIP

Distinction between transit and transhipment is that in 'transit' goods continue to be on same vessel, while in transhipment, goods are transferred to another vessel / vehicle. Hence, procedures are also different.

Coastal Goods

Coastal goods means goods transported from one port in India to another port in India, *but does not include imported goods*. Thus, coastal goods means goods taken by ship from one Indian port to another. No export or import is involved, but control is necessary to ensure that coastal goods are not diverted illegally for export.

LOADING OF COASTAL GOODS

The Consignor should submit bill of coastal goods to Customs Officer (section 93). Form of the bill has been prescribed. These will be loaded by master of vessel only after 'bill of coastal goods' is passed (section 93). Master of Vessel will carry an 'Advice Book' where entries will be made by Customs Officer. This 'Advice Book' has to be presented for inspection of Customs Officers, if called for. After loading, the vessel can leave only after obtaining written order from Customs Officer. As per notification No 15/98-NT dated 27.2.1998, exemption has been granted for delivery of 'Advice Book' at each port of call. However, the 'Advice Book' will have to be submitted for inspection on board of vessel, when called for.

UNLOADING OF COASTAL GOODS

Unloading of coastal goods should be done only at Customs Port or coastal port appointed by CBEC under section 7 of Customs Act. On arrival, all bills relating to goods which are to be unloaded will be delivered to Customs Officer. Unloading can be done only after obtaining permission from Customs Officer. Customs Officer can inspect goods and ask for questions and documents relating to goods. Goods will be unloaded at approved place under supervision of Customs Officer.

2

Methods of Payment

DIFFERENT METHODS OF PAYMENT

The method of payment determines how payment is going to be made, *i.e.*, the obligations that rest with both buyer and seller in relation to monetary settlement. However, the method of payment also determines - directly or indirectly - the role the banks will have in that settlement. Methods of payment can be categorized in different ways, depending on the purpose. This is often based on the commercial aspect seen from the exporter's perspective in terms of security. In security order, the basic methods of payment could be listed as follows:

- Cash in advance before delivery;
- Documentary letter of credit;
- Documentary collection;
- Bank transfer;
- Other payment mechanisms, such as barter or counter-trade.

However, as can be seen in the following text, the security aspect is usually not that simple to define in advance. In reality, there are many different variations and alternatives that will affect the order of such a listing; for example, if the open account is supported by a guarantee, a standby letter of credit or separate credit insurance, or how a barter or counter-trade is structured.

Even the nature and wording of the letter of credit will eventually determine what level of security it offers the seller. Seen from a more practical point of view of how the payment is actually made and the role of the commercial parties and the banks, there are, in principle, only four basic methods of payment that are used today in connection with monetary settlement of international trade. One of these methods is always the basis for the terms of payment:

- Bank transfer;
- Cheque payment;

- Documentary collection; and
- Letter of credit.

BANK CHARGES AND OTHER COSTS

The costs of the alternatives are mainly governed by what function the banks will have in connection with the execution of payment. Other forms of fees, which can have an indirect connection to the payment, do sometimes arise, such as different charges related to the creation of the underlying documents, for example consular fees and stamp duties. However, such fees are related more to the delivery than to the payment and are normally borne by the party that has to produce these documents according to the terms of delivery. Other costs, such as payment of duties and taxes, are also governed by the agreed terms of delivery. Bank charges will arise not only in the seller's but also in the buyer's country; they can vary hugely between different countries, both in size and, more importantly, in structure. In some cases they are charged at a fixed rate, in others as a percentage of the transferred amount. Sometimes they are negotiable, sometimes not, and these differences occur not only between countries but also between banks.

The best solution for both parties is often to agree to pay the bank charges in their respective country, but whatever the agreement, it should be included in the sales con-tract. However, such a deal would probably minimize the total costs of the transaction since each party would have a direct interest in negotiating these costs with their local bank. Bank charges in one's own country are more easily calculated and, even if the difference between banks in the same country is relatively small, they are often negotiable for larger amounts. Bank charges are often divided into the following groups:

- Standard fees for specified services - normally charged at a flat rate;
- Handling charges, *i.e.*, for checking of documents - normally charged as a percentage on the underlying value of the transaction;
- Risk commissions, *i.e.*, the issuing of guarantees and confirmation of letters of credit - normally charged as a percentage of the amount at a rate according to the estimated risk and the period of time.

Detailed fee schedules, applicable in each country and for each major bank, can easily be obtained directly from the banks or found on their websites, but as pointed out earlier, for larger transactions, fees, charges and commissions are often negotiable.

BANK TRANSFER (BANK REMITTANCE)

Most trade transactions, particularly in regional international trade, are based on so-called 'open account' payment terms. This means that the seller delivers goods or services to the buyer without receiving cash, a bill of exchange or any other legally binding and enforceable undertaking at the time of delivery, and the buyer is expected to pay according to the terms of the sales contract and the seller's later invoice. Therefore, the open account involves a form of short, but agreed, credit extended to the buyer, in most cases verified only by the invoice and the specified date of payment therein, together with copies of the relevant shipping or delivery document, verifying shipment and shipment date. When the terms of payment are based on open account terms and the seller receives no additional security for the buyer's payment obligations, the normal bank transfer is by far the simplest and most common form of payment.

The buyer, having received the seller's invoice, simply instructs the bank to transfer the amount, a few days before the due date, to a bank chosen by the seller. This can be done either directly to the seller's account at a bank in their country or to a separate collection account that the seller may have at a bank in the buyer's country.

PAYMENT STRUCTURE FOLLOWS THE TRADE PATTERN

Bank transfers are a method of 'clean payments', which predominate both in size and in number; more than 80 per cent of all commercial international payments are estimated to be in this form. The main reason is not only that it is a simple method of payment, cheap and flexible for both buyer and seller, but that it is also an indication of the underlying general trade pattern. The majority of all international trade is regional, where the commercial risk is generally regarded as low and open account terms traditionally used.

Such trade has the advantage of short shipping distances and often regular business patterns between well-known companies, even between companies belonging to the same group, or companies that can be properly evaluated from a risk assessment point of view. In these cases it is also quite normal that there exist established market practices, where open account trading settled through a bank transfer is the most common form of payment. Even in individual cases where the seller would have preferred a safer method of payment, this can often be difficult to achieve owing to competition or established practice.

Instead, many sellers use export credit insurance covering the risk on different customers or even their whole export; with this cover, bank transfer may be the best payment alternative.

THE SWIFT SYSTEM

Nowadays, most bank transfers are processed through an internal bank network for international payments and messages, the so-called SWIFT system, in which more than 8,000 financial institutions around the world participate. This network is cooperatively owned by the participating banks, which have created a low-cost, secure and very effective internal communication system for both payments and messages. As a consequence of the introduction of SWIFT, bank transfers between countries and banks are now completed much faster than before. When the instructions are fed into the system by the buyer's bank it is normally available at the seller's chosen bank two banking days later, and usually available for the seller the next day or according to local practice. Urgent SWIFT messages are processed even faster, but at a higher fee.

However, it should be stressed that even if the speed of processing has increased through SWIFT, this happens only when the payment instruction has been com-municated to the network. The seller is, as before, dependent on the buyer giving correct instructions in time to their bank and it is still up to the seller to maintain a high standard in their own systems and routines for close monitoring of outstanding payments. It is also of great importance to use the correct address code system developed by SWIFT, the bank identifier code. This code is a unique address which, in telecommunication messages, identifies the financial institutions to be involved in the transaction. The BIC code consists of 8 characters identifying the bank, the country and the location. This code, often called the SWIFTBIC, must therefore be correctly included in the terms of payment and later in invoices and other correspondence with the buyer.

Irrespective of where the payment originated, or where it is to be sent, it is up to the seller to provide the buyer with the correct and necessary information to pass on to their bank, information which must also appear in the terms of payment and in the invoice. Many receiving banks today process these payments automatically, but they have to do it manually if incorrect or incomplete information is given, and will in such cases charge a higher fee.

SWIFTnet Trade Services Utility (TSU)

After order confirmation, shipment and invoicing, the bank transfer is the final step in open account trading, but it contains no form of guarantee for its timely execution. In the documentary methods of payment, however, in particular the letter of credit which will be described later in this chapter, the banks are involved in the supply chain from shipment to payment. This makes documentary payments safer but generally more time consuming, inflexible and expensive, while expanding global trade calls for more open account trading with reduced transaction costs and increased efficiency and flexibility.

In order to enable banks to offer risk management and information services appropriate to today's corporate supply chain and to fill the gap between open account and documentary payments more effectively, SWIFT is currently testing a 'semi-open account' trading solution, the SWIFTnet Trade Services Utility. This is basically a central trade data information-matching database, which will provide both banks and their customers with a tool for monitoring the supply chain of individual transactions, thereby increasing transparency and reducing the uncertainty of the transaction. The introduction of the TSU should also form the basis for new financial services, not least in the area of trade finance, resulting in cheaper and more readily available pre-shipment finance for the exporter and/or post-delivery finance for the buyer. The TSU will be introduced in separate phases and is presently being pilot-tested by some of the world's leading trade banks.

In short, the system, streamlined for ordinary and not too complicated transactions, should work as follows. Both buyers and sellers will send highly standardized purchase order confirmations to their banks as input into the SWIFT database. When matched successfully against each other, that fact will be certified not only to the commercial parties but also to their banks, which could form the basis for the financing of the transaction at an early stage.

As the deal progresses, the sellers' bank will add invoice, transport and other required information to the database, enabling the banks to supervise the proper fulfilment of the contract, and accordingly, also the buyer's payment obligations according to the agreed database information. If and when the SWIFTnet Trade Services Utility becomes fully operational and commonly used, a new support structure for increased usage of open account trading will have been created, including vital elements taken from both the ordinary bank transfer and from the documentary methods of payment.

COLLECTION ACCOUNTS ABROAD

The bank transfer has, so far, been described as a payment between two countries, arriving directly from the buyer's bank to that of the seller, and that is usually the case. However, it is increasingly common for the seller to choose to open an account in local currency in the larger OECD countries, where they already have, or can expect, larger flows of payments within one and the same country. The buyer will then make a domestic, not an international, payment to this account, which is both easier and usually cheaper - and the seller will have direct access to the payment when it has reached that account.

These accounts are often established with branches of the seller's bank abroad or in cooperation with one of their banking partners. The structure can vary depending on if and how these accounts are integrated in the seller's cash management system, and the cost will depend on the set-up and the service level required.

The use of collection accounts has also been accelerated by other developments within the banking systems in some countries. For example, a quicker or even online reporting of transactions and balances, whereby it is possible for the seller to monitor individual transactions on these accounts on a daily basis, through their own terminal connected to the bank. The balance can then be used for local payments within that country, for intra-company transfers or for direct transfer back to the seller's head-office account.

PAYMENT DELAYS IN CONNECTION WITH BANK TRANSFERS

Since the main role of the banks in connection with bank transfers is to provide an intermediary function, the responsibility for correct and timely payment rests with the commercial parties. It is the buyer who has to give correct payment instructions to their bank, but this obligation does not normally arise until the seller has fulfilled their delivery obligations according to the contract.

Delays in payment are common, not only with different countries but also with indi-vidual buyers. Sometimes the reason may be non-acceptance of delivery, or other related claims, but in these cases an ongoing dialogue should already have been established between the parties and the seller can be expected to be fully aware of the situation and the reason for the delay in payment. However, in some cases the seller may not be aware of any such open payment disputes with the buyer, and will not have received payment in time - this may be for many different reasons:

- In some countries or companies it may be established practice to delay local payments, and international payments are then treated in the same way.
- Bank credit limits or the interest level in local currency could make it advantageous or necessary to delay all payments, including payments to suppliers.
- Supplier payments are often based on open account payment terms, ie without a bill of exchange or similar instrument. Such payments could then have a low priority among other debts.
- The buyer may want a self-liquidated deal in order to improve liquidity, and may prefer to delay the payment until they have been paid by their customer.
- The buyer may see currency advantages in delaying the exchange from local currency into the currency to be transferred to the seller.
- Larger corporations often have internal payment systems with batch payments made at certain intervals during the month.
- In the worst case, the delay may be due to liquidity or solvency problems on the part of the buyer, or if applicable, the buyer's country.

REDUCING PAYMENT DELAYS

Even if it is not possible to establish the exact cause of the delay in payment, there are always some steps the seller can take to reduce such delays.

First, the seller must have an agreement or a sales contract with clear terms of payment. This should include detailed instructions on how to pay and the invoice to be issued after delivery should specify the same information, a fixed due date, full bank name and address, account number and SWIFTBIC references. It could also prove advantageous to stress the right, according to the contract, for a late payment interest charge and to specify the applicable rate. Even if it may be difficult to collect interest afterwards, the mere indication of it could have a positive effect on the speed of payment.

The most important and effective way to speed up payments related to open account payment terms lies within the structure and efficiency of the internal system implemented within the company in order to treat outstanding and overdue payments. The seller must have clear internal rules and guidelines with a limit for amounts, timing and frequency of individual overdue payments, together with instructions on reporting and how to deal with such matters. It is equally important to have functional internal communication between the sales and administrative departments within the company so that the salesperson responsible for that particular buyer becomes aware of any late payments.

This person might have additional information and can contact and get support from their opposite number at the buyer, who is not normally the person responsible for payments and may be totally unaware of the delay. Above all, the seller should not let the matter linger too long. If the buyer has financial problems, the seller will often learn about it once it has become common knowledge among local business partners, who will then be the first to press for payment. The buyer might also be more dependent on them than on a foreign supplier for ongoing business, and might act accordingly in their payment priorities.

E-COMMERCE

The rapid pace of technology and the explosive growth of the internet are having a profound effect on many markets, and there are huge opportunities for companies in most countries to develop new products and services in the area of international trade. In order to support this development and to strengthen their e-commerce industry, governments in many countries have established policies for creating a stable regulatory environment that supports and underpins competition in both the network and service sectors. This development is also supported on the supranational level by guidelines set by the OECD for business-to-consumer e-commerce.

These guidelines were developed in order to set a level playing field for businesses and to protect customers, for example in matters relating to transparency, fair business and marketing practices, online disclosures, information obligations and payment practices, and are incorporated into rules in most countries involved in e-commerce.

The problem with e-commerce in general has always been the security aspect and the risk of unauthorized use of customer and account information, spread over an open system - not least for international payments. Many e-commerce transactions are still made on open account terms with payment after delivery, either by ordinary bank transfers or by cheque, even if such payments could be proportionately expensive for small payments. When it comes to international payments, most e-commerce businesses want to see the actual money being transferred before shipping the goods. However, new technology and the creation of separate worldwide e-commerce payment systems that are both secure and reliable have created the background for a rapid increase in e-commerce transactions in international trade. These are based on payments through debit/credit cards, particularly in areas such as leisure, travel and most segments of the retail market where card payments have been the norm for many years.

When it comes to business-to-business transactions, the picture is somewhat different. Customer relations are often more established, the amounts involved are normally larger and the payment terms are often based on open account or documentary payment terms. Even when marketing and sales are based on e-commerce as an alternative or complement to other sales channels, actual trade payments between companies are generally done through the banks, based on the established SWIFT system.

CHEQUE PAYMENTS

Paying by cheque was once a common form of payment, but following the introduction of more cost-effective and faster ways of processing international bank transfers, this is no longer the case. Perhaps not more than a few per cent of all international payments are now processed by cheque. In countries where this form of payment is commonly used in domestic trade, for example in the UK and the United States, the situation may be different, and cheques may for that reason be more frequently used for payment in international trade. Sometimes the buyer prefers to pay with their own cheques for cash management purposes, as opposed to through a 'bank cheque'.

The corporate cheque will not be paid to the seller until it is received and presented to the seller's bank, usually with a considerably delayed value date. This will delay the receipt of liquidity for the seller and often incur additional fees, but the payment will also be subject to the cheque being honoured later on by the buyer's bank when sent back to them for reimbursement. Only at that late stage will the cheque be charged to the buyer's own account - with a profit for the buyer of many interest-free days. In some countries it may take weeks to get a corporate cheque from abroad cleared between the banks, during which time the cheque has to be sent to the account holding bank for collection.

In such cases, both banks involved may charge collection commissions with high minimum charges, which could add up to large amounts for the exporter, not to mention the liquidity disadvantages. These procedures vary between countries and, if uncertain, the seller should always check in advance with their bank before agreeing to accept a corporate cheque as payment in international trade. The seller should also be aware that if payment by cheque is agreed, and no other stipulation is made, then it is likely that they will receive a corporate cheque, with the liquidity and cost disadvantages mentioned above. However, larger companies may have this payment procedure as a policy, which the seller then may have to accept but, in such cases, this may be of minor importance compared to other aspects of the transaction.

Figure shows how the handling of cheques is different from bank transfers. However, as a form of clean payment with no direct connection to the underlying trade documents, the level of security for the seller is almost identical to that of the bank transfer and with the same disadvantages as described earlier.

There is, however, one further risk aspect relating to cheques in general, which is the postal risk. If lost in transit to the seller, or delayed because of strikes or any other reason, the buyer can claim that they have paid by sending the cheque, but the seller has not received payment. The terms of payment should decide which of the parties has to carry this risk but this is often not the case. If the terms clearly state that payment should be made through a bank transfer, that risk is normally eliminated. The conclusion is that if payment is to be made by cheque, the terms must clearly state whether this will be a corporate cheque or a bank cheque. Then both parties will know what has been agreed and the exporter is aware of the risks involved. As shown in Figure 2.3, the front of the bank cheque is crossed. This is often done as a safety precaution; such a cheque will not be paid in cash but will only be credited to an account of the payee, in this case the seller, in the bank where it is cashed.

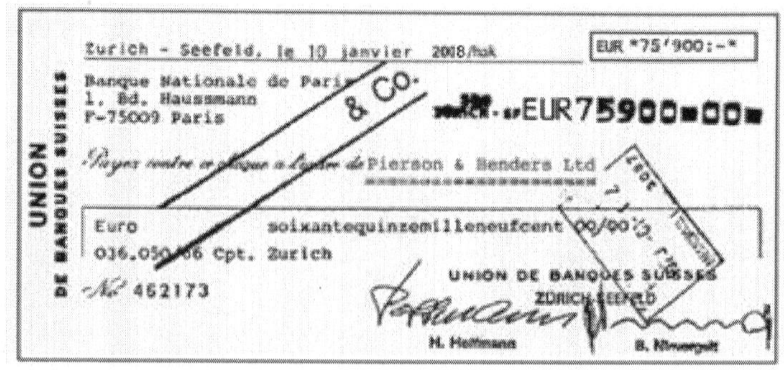

Figure Sample bank cheque

DOCUMENTARY COLLECTION

Documentary collection, also sometimes referred to as bank collection, is a method of payment where the seller's and buyer's banks assist by forwarding documents to the buyer against payment or some other obligation, often acceptance of an enclosed draft. The basis for this form of payment is that the buyer should either pay or accept the draft, before they gain control over the documents that represent the goods.

The role of the banks in a documentary collection is purely to present the documents to the buyer, but without the responsibility that they will be honoured by them. The collection contains no guarantee on behalf of the banks, which act only upon the instruction of the seller, but it is nevertheless a demand against the buyer, performed by a collection bank at their domicile, often their own bank. It is, in most cases, a more secure alternative for the seller, compared to trading on open account payment terms. The collections are often divided into two main groups:

- Documents against payment -when the bank notifies the buyer that the documents have arrived and requests them to pay the amount as instructed by the seller's bank.
- Documents against acceptance -when the buyer is requested to accept a term draft that accompanies the documents instead of payment. The seller's risk deteriorates by handing over the documents against a bill of exchange instead of receiving payment and is dependent on the buyer's ability to pay the bill at a later stage, but the seller has lost the advantage of having control of the documents related to the goods.

DOCUMENTARY COLLECTION AND CONTROL OF GOODS

The general advantage with this method of payment is that the buyer knows that the goods have been shipped and can examine the related documents before payment or acceptance. From the seller's perspective, the documents are not placed at the disposal of the buyer until they have paid or accepted the enclosed draft.

Scenario 1

The goods are being sent by air to the buyer, who will be able to get hold of them on arrival, without presentation of the relevant air waybill. The goods will generally have arrived at the buyer's destination long before the documents have arrived at the bank.

Scenario 2

The goods are sent by sea to the same buyer who, in this case, cannot get hold of them until the corresponding shipping documents, ie the bill of lading, can be presented; the bill of lading is among the documents under collection at the bank. The main difference between the two cases is the mode of transport and related documents. The air waybill is simply a receipt of goods for shipment, issued by the airline company, similar to a rail waybill or a forwarding agent certificate of receipt. Sometimes a multimodal transport document is used, providing for combined transport by at least two different types of transport, which is also a receipt of goods but not a document of title to the goods. A bill of lading is not only an acknowledgement that the goods have been loaded on board the ship, but also a separate contract with the shipping company, which includes the title to the goods. The buyer cannot get access to the goods under a bill of lading without possession of this document. If other transport documents are used and the seller is anxious to have control of the goods until the buyer honours the presented documents at the bank, then this has to be arranged in some other way. For example, the goods may be addressed to a consignee other than the buyer, perhaps the collecting bank or alternatively to the forwarding agent's representative at the place of destination. To address freight bills or forwarding agent receipts to someone other than the buyer or to insert restriction clauses about the release of the goods could cause problems, or even be prohibited in some countries. Before taking such action, the seller should get prior approval from the bank or shipping agent.

INSPECTION OF THE GOODS

So far, our description has mainly been given from the seller's viewpoint; however, the use of documentary collection could have certain disadvantages for the buyer. Perhaps the most important of these is that there are no opportunities to examine the goods before payment; the buyer has to rely solely on what can be seen from the documents presented. There are, however, some actions that the buyer can take to help deal with this drawback. The buyer or the buyer's agent may have the opportunity to inspect the goods before shipment or may use a company specializing in such inspections to do so, as part of the agreement.

Such a certificate could then be included in the set of documents sent for collection. This procedure is described later in this chapter. Other ways for the buyer to increase security in connection with documentary collections could be to have the contractual right to postpone payment/acceptance until the goods have arrived and then to have the right to inspect them or to take samples. Measures like this have to be approved by the seller but there are often considerable practical and logistical problems with such procedures. Another solution could be to avoid collection altogether and instead agree on a bank guarantee or a standby letter of credit in favour of the seller, thus covering the buyer's payment obligations.

The parties can then agree on open account payment terms and use bank transfer instead of collection as the method of payment and the buyer can inspect the goods upon arrival before payment, knowing that the guarantee can only be drawn upon by the seller if and when they have fulfilled their delivery obligations. The buyer is then obliged to pay anyway under the terms of the contract. The disadvantages for the buyer are of course the costs involved and that such a guarantee has to be issued under available credit limits with their bank. If the buyer does not accept documentary collection but only open account terms without any guarantee, one alternative for the seller could be to agree to such terms, but in combination with separate credit risk insurance covering the payment obligations of the buyer. However, if no such insurance can be obtained, the seller should probably opt for a safer method than documentary collection, ie a letter of credit.

DOCUMENTARY COLLECTION DOCUMENTS

It is important that the documents required under a collection are specified in the terms of payment in order to avoid disputes with the buyer later on, which will only delay the collection procedure. Documents often used include:

<table>
<tr><td>Drawer's reference number:
EA 2891-83</td><td>Date of issue
12/02/07</td><td>Maturity
At sight</td></tr>
<tr><td>Payable at:
Overseas Chinese Banking Corp Ltd,
261 High Street, Singapore</td><td colspan="2">Pay against this Bill of Exchange to:
Pierson & Henders Ltd</td></tr>
<tr><td colspan="2">Amounts in words and currency:
Five thousand and three hundred US dollars only</td><td>Currency and amount in figures:
USD 5,300.00</td></tr>
<tr><td colspan="3">For:
Value received in goods as per invoice no. 2891-83 of February 12th, 2007</td></tr>
<tr><td>Accepted by Drawee:
[Signature of Drawee along with full name and address]</td><td colspan="2">Drawer's Signature:
Pierson & Henders Ltd
[Drawer's signature along with full name and address]</td></tr>
</table>

- Draft/bill of exchange, issued at sight or as a term bill;
- Invoice, sometimes also separate consular invoices;
- Specifications and separate packing or weight lists;
- Relevant transport documents;
- Certificate of origin;

- Other certificates, such as health test or performance certificates;
- Inspection certificates, verifying quality or quantity of the goods;
- Insurance documents.

1. The bill of exchange, often also called a documentary draft, is similar to a cheque when signed by the buyer, constituting a legal undertaking in accordance with the terms of the bill. The wording varies between countries; often the term 'draft' or 'term draft' is used when issued by the exporter, but 'bill' or 'bill of exchange' only after it has been accepted by the buyer.

   Documents to distant countries are sometimes sent as duplicates in two different mails, one bill marked 'First Bill of Exchange and the other marked 'Second Bill of Exchange'. But otherwise only one bill of exchange is issued, as in this case.
2. The date of issue should normally be the same as the invoice date, shipment date or any other specified date related to the underlying contract or agreement.
3. The example is due at sight, which means that this draft is not supposed to be accepted but paid by the buyer at first presentation. If it is to be accepted as a term bill, the maturity date could be a fixed future date or at a certain date after presentation to the buyer, for example 90 days' sight, or from the date of issue.
4. The draft is normally payable to the drawer, as in this case, but, as a term bill of exchange, it could also be endorsed on the back in order to have its title and its rights transferred, either in blank or to a specific order, the collecting bank or a refinancing institution.
5. The place of payment specifies the obligations of the drawee. If not specified in some other way, a bill should be presented at sight or at maturity either at the debtor's bank or to the debtor personally, which is normally executed as a part of the original instructions in the documentary collection.
6. Commercial trade bills should have the statement that value has been received, referring to the invoice and/or the underlying contract, in order to specify its origin as a trade instrument.

If import or currency licences are required in connection with a documentary collection, this must always be part of the contract, together with a statement of the buyer's responsibility to produce these documents prior to shipment.

However, if this is the case, that is in itself a sign of a considerable political risk involved in the transaction and the seller should then consider if collection really is the most suitable form of payment, or if a letter of credit would not be more appropriate. If the documents are to be released against acceptance, a term draft/bill of exchange issued by the seller should also be included. But even if the documents are to be released against payment it is still common that an 'at sight' or 'on demand' draft is included for the following reasons:

- It will show the total amount due for collection, which will avoid misunderstandings where several invoices and credit notes are included.
- It will show the name of the company to whom presentation should be made, which is not always the same as in the documents.
- It is in itself a request for payment, with a reference to the underlying contractual obligation of the buyer as shown in the enclosed documents.

LETTER OF CREDIT

The letter of credit is a combination of a bank guarantee issued by a bank upon the request of the buyer in favour of the seller and a payment at sight or at a later stage against presentation of documents which conform to specified terms and conditions. This is more strictly defined in the new 2007 revision of ICC Uniform Customs and Practice for Documentary Credits, under which rules practically every L/C is issued. According to these rules, the documentary credit/letter of credit means any arrangement, however named or described, that is irrevocable and thereby constitutes a definite undertaking by the issuing bank to honour a complying presentation. This sentence involves two major expressions which will be described in detail later in this chapter, namely:

- The expression 'complying presentation', which means that the documents pre-sented should be in accordance with the terms and conditions of the L/C, but also in accordance with the UCP 600 rules and with international standard banking practice;
- The expression 'honour', which allows three different possibilities for payment to be made upon presentation of compliant documents, either at sight, by deferred payment or by acceptance of a bill of exchange.

The L/C is normally advised to the seller through another bank but without engagement for that bank, unless instructed otherwise. The advising bank is usually located in the seller's country and its role is to take reasonable care to check the authenticity of the L/C and to advise the seller according to its instructions. The L/C has many advantages for the seller. Payment is guaranteed and there are fewer concerns about the buyer's ability to pay or about other restrictions or difficulties that may exist or arise in the buyer's country - but only if the seller can meet all the terms and conditions stipulated in the L/C.

There are also advantages for the buyer when using an L/C. While it is considerably more expensive than other forms of payment and has to be issued under existing credit limits with the buyer's own bank, the buyer is assured that the stipulated documents will not be paid unless they conform to the terms of the L/C. This may be very important for the buyer in some cases, particularly in connection with goods where fulfilment of special shipping arrangements is essential or in the case of deliveries where timing may be the crucial factor.

With regard to cost, an L/C is sometimes of such importance to the seller that the buyer may be able to obtain fair compensation or even a better deal overall, if able to offer a form of payment that, in principle, eliminates the seller's commercial and political risks. The L/C can be issued in many ways, depending on how it is going to be used, and the design will vary in each case. However, an L/C has certain general features that must be included in each case, particularly with regard to:

- Period of validity;
- Time for payment;
- Place of presentation of documents;
- Level of security; and
- Documents to be presented.

PERIOD OF VALIDITY

According to the old ICC rules, an L/C could be either irrevocable or revocable, but under the present rules in force since July 2007, L/Cs governed by these rules are always irrevocable, which means that they are without exception binding undertakings on behalf of the issuing bank to honour complying documents presented to either the issuing bank or any nominated bank within the stipulated period of validity.

It is therefore no longer necessary to specify that the L/C is irrevocable, but on the other hand there is no harm in doing so either. The nominated bank where the documents must be presented within the validity of the L/C can be any bank specified as such in the L/C.

In most cases it is the advising bank, but that does not mean that this bank is under an obligation to pay. Only the issuing bank is under such obligation, unless this undertaking is also guaranteed by some other bank, which will be described later.

TIME FOR PAYMENT

An L/C must stipulate when payment is to be made to the seller. It can be payable either at sight or at a specified time thereafter, by deferred payment or by acceptance. An L/C at sight will be paid on presentation of documents, either at the issuing bank, the advising bank or any other nominated bank. If payment is to be effected at a later stage, normally a specified time after shipment or after presentation of documents as specified in the L/C, this can be done either through presentation of a bill of exchange or by a stipulated deferred payment in the terms of the L/C, which allows that bank to effect payment at the later specified date. In the case of both acceptance and deferred payment, the issuing bank is guaranteeing payment on the due date and based on that guarantee; the seller may generate instant liquidity through discounting or through advance payment from their bank while finance is provided to the buyer during the same period.

Apart from the extended period of risk on the issuing bank, the difference for the seller between an L/C at sight and a term L/C is then mainly a question of interest for the credit period and related bank charges and commissions.

PLACE OF PRESENTATION OF DOCUMENTS

When referring to the place of presentation of documents under an L/C, this is a question of the place where the documents are to be payable. Unless the L/C is payable only with the issuing bank, this bank must authorize another bank to pay, incur a deferred payment or accept drafts - if all terms and conditions have been complied with. In the case of a freely negotiable L/C, any bank is the nominated bank and presentation of the documents can then be at any place.

Seen from the seller's perspective, the best place to present the documents is at the advising bank in their country, for reasons explained below. As pointed out above, unless it has also confirmed the L/C, the advising or nominated bank is under no obligation to take up the documents when presented by the seller, if at that time this bank - at its own discretion - is uncertain whether the issuing bank will be able to fulfil its obligations to reimburse them for such payment. On the other hand, if the L/C is only payable with the issuing bank, usually but not always domiciled in the country of the buyer, that bank will make payment or accept the term bill of exchange if the terms and conditions are complied with.

But, even in this case, the advising bank, or any nominated bank, where the documents are presented before they are forwarded to the issuing bank, may still negotiate the documents at presentation and advance funds to the seller, but such negotiation is then made with recourse to the seller until the issuing bank has approved the documents and reimbursed the negotiating bank. There are thus many reasons why it is more advantageous for the seller to have the documents under the L/C payable with the advising bank at their domicile, because:

- The payment/acceptance will take place at the earlier stage when the documents are delivered to and approved by the advising bank.
- In case of discrepancies or other faults in the documentation, it may be much easier and quicker to remedy these directly with the advising bank before the documents are forwarded to the issuing bank.

- The seller avoids any postal risk and other delays from the issuing bank until payment is made and effectively transferred to the seller.

However, what is an advantage for the seller could also be a disadvantage for the buyer, who normally, for the same reasons as above, often prefers the L/C to be payable with the issuing bank only. This question has to be decided in each case but, in many countries, local practice will influence this outcome. In some countries this matter may be subject to specific rules or established practice, mostly working in the buyer's favour.

If it is agreed in the terms of payment that the L/C should be payable at the advising bank, that should also be openly stated in its terms and appear in its reimbursement instructions to the advising bank, to enable this bank to make it payable at its counters. But, if nothing is stated to that effect, the L/C might be deemed payable at the issuing bank only. The seller's own bank will know what local practices, if any, are applicable in different countries.

LEVEL OF SECURITY

The issuing bank always guarantees an L/C for the entire period of its validity without exception. However, many countries have such economic and/or political problems that the seller may be uncertain if the issuing bank can fulfil its obligations and/or is able to transfer the amount out of the country in a freely convertible currency. New and deteriorating events may also take place in the country during the validity of the L/C and, in such cases, the advising bank may refuse to take up the documents until reimbursement is first received from the issuing bank. To cover the payment obligations of the issuing bank, the seller can also have the L/C confirmed by the advising bank. This is usually made upon request from the issuing bank based upon instructions from the buyer, according to the agreed terms of payment in the sales contract.

Such confirmation may occasionally, although more often as an exception, also be made directly by the advising bank upon request of the seller, without the issuing bank being aware of it. This silent confirmation is also sometimes given by separate forfaiting or other financial institutions in the form of a payment guarantee, if the advising bank for some reason is not willing to do so. The request for confirmation involves a potential risk to the issuing bank or their country, which the seller's bank may or may not be prepared to enter into without additional cover.

The reason may be that the risk to the buyer's bank or the country is not acceptable, or that the seller's bank already has such a high level of exposure to that bank or country that their internal limits are fully used. In such cases, the bank may sometimes be able to apply for a bank letter of credit cover to either a private insurance company or mostly to the domestic export credit agency, which is established by governments in the larger trade countries. Such guarantees are based on the assessment made by the insurer of the commercial/political risk to the issuing bank and the risk period involved. The guarantee normally provides cover to the confirming bank of between 50 and 1

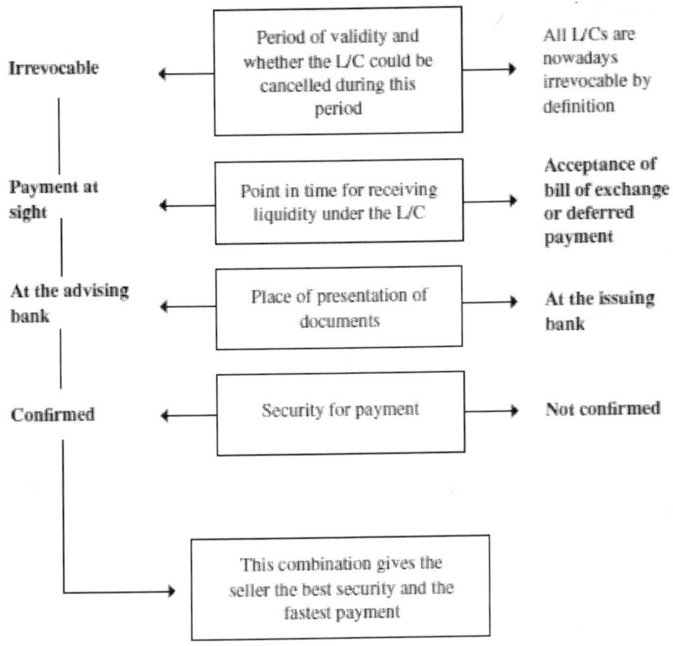

Fig. Key Aspects of a Letter of Credit

In some countries L/Cs are more or less always confirmed in principle, whereas in other countries that is not normally the case. However, between these two categories there are also many other countries where both alternatives are used. The cost for a confirmation is normally calculated per quarter and varies depending on the assessed risk involved and the length of such confirmation. The buyer and seller have to agree whether the advising bank should confirm the L/C or not. In some cases, agreeing on a more internationally recognized bank as the issuing bank might provide enough additional security for the seller without the need for a confirmation. In some cases an international bank may be necessary in order for the advising bank to be willing to add its confirmation. Regarding more 'problematic' countries, this is something the seller should discuss with their bank prior to negotiations with the buyer, and if needed, get commitment from this bank to confirm any L/C that may be the outcome of the negotiations. Such commitments are often issued by the banks against a commitment fee.

OTHER COMMON FORMS OF LETTERS OF CREDIT

It is relatively common that someone other than the seller makes the actual delivery, for example when they are acting as agent, using independent suppliers or having an intermediary function in the transaction. In these cases it can be advantageous to have the L/C expressly stated as being transferable, which permits the seller to transfer the rights and obligations under the L/C to another beneficiary, a business partner or some other supplier who will make the actual delivery. The transferable L/C can be transferred only when it relates to identical goods and with the same terms and conditions as in the master L/C, with the exception of amount, unit price, shipping period and expiry date - or any earlier date of presentation - which may be reduced or curtailed.

When later presenting the documents under the master L/C, the seller is also allowed to exchange the suppliers' invoices for their own. However, if the goods to be delivered by other suppliers need to be changed, upgraded or altered before delivery to the ultimate buyer, then the goods may no longer be identical and the L/C may not be used as transferable. In such cases it can nevertheless often be used as supplementary security against which one or more new L/Cs, so-called 'back-to-back credits', can be issued by the advising bank on the seller's behalf in favour of their suppliers and with payment out of documents to be presented under the master L/C.

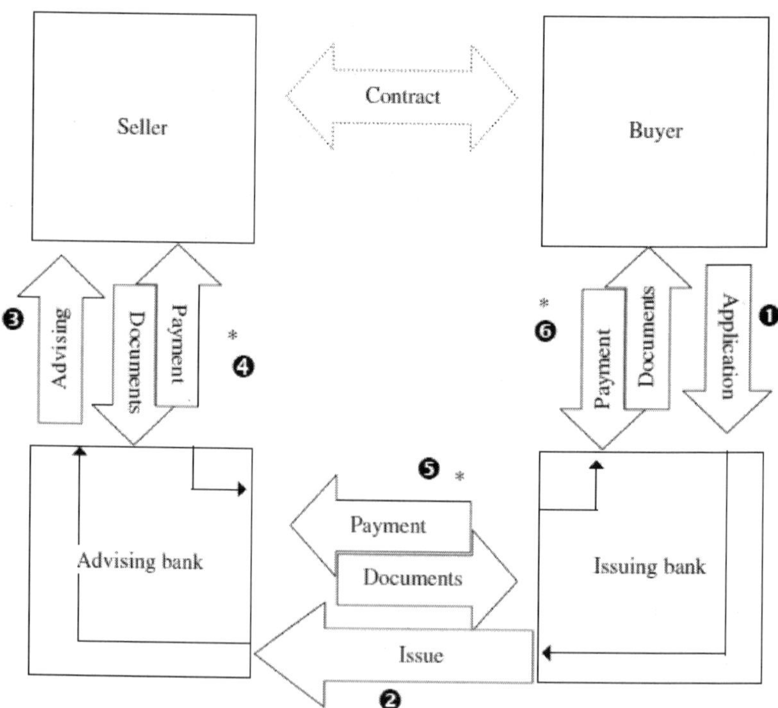

*Payment could also alternatively be acceptance or deferred payment, depending on the stipulations in the L/C.

1. After signing the contract, it is up to the buyer to take the first step by applying to their bank to issue the agreed L/C.
2. The issuing bank must process a formal credit approval of the application and check that local permissions, import licences or currency approvals, if needed, have been granted. When all formalities and procedures have been dealt with, the L/C is issued, hopefully as stipulated in the terms of payment, and forwarded to the selected advising bank.
3. Upon arrival of the L/C from the issuing bank - by letter, fax or mostly nowadays as a SWIFT message - the advising bank will assess its contents and determine where it should be made payable. If the advising bank is instructed to add its confirmation, this involves a separate credit decision in this bank, after which the seller is notified of the L/C and its details, including information about where it is to be honoured for payment acceptance or deferred payment, and whether it has been confirmed by the advising bank.

   At this point, it is vital that the seller checks the terms of the L/C against the agreed terms of payment to make sure that all the details and instructions can be met at a later stage when the documents are to be produced and delivered. If not, the seller must immediately communicate directly with the buyer so that the necessary amendments are made and confirmed to the seller through the banks. Only then does the seller have the security on which the whole transaction is based.
4. After shipment the seller receives the transport documents and prepares the other documents required. Checks are also made to ensure that they conform to the terms of the L/C, but equally important, that the contents of the documents presented are consistent between themselves.

   The documents are then forwarded to the advising bank, which checks their conformity with the terms of the L/C. The seller is contacted about any discrepancies. Discrepancies that cannot be corrected at this late stage, for example wrong shipping details or late presentation, will be subject to later approval by the buyer, and any payment made by the advising bank will then be with recourse, subject to this approval.
5. The issuing bank will also check the documents and the buyer has to consider any discrepancies. When approved, or if the documents are compliant, the buyer has to pay. If not approved, the documents will be held at the disposal of the advising bank, pending any new negotiation between the buyer and the seller of the terms for such an approval, or ultimately returned to the advising bank against

repayment of any earlier payment made with recourse to the seller.

6. The documents are released to the buyer against payment at sight or at any later date as stipulated in the L/C.

Sometimes the expression 'red clause letter of credit' is used in international trade, referring to a special clause that can be inserted in the L/C. Through such a clause the seller can receive an advance payment for part of the value of the L/C before presentation of shipping documents enabling them to purchase raw material or to meet other costs prior to receiving full payment upon presentation of conforming documents. However, such a clause creates an additional risk for the buyer who cannot be sure that final documents will be presented under the L/C, and a red clause arrangement is now seldom used other than as part of the overall agreement between the parties when forming the sales contract. If the L/C is to be used for repeat shipments under a long-term contract or for similar shipments to the same buyer over longer periods, it could be practical to have it issued as a 'revolving letter of credit', which is automatically reinstated to its original value after each presentation of documents or when reaching a certain lower level. However, this L/C must have a final due date and/or limits for the number of times it can be revolved.

ISSUING AND ADVISING LETTERS OF CREDIT ELECTRONICALLY

Nowadays, it is common practice in most countries that L/Cs are issued as SWIFT messages in a standardized format. This procedure facilitates both the issue of the L/C and authentication at the advising bank, which will then be able to advise it immediately to the seller. The box on pages 57-58 shows a standard SWIFT format. This example shows a freely negotiable L/C, available at sight with the issuing bank, and advised to the seller without the advising bank's confirmation.

Many major banks also advise L/Cs to the seller through their internet-based advising services, which means that the seller can expect to receive the L/C almost immediately after the bank receives it. In this form the L/C can then easily be distributed in a standardized electronic format to and within the company, thus increasing its effectiveness and reducing possible errors in transmission. The next phase in the chain, the presentation of documents, can also be completed electronically in some cases, but only if the L/C indicates that it is subject to the eUCP rules, which form a supplement to the new UCP 600 rules.

These rules should be seen both as a guide to how electronic presentation of documents should take place and how some often-used documents should be structured to conform to these rules. The main limitation in presenting all documents in this form seems to be the transport documents, which are not always available in an electronic format.

PRESENTATION OF DOCUMENTS

The characteristic feature of the L/C in international trade is that the undertaking of the issuing bank is only valid if the specified terms and conditions are fully complied with within the period of its validity. If this is not the case then the issuing bank and the buyer have the right to refuse payment. From the seller's perspective, not complying with all the terms of the L/C could reduce what was originally a bank guaranteed payment to a documentary collection without any such guarantee. This is the main reason why due fulfilment of all terms and conditions specified in the L/C is so important, and why this subject is discussed in such detail below.

As stated earlier, when the seller receives the L/C it is up to them to decide if it is in accordance with the contract and its terms of payment. However, the seller must then also ensure that all details specified in the L/C can be complied with when the documents are to be prepared for presentation at the bank. This requires both experience and caution for, if not accurately scrutinized and, if necessary, amended when the L/C is first received, it may be difficult to make corrections later. On the other hand, having an uncomplicated L/C and including only the essential documents and specifications, together with a reference to the underlying contract, is normally advantageous for both parties.

The documents most commonly used in connection with L/Cs are basically the same as were mentioned earlier in connection with documentary collections even if the stipulations in the L/C are usually more detailed as to how, and by whom, they should be issued. As can be seen in the examples in Chapter 8, wording may also be inserted in the terms of payment to the effect that the L/C should be issued 'in form and substance acceptable to the seller according to contract'. This wording is suggested in order for the seller to have a stronger case when arguing for amendments, should the L/C technically be issued according to the contract but, at the same time, contain additional details or stipulations that will restrict or potentially prevent the seller from fulfilling all conditions at a later stage when the documents are presented to the bank.

THIRD-PARTY DOCUMENTS

One general aspect that must be commented on at this stage is the importance of the seller being particularly observant with regard to documents that are to be produced, verified, stamped or signed by a third party, and also other terms and conditions in the L/C over which the seller may not have full control. When it comes to the documents, some of them, often the invoice, may have to be certified or legalized by a third party, often a chamber of commerce and/or the embassy of the importing country. If so, the seller has to make certain not only that such a procedure can take place, but that it can be done in time to comply with the dates of the L/C, primarily with regard to the due date of shipment or presentation of documents. The same check has to be made for any other third-party documentation, such as test certificates and inspection records.

The seller should also be aware of the interaction between the terms of delivery and the documents related to the L/C. Some terms of delivery stipulate that it is up to the buyer to arrange transportation, after which the transportation documents, for example, the bill of lading, can be released. Some buyers often try to arrange transportation themselves, in some cases with ships from their own country, perhaps because they have established contacts with the local shipping company, because import regulations need to be followed in order to support the country's shipping industry, or simply because it is cheaper and payment may be made in local currency.

For these reasons, the buyer might prefer FOB as their choice of terms of delivery; however, the buyer does not always have control of the shipping schedules, which might change, or the designated ship may re-route at short notice. Should this happen, the seller would not be able to load as planned and will conse-quently not be able to produce the bill of lading stipulated in the L/C - or will receive it too late to comply with the stipulated time frames. There are ways the seller can eliminate such risks if the parties cannot agree on more suitable terms of delivery, but they have to be agreed beforehand as part of the terms of payment and thereafter form part of the L/C. For example, the seller might stipulate an alternative to the bill of lading, such as a warehouse or other certificate, which they know can be arranged.

INSPECTION OF THE GOODS IN CONJUNCTION WITH DOCUMENTARY PAYMENTS

With regard to both documentary collections and L/Cs, the buyer has to honour the documents as presented, but normally without having seen the actual delivery. The documents may be scrutinized when presented for collection and the banks check their correctness under the L/C, but they have no responsibility for the genuineness or correctness of the information contained therein.

In many cases this may not be important; the parties may know each other through earlier transactions, the goods delivered can be standardized or well known to the buyer, and they can always claim compensation after delivery, whatever value that may have. But in other cases this question may be of greater importance to the buyer.

In particular, the seller must then find other ways to satisfy the buyer in order for them to agree to an L/C. This can be done through the inclusion of a separate certificate of inspection in the documentation, issued by an independent surveyor who verifies the goods before delivery through samples or production surveys. Such arrangements must form part of the contract and the certificate should be included in the required documents in the terms of payment.

FREQUENT DISCREPANCIES IN DOCUMENTATION

Apart from genuine mistakes in preparing the documentation, some of the more frequent discrepancies include:

- The expiry date of the L/C has passed.
- Late presentation, ie the specified period of time after the date of shipment during which presentation should be made, has expired.
- Late shipment, ie the shipping document is signed too late or indicates shipment after the stipulated time of shipment.
- A document has not been presented or, if presented, has not been issued by a correct company or authority.
- Stipulated tolerances in credit amount, quantity, unit price or other variables have not been met.
- The shipping documents are not in accordance with the terms, for example loading/unloading in the wrong port or not on the specified ship, issued to the wrong order or wrongly endorsed.
- The insurance documents are incorrect, for example not covering the risks required or showing an incorrect insurance value - incorrectly endorsed or not explicitly indicating explicit statements as required in the L/C.
- Shipping details are incorrect, for example showing part shipments or transhipment, if not allowed, or the packing/marking is not in accordance with the terms.

Finally, not only must each document be issued as stipulated, but they must be consistent between themselves with regard to description of the goods, markings, etc. In practice, however, it is relatively common that this is not the case, owing to carelessness, last-minute changes or lack of documentary knowledge, but it should always be possible to avoid such potential discrepancies.

HOW TO AVOID DISCREPANCIES IN THE LETTER OF CREDIT

L/Cs that do not totally comply with the terms of the credit are dependent on the approval of the buyer and will, therefore, contain an additional risk that the seller did not anticipate when entering into the deal - if this risk had been known beforehand, the seller might not have entered into the transaction at all. As pointed out earlier, the bank guarantee incorporated in the L/C will then disappear and the L/C will, in practice, be transformed into a documentary collection.

In smaller trading companies, with high volumes of export sales with small margins, such an added risk is unacceptable and one such default could lead to bankruptcy. It is also among these trading companies that you often see real professionalism in dealing with L/Cs and the banks very seldom find discrepancies in their documents. Based on that experience, which can be achieved by all companies, there are at least some measures that can be taken to avoid such discrepancies:

- Many banks have letter of credit checklists, which contain valuable information on how to check the L/C and its required terms and conditions, both when the L/C is received and later on when the documents are presented.
- The new ICC rules contain detailed information about the more commonly used documents in international trade and what they generally should contain in order to be approved under the L/C, but should be read in connection with the new International Standard Banking Practices describing in detail the procedures for examining L/C documents.
- It is at the time of receipt of the L/C by the seller that it can be amended. Someone in the company must have direct responsibility for such internal approval so as to ensure that there are no problems now or in the future that might prevent the seller from delivering documents without discrepancies.
- The L/C should be payable at the advising bank if possible and the documents should be sent to that bank directly after shipment. This bank will then advise on any discrepancies and the seller will have time to amend the documents if and when it is possible to do so. Should that not be the case, it is usually an indication that the seller's own approval of the L/C when it was issued was incorrect; it should have been amended at that earlier stage.
- Timing is essential; always allow a longer period than expected for issuing the L/C and for shipment, presentation and expiry dates. Deliver the documents in good time before expiry in order to be able to make amendments, or deliver completely new documents, if necessary.
- Finally, the banks not only offer practical help on an ad hoc basis but some also offer additional services which could help the seller avoid discrepancies in the documents altogether, for example freight management and even export document preparation.

THE LETTER OF CREDIT AS A TOOL IN THE BUSINESS PROCESS

The advantage of using an L/C is not only the security it gives to the seller, but also its flexibility and adaptability in helping to solve complicated business problems and, thereby, creating the base for additional business. This enables the seller to offer reasonable advantages to the buyer in return for acceptance of an L/C, for example extended credit on favourable terms, or sharing bank charges. It is true that once a contract has been signed and the L/C issued, any later amendments will demand corresponding amendments in the L/C as well, and that may take time and involve additional costs for the transaction as a whole.

But before that time, almost any transaction can be structured in a way that allows the L/C to function as the glue which holds the deal together and protects the interests of both parties. When the L/C is thereafter correctly issued, both the seller and the buyer know in advance that they are safeguarded in a way that can be controlled by one and the same payment instrument and guaranteed by at least one of the participating banks. Some examples of how the L/C can be used as part of a more complicated business transaction are given below:

- Clauses can be included whereby the seller can arrange necessary start-up prepara-tions for the forthcoming delivery, either at home or in the buyer's country.
- Separate procedures can be arranged to secure the fulfilment of the obligations of the buyer in connection with installation and other necessary arrangements prior to delivery.
- If required by the buyer, both tests and samples as well as the process of production and final delivery of the goods can be monitored or verified by using independent inspection certificates under the L/C.
- The transferability of an L/C makes it possible for the seller to arrange for multiple or combined deliveries without added security or liquidity.
- Arrangements for different types of barter-trade transactions can also be connected to the underlying contract and covered by a combination of L/Cs.
- Arrangements for different supplier or buyer credits with repayment with or without coverage under the L/C can be arranged, at the same time giving credit to the buyer and cash payment to the seller.
- Increased business opportunities are generally available to the seller when using the L/C as supplementary security for pre-financing during the period of purchase, production and delivery.

THE LETTER OF CREDIT AS A PRE-DELIVERY FINANCE INSTRUMENT

As a guaranteed payment, subject to fixed and known terms and conditions in the individual case, the L/C can also be used as part of the pre-financing needed in order to produce and deliver the goods. This may be particularly important in cases of longer production and delivery periods or in single large transactions, when the pre-delivery period often is the most difficult to finance, a period before a clear claim on the buyer normally can be obtained. Many such transactions may require pre-financing on a scale that could exceed the seller's ordinary credit limits, even when ignoring any supplier credit given to the buyer, and the L/C may be the tool to close this gap. The financial consequences of each transaction are directly connected to its size, structure and time of payment, combined with additional demands on the seller for credits and guarantees, perhaps starting several months before delivery and payment, for example:

- demand for performance and/or advance payment guarantees;
- acquisition of raw material or additional/changed production facilities;
- additional contracts with suppliers or subcontractors with a payment structure independent of the underlying contract;
- additional bonds or guarantees covering shipment obligations or insurance;
- additional running costs covering production and delivery.

These additional expenditures, including the costs for insurance cover and necessary reserves for unforeseen events, have to be taken out of the seller's own resources and existing credit limits, but often the financial advantages that the L/C in itself can generate may be needed as well. In these circumstances, it is particularly important to get the buyer to accept the L/C as the method of payment, in order for the seller to be able to arrange the supplementary financing that the transaction will require - even if the seller has to compensate the buyer by taking part of the bank charges involved or giving concessions in other areas of the contract.

With this in mind, the advantage of having the L/C transferable is obvious; the possibility of transferring it on to other suppliers will relieve cash-flow pressures from the seller and these suppliers will get the same pre-delivery advantages of knowing what terms and conditions will apply in order to receive payment. Even if the L/C is not made transferable, it could be used as a master L/C and supplementary security for new back-to-back L/Cs in favour of the suppliers, with the same advantage to them as a transferable L/C would have had. Even without such an arrangement, or if it is already used for additional finance elsewhere, its mere existence may indirectly help the seller in obtaining new or extended credit from the suppliers involved in the transaction.

Many banks, acting as advising banks, offer special export loans or similar facilities, with a percentage of the value of the L/C as additional working capital, to be repaid from the proceeds upon presentation of documents. Such loans are often backed by a pledge on the underlying L/C. The L/C may also be used as an important tool in arranging different forms of pre-delivery finance, not least when combined with pre-shipment credit insurance policies. Such policies cover the commercial and/or political risks of the transaction from the time when the sales agreement is signed, but may be dependent on the seller having received some form of additional security, for example an L/C, covering at least part of the buyer's obligations. These policies, covering the entire transaction, would strongly facilitate the seller's pre-delivery financial requirements.

COUNTER-TRADE

So far, the assumption has been that goods are delivered against payment, at sight or at a later date. But there are other forms of transactions, where payment or settlement, wholly or partially, is made in some other way. The word 'counter-trade' is in itself a general term, representing various types of connected transactions or reciprocal arrangements that are linked to each other in a larger structure, necessary for the completion of the individual transactions. The terminology may vary, but the following terms are often used to describe the most common forms of alternative trade transactions:

- barter trades - with payment in other goods;
- compensation trades - with payment partly in money but also in other goods or services to balance the transaction, agreed between the parties;
- repurchase agreements - in which payment is made through products, generated by the equipment or goods delivered by the seller;
- offset counter-trades - mostly with settlement in money, but with the transaction being dependent on corresponding sales/purchase transactions to balance the payment stream.

There are many reasons why these alternative trade transactions are used, but at least four main reasons are often referred to, namely:

- To enable trade to take place in markets which are unable to pay for imports. This can occur as a result of a non-convertible currency, a lack of commercial credit or a shortage of foreign exchange.
- To protect or stimulate the output of domestic industries and to help find new export markets.
- As a reflection of political and economic policies which seek to plan and balance overseas trade.
- To gain a competitive advantage over competing suppliers.

Pure barter trade or other forms of counter-trade are the oldest forms of trade, today often associated with countries with a state-regulated economy. But it is also commonly used in many other countries around the world; some estimates indicate that up to a quarter of all world trade is in this form, even if no one really knows the exact figures. Apart from extremely large or complex transactions, particularly within the areas of defence, nuclear installations and complete production plants, large aircraft deals or similar transactions, most other counter-trade transactions are made with or between developing countries - or other countries with a non-competitive or regulated trade system or a non-convertible currency. But sometimes it is the character of the deal itself, its size and complexity, rather than the importing country, that necessitate these transactions, often structured through specialized trading houses that have the overall knowledge and expertise for creating new trading combinations that would otherwise probably not have made the export part of the combined deal possible.

The terms of payment in these transactions are dependent on the structure of the deal, and the participation of the banks may be totally different compared to ordinary transactions with payment in currency. In real barter-trade situations, only a designated clearing account may be needed in order to register the value of the transactions and the net balance of the flow of goods. When it comes to other forms of counter-trade, the banks often have a more central role, often through the use of L/Cs, all of them being structured to come into force simultaneously when all other arrangements are in place and approved by the individual trading partners. But thereafter, they could often be handled as individual transactions, with each L/C being settled separately.

EXAMPLE OF A SIMPLE COUNTER-TRADE TRANSACTION

As an example of how the mechanism of a simple counter-trade could work, a US seller of machine equipment has made a deal with a buyer in Honduras. In order to finance the deal, a US trading house has arranged with a Hong Kong company to buy raw sugar from another company in Honduras for the equivalent amount, which the Hong Kong company plans to sell to an African buyer. In this example, the Hong Kong company has to take the first step by instructing their bank to issue an L/C in favour of their seller in Honduras, but its validity has to be conditional upon a second L/C being issued by a bank in Honduras in favour of the US seller. Such a clause could have the following wording in the first L/C to be issued, in order to create the security for the combination of transactions that form the counter-trade:. This letter of credit is not operational until:

- Banco Central, Honduras, has issued through US Commercial Bank, New York as advising bank, a letter of credit for the amount of USD 1,000,000, covering shipment of coffee grinding equipment, in favour of US Grinding Machinery Inc., Boston. The letter of credit should be payable at sight with the advising bank and contain instructions to this bank to add its confirmation.
- The advising bank has confirmed that US Grinding Machinery has approved the terms and conditions of the letter of credit above.

When both L/Cs are issued, they will become operative at the same time, but can thereafter be settled as separate transactions, or alternatively be structured in such a way that payments received under one L/C can be used as outgoing payments under the other in order for the transactions to be liquidity and currency neutral. It is then advantageous if both L/Cs are payable at the same bank, which, in this case, will use the payments from the Hong Kong buyer to pay the US seller upon due fulfilment of the terms and conditions under the L/C. In the same way, the payments between the companies in Honduras are settled between their banks, often in local currency.

COUNTER-TRADE ARRANGEMENTS - A SUMMARY

Counter-trade transactions are by definition a complex area of trade. This is largely due to the fact that the seller often lacks the overall knowledge of potential goods or products suitable or available to arrange the total deal and also because they often do not have direct contact with other potential commercial parties. The structure becomes more complicated in these combined transactions and the risk involved more difficult to assess and to cover. Counter-trade transactions also often involve countries with a potentially high risk profile, including both convertible and non-convertible foreign currencies.

Such transactions demand longer arrangement periods and incur higher transactional costs. The risk of outside pressure for illegal practices, such as bribery or facilitation payments, may also be higher compared to more standard trade transactions. Equally, the reward could be high to compensate for all these real or potential risks.

The seller therefore seldom acts alone in this type of trade, but normally through or in cooperation with specialized trading houses or international banks that have this expertise. There are also a number of domestic or regional counter-trade associations offering the same services, but the trading parties are generally advised to check with their bank or their trade council or export organization to find a partner that has the relevant knowledge and reputation.

3

Export Management

INTRODUCTION

Management is a term commonly used in every activity. It means planning, organizing, directing, controlling and coordinating the specific activity so as to achieve its objective. Such activity may be related to purchase, production, and marketing and as well export. Export management means conducting the export activity in an orderly, efficient and profitable manner. Since the heart of each business is marketing, export management can be termed as export marketing management.

Because if needs to be managed efficiently so that the export should increase and exporter should get more profit and importer should get more satisfaction. Therefore export management activity is growth oriented and dynamic in nature. Export marketing management and domestic marketing management are two aspects of the same coin *i.e.* total marketing management. However export marketing management is more difficult and complicated as compared to domestic marketing due to several factors such as, three faced competition, varied regulations of different countries, language, etc. If requires systematic approach for comprehensive oversea, marketing research: therefore export management involves the study of foreign markets, requirements, of foreign buyers, potential marketing opportunities and using and them tactfully for large-scale exporting. Export management is basically planning, organizing, coordinating and controlling all activities relating to export of goods and services to other counties.

It involves various activities such as production of exportable good, collection of orders from foreign buyers and their execution, publicity in abroad, adoption of sales promotion techniques, price fixation and looking after various procedures and formalities relating to exporting of goods. It is rightly said that export management involves functions and activities undertaken by the department/ division of a large manufacturing enterprise. The scope of export management is vast as everything concerned with exporting comes within the scope of export management. It is also argued that export management means what an export manager does.

DEFINITIONS OF THE EXPORT MANAGEMENT

The term export of management is rather difficult to define precisely as it is dynamic in scope. Secondly, standard definition of the term export management is not available as it is an applied subject. Here, the principles of management are applied to the management of export trade/ marketing activities. However, it is possible to note some simple definition of export management.

Such definitions are as noted below:

- Export management means managing export marketing activity efficiently, smoothly and in an orderly manner.
- Export management means finding at opportunities for marketing goods & services in foreign markets and exporting such opportunists for the benefit of an exporting firm, subject to existing export rules and regulations.
- Export management is one specific area of business management and it is concerned exclusively with exporting goods abroad. It is concerned with international marketing activities and operations.
- Export Management means planning, organizing, coordinating and control export efforts or activities to achieve desired export objectives smoothly and with continuance.
- According to B. S. Bathor, "Export Marketing includes the management of marketing activities for products across the national boundary or a country".

NEED FOR EXPORT MANAGEMENT

Increase in exports provides several benefits to exporter as well as the Nation, Export sector has been termed as a priority sector for Indian Economy. It is treated as an engine of economic growth and an instrument for employment generation. Government has made every effort to increase export, and raise the volume and value of exports. Better export, performance leads to do industrial development, economic development, foreign Exchange reserves, favourable balance of payment etc. All these benefits will be available only when exports are made at large scale.

In the early 1960s the slogan "Export or Perish" was coved by the then Prime Minster of India Pandit Jawaharlal Nehru. It is applicable even to present economic condition of India with a little change *i.e.* "Globalization or Perish". Therefore export promotion is rightly heated as a national challenge.

Therefore export management is receiving top priority in the country to take effective steps in the right direction for economic growth and prosperity.

We can discuss the need for export management at two different levels:

1. At the National level.
2. At the Business level.

NEED FOR EXPORT OR EXPORT MANAGEMENT AT THE NATIONAL LEVEL

Earning Foreign Exchange

Export management enables the country to earn foreign exchange.

The foreign exchange can be utilised for following purposes:

- Import of consumer good
- Imports of Raw materials, spares and components
- Import of capital goods and technology
- Servicing of External Debts.

International Relations

Export helps to develop international ties with importing countries due to the following reasons:

- The international trade brings together the exporters and importers of various countries.
- Trade talks take place between nations at international forums like WTO.
- Also, trade agreements are singed between Governments of participating counties.

Balance of Payments

A country's external economic strength depends upon its balance of payment position. Naturally, every country would like to have a strong and favourable balance of payments position since exports bring in foreign exchange, it helps a country to solve and improve its Balance of payments position.

Reputation in the World

Exports bring reputation and goodwill for a nation in the international markets.

For instance:

- Japan commands reputation for electronic products.

- India has goodwill for handicrafts including germs and jewellery.
- Germany is famous for engineering of goods.

Employment

Exports help to generate employment in the country Export facilitates:

- Direct Employment in the export sector
- Indirect Employment in the supporting sectors such as banking, insurance, transport etc.

Research and Development

In international markets, quality of products is of at most importance. Therefore, government provides assistance to exporters to undertake R&D.

R&D helps to:

- Reduce costs
- Develop new products
- Improve quality of existing products

The fruits of R&D benefit the consumers not only in the overseas markets but also in the domestic market.

Regional Development

Exports facilitate regional development of instance, about 1/3rd of India's exports are from small sector. The small units are located throughout India. (for instance, in India, The maximum number of small units, is located in the industrially backward state of Uttar Pradesh). Therefore, export sector contributes, towards regional development of a nation.

Optimum Use of Resources

Exports facilitate, optimum use of resources in the country, such as:

- Physical resources such as materials, machines, etc.
- Capital resources
- Man power

For instance, Gulf countries have enough supply of petroleum, which is exported, thereby making optimum use of resources.

Standard of Living

Exports increase demand, which leads to higher production and distribution. Increase in production and distribution generates more employment. Increase in employment leads, to higher purchasing power with the people. Therefore, people can enjoy new and better products, which improves standard of living

Economic Growth

Due to export, the demand increases. Increase in demand leads to higher production. Higher production increases the GDP of the country which leads to economic growth.

Spread Effect

Due to increases in export trade in the country service sector also expand, like banking, transport, etc. Similarly other ancillary industries are established to support the export activities.

NEED FOR EXPORT OR EXPORT MANAGEMENT AT BUSINESS LEVEL

Export Obligation

It means the firm which intends to import capital goods at concessional rates has to export the goods, under EPCG scheme. Thus the firm can fulfill its export obligation. In India, units operating in the SEZ are expected to honour export obligation against special concession offered to them.

Increase Production Capacity

For every business unit increase production is necessary, in order to meet domestic demand and export order. Exports are possible when surplus production is available after meeting domestic demand.

Organizational Efficiency

Export management enables a firm to improve its organizational efficiency. *E.g.* firms have to emphasize on training and development of employees. This helps to improve knowledge, attitudes, skills and social behaviours. Therefore, the over all efficiency of the organisation improves due to training, research and other much activities which are encouraged by export management.

Higher Profits

Export management enables a business unit to export quality goods at higher prices and there by raise the profit margin.

Reputation and Goodwill

Exports bring reputation to the export firm in international market as well as in the domestic market. It is assumed that export firms. Produce quality goods which help to develop goodwill. *e.g.* some of the world famous firms include.

- Microsoft for computer and Nike for Sports.
- Sony for Electronics etc.

Economies of Scale

Because of increase in export there will be large scale production and distribution.

This will result in:

- Economies of large scale production like discount in bulk purchase of material and reduce cost.
- Economies of large scale distribution such as freight concession on bulk shipment of goods.

Technological Up Gradation

Continuous research and development activities lead technological development and improvement in other organisational activities which help in improvement in quality standards which is beneficial to the form and customers both.

Imports are Liberalized

Business organisations exporting on a large scale collect huge foreign exchange which can be utilised for the import of new technology machinery and component. This also raises their competitive capacity.

Spreading of Marketing Risk

A firm engaged in domestic as well as export marketing activities can spread its marketing risk. The loss in domestic market can be compensated by the profit, earned in export market and vice versa.

Government Incentives

Exporter gets various assistances and incentives for export promotion. These are Duty Drawback, Octroi exemption, Excise duty exemption, Income tax exemption, liberal finance etc. These incentives make export marketing attractive and profitable. In present global trade, all countries developed as well as developing take special interest and initiative in making export trade at a very large scale. Thus large scale exports are necessary for survival and growth of developed as well as developing countries. Presently U.S.A., European counties, China, Japan, India, and many other countries, take special measure, for promoting export. This suggests the significance of exports to all counties developed, developing and even to poor counties. Therefore it is correct to say that, "Exports are necessary not only for developed counties but also for developing countries like India".

NATURE /FEATURES OF EXPORT MANAGEMENT

LARGE SCALE OPERATIONS

Export management involves large scale marketing and production operations of goods and services. Because of large scale business operation the firm gets the benefit of economics of scale and increase profit margin. Import, of other counties also prefer in placing large orders. Exporters get advantage of reduce cost and quoting competitive prices in the increase market.

SYSTEMATIC PROCESS

It is a systematic process became the export manager under takes various marketing activities such as marketing research, product design, branding, packaging, pricing, promotion etc. All these aspects require collection of data, analysis of data, then in perpetration of data in order to take systematic export marketing decisions.

THREE FACED COMPETITION

Foreign trade market is highly competitive in nature.

The competition is three dimensional i.e.:

- Competition from Indian exporters
- Competition from local producers of Importing country.
- Competition from exporter of other nations

TRADE BARRIERS

Export trade is subject to trade barriers tariff and nontariff barriers. The trade barriers are the restrictions on free movement of goods between countries. Normally countries impose trade barriers in order to restrict import. The export marketing manager must have a good knowledge of trade barriers imposed by importing counties.

DOMINATION OF MNC

Multinational Corporation has huge investment and conduct business operation all over the world. Major share of foreign trade is captured by MNCs, and TNCs, (Transnational corporations). Therefore they dominate in export management activities of the world. Due to large scale business they get the benefit of economies of scale.

DOMINATION OF DEVELOPMENT COUNTIES

Most of the MNCs belong to industrially developed countries. Such countries like USA, Japan, Germany etc. produce and sell good quality of goods at low cost on massive scale with the help of advanced technology. In this way rich and developed countries always dominate in international business activities.

FOREIGN EXCHANGE REGULATION

Export trade is subject to foreign exchange regulations imposed by countries. These foreign exchange regulations relate to payment and collection of export proceeds.

In addition, export marketing is subject to other rules and regulations relating to health and safety, environment protection, etc. All such regulation affect free movement of good among the countries.

DOCUMENTATION FORMALITIES

Export marketing is subject to various documentation formalities. Exporters require various documents to submit them to various authorities including customs, port trust, etc.

The documents include Bill of lading, Commercial consular invoice, Shipping bill, Certificate of origin etc:

- Shipping Bill
- Consular Invoice
- Certificate of Origin etc.

MARKETING MIX

Export marketing requires the right marketing mix for the target market, *i.e.* exporting the right product at the night price, at the right place and with the right promotion, the exporter can adopt different marketing mixes fro different export markets, so as to maximize exports and earn higher retunes.

INTERNATIONAL MARKETING RESEARCH

Knowing more about customers, dealers, and competitors is a must not only in the domestic markets but also in the export markets. Marketing research is a must in export business due to various factors, such as diversities on social, economic, and political environments of distant markets.

ADVANCE TECHNOLOGY

Export marketing is highly competitive. An exporter should be able to sell quality articles at competitive price. Use of advanced computer – oriented technology is a must for making the goods globally competitive. World markets are dominated by developed countries due to intensive use of computer technology.

GLOBALISE OR PERISH

Foreign trade is the need of each country. Because some important goods a country has to import like technology and goods which are not available in domestic market to export to get foreign exchange, otherwise it will perish economically.

SUBJECT TO REGULATION

Foreign exchange regulation may be imposed by importing countries. These may relate to payment and collections of export proceed. Similarly export trade is subject to other rules and regulations relating to health and safety, environment protection etc. All such regulations affect free movement of goods among the countries.

DIVERSE CUSTOMS AND TRADITIONS

The export markets differ in languages, customs and traditions. The exporter may not be able to cope up with these diversities. Therefore, he has to be selective, he should be deal in only such markets where he can easily handle or overcome such differences or diversities.

HIGH AMOUNT OF RISK

Export business is profitable than domestic business. But it is more risky also. Such as cancellation of order, non-collection of document, non-payment, transport risk, foreign regulation risk etc. these risk can be reduced by taking various insurance cover form ECGC and insurance agents. Risk can be spread also by exporting goods to many countries, so that loss in one market is compensated by the project other market.

SENSITIVE AND FLEXIBLE CHARACTER

An exporter has to identify the specific requirement or foreign buyers and design the goods accordingly, but some times because of technological development new design of good may be supplied by other exporters due to which demand for this goods may go down. Therefore exporter has to offer continuous support and loyalty.

FUNCTIONS OF AN EXPORT MANAGER

- To decide export objectives of the organization and prepare comprehensive short term and long term plans and progammes to achieve such objectives.
- To conduct marketing research so that export efforts will be concentrated on certain commodities and on foreign markets which are highly promising.

- To introduce product development and to produce quality goods as per specific needs of foreign markets/buyers.
- To execute long-term export promotion programmes for the products with promising overseas demand.
- To fix up the prices of exportable items with proper care.
- To find out new designs for packaging of export items.
- To look after the advertising and publicity abroad and to maintain effective communication with prospective buyers.
- To look after prompt execution of export orders so as to avoid inconvenience to foreign buyers.
- To analyze the EXIM policy of the government and the current export regulations and procedures.
- To look after the opening of new branches/offices aboard.
- To face the challenges of international competition and changing marketing environment.
- To evaluate export incentives/facilities offered by the government and to secure benefits from them.
- To look after the accounting and financial aspects of export transactions.
- To look after the training of staff working in the export division, to motivate them and to develop human relations.

In brief the functions of an export manager are to develop export markets for which he should plan, organize, direct and control the export marketing activities. Therefore the export manger should have a clear understanding of there major export marketing functions. Planning the export marketing activities is very important in order to avoid bottleneck, which may be proved expensive in foreign market. Organizing expert marketing system requires and understanding of fundamental organizational concepts.

EXPORT ORGANIZATION STRUCTURAL DESIGNS

Marketing system required an understanding of fundamental organization concepts and basic organizational principle. The organisational system must be capable of carrying out the export marketing plan, while the plans can be easily adjusted, taking into consideration the latest development most organizations are not that flexible while in the U. S. A. adjustments all made much more easily, these are almost impossible in Europe. This is even more true in Japan the organizational export marketing system might be viewed as a legal organizational structure, a formal organi-zational structure, formal organizational structure and an informal organizational. The foreign legal aspects and cultures setting of the export firm play an important role here.

The export manager may also keep in mind the following basic ways or organizing export marketing operations:

- Organizing the export marketing operations by sub-functions such as pricing, promotion and transportation.
- Organizing the export marketing activities by product groups.
- Organizing the export of marketing effort according to the uses of he product, the customer.
- Organizing the export marketing systems geographically.

Export organizations very often use a combination of these basic methods. Once the export marketing activities are planned and the export marketing system is organized the export manager faces the task of direction the export marketing operations and controlling the export marketing efforts. Directing sales forces in Kuwait is quite different from directing a sales force in the U.S.A. understating of foreign culture and sociological structure is vital. While autocratic approach might work in federal republic of Germany, it is the motivation, approach which is successful in U.S.A A well developed marketing plan might serve as a controlling device.

Probably, the most important task for the export manger is the development of an export marketing strategy. If we define strategy as a system of plans, then it requires a careful coordination and integrations of the various sub-plans must be developed for each major export marketing instrument. These sub plans must be co-ordinate and integrated into an export marketing plan for a given market abroad. Besides horizontal integration, a vertical co-ordinate sub-plans and area marketing plans must be brought together in an overall global marketing plan for the company. An exporter can adopt any of the following types of organizational structural designs-

IN-BUILT EXPORT DEPARTMENT

In this type, organization's activities are divided into various units like purchase, production, finance, domestic marketing and export marketing also. The export marketing unit is headed by export manger. He explores export opportunities, for the organization. He can also take helps of other departments for arranging the good in export market like production, finance, advertising, distribution etc. Since this structure is at the initial stage of export, the organization does not have adequate and efficient staff for export.

INDEPENDENT EXPORT DIVISION

This may be second stage or organize structure for export. In this case the business organization may have a separate export division. It will have its own full fledged competent staff. All the activities of export are handled by the export division. The export division may be located near the port so that all the necessary formalities like clearing forwarding of documents can be easily done. The export division can also take help from export promotion organisations and other government officers.

EXPORT SUBSIDIARIES IN SEVERAL MARKETS

Where the exports are on a large scale and more of long term nature, then the exporter may start an export subsidiary to undertake export activities in connection with marketing research, product planning and development, pricing, promotion, physical distribution as well as marketing of export goods. However a subsidiary can be introduced only for the purpose of export marketing.

EXPORT SUBSIDIARY IN IMPORTER'S COUNTRY

When the organization has been developed in MNC. It has large investment and technology then it will be suitable to establish an export subsidiary in the foreign country to undertake export marketing. The foreign subsidiary may undertake production and marketing activities or only export marketing which ever is suitable.

GEOGRAPHIC STRUCTURE OF EXPORT ORGANIZATION

This is again one step forward. The export organization can be divided into various department *e.g.* there can be departments looking after export marketing in specific export areas, like departments looking after export to ASEAN countries EEC countries, Middle East countries etc.

PRODUCT ORGANIZATION STRUCTURE

In this case the export organization can be decided on the basis of product levels. Thus there can be separate, department for each product line. *E.g.* there can be a department monitoring exports of engineering goods, readymade garments etc.

SUMMARY

Export management means conducting the export activity in an orderly, efficient and profitable manner. Exports provide several benefits to the exporter and the Nation. Export is essential for the Nation for: Earning foreign exchange, developing international relations, Balance of payment, reputation, employment, research and development, regional development, optimum use of resources, standard of living, economic growth etc. Export is essential at business level also for: increases production capacity, improve organizational efficiency, higher profit, reputation and goodwill, large scale of production and distribution, technical up gradation, spreading of marketing risks, getting government incentives etc.

The main features of Export management are: large scale operations, systematic process, three faced competition, trade barriers, domination of MNCs, domination of developed countries, foreign exchange regulation, various documentation formalities, right marketing mix, international research, advance technology, globalize or perish, diverse customs and traditions, high amount of risk sensitive and flexible character etc. There are different organization structures such as In-built export department, Independent export division, Export subsidiaries in several markets, Export subsidiaries in Importer's country, Geographic structure of Export organization, Product organization structure.

4

Documentation and Preparation of Vouchers

DEFINITION OF DOCUMENT

A document is a bounded physical or digital representation of a body of information designed with the capacity to communicate. A document may manifest symbolic, diagrammatic or sensory-representational information. To document is to produce a document artifact by collecting and representing information. In prototypical usage, a document is understood as a paper artifact, containing information in the form of ink marks. Increasingly documents are also understood as digital artifacts. Colloquial usage is revealed by the connotations and denotations that appear in a Web search for document.

From these usages, one can infer the following typical connotations:

- Writing that provides information person's thinking by means of symbolic marks.
- A written account of ownership or obligation.
- To record in detail; "The parents documented every step of their child's development".
- A digital file in a particular format.
- To support or supply with references; "Can you document your claims?".
- An artifact that meets a legal notion of document for purposes of discovery in litigation.
- Document is the practical construct for describing matter in different forms which retain information for a reasonable period of time wherein it can be perceived by a sentient observing entity.

The variety usage reveals that the notion of document has rich social and cultural aspects besides the physical, functional and operational aspects:

- Document is just a practical concept which presently would be defined narrowly based on human understanding and perception of the external world.

- Document in its wider connotation could include matter in all its forms, even a universe could be perceived as a document on a wider scale.
- The practical construct requires the retention of information but the relevance of the information
- The information must also be with reference to the observing entity be retained for a reasonable period of time wherein it can be observed. Fleeting images which cannot be seen are almost as if never observed.

CONCEPTUALIZATION IN ANALYTICAL PHILOSOPHY

The notion of document admits both an empirical and analytical characterization. The analytical characterization hinges on the semantic character of the word document, as well as the use of a primitive notion of document in accounts of larger communication constructs such as discourses, or related constructs such as language games. The nominal 'document', like other nominals, exhibits familiar patterns of polysemy.

For example, "document" might be used on an occasion to denote a certain body of information independently of how that information is physically rendered, or it might be used to denote a particular physical instantiation of a body of information. This kind of polysemy bears some similarity to what Nunberg, 1979 termed "container/contents polysemy". These patterns of polysemy exhibited by 'document' matter for the following reason.

A certain document qua body of information will have different properties than a document qua physical rendering of a body of information. Importantly, the latter would have the property of being a static, physically bounded thing. The former would have the properties of being able to evolve over time, being susceptible of certain changes to information content, and being capable of supporting multiple physical instantiations that have allowable differences in information content. This distinction is relevant to the discussion of aspects and history of documents below.

EMPIRICAL CHARACTERIZATION

In light of the polysemy of the core concept of document, it is useful to note a number of examples ranging from instances commonly understood as prototypical documents, to instances that are understood as documents only in specialized or rare situations.

- *Prototypical Documents*: Letters, memos, legal forms, owners manual
- *Documents of Record*: Newspapers, magazines
- *Books*: Textbooks, novels, cookbooks, encyclopedias, comic books
- *Canonical Documents*: Code of law, statute, constitution, religious text

- *Transactional Documents*: Cheques, contracts, medical prescriptions, receipt, forms, Postage stamps
- *Functional Documents*: Portable Document Format files, PostScript files, XML files, e-mail
- *Non–Prototypical Documents*: Post-it notes, fortune cookie strips, maps, paintings, milk cartons, cereal boxes
- *Non–Classical Digital Documents*: Web pages, blogs, wikis
- *Boundary Examples*: The Pioneer plaque on the Pioneer 11 spacecraft, designed by astronomer Carl Sagan, and using information assumed to be universal is an extreme example of a document that is intended to communicate with aliens. Conversely, the recorded and printed signals of the SETI project would constitute documents if they were discovered to contain alien communication.

SOCIAL ASPECTS OF DOCUMENTS

Documents play a key role in the construction of social reality and therefore play a part in accounts of every important aspect of human society and culture. An example of this type of account is in the seminal account of the role of print in political evolution, Imagined Communities. More direct examples include the works of Marshall McLuhan. Many key social aspects of documents arise from their historically unchanging character.

This aspect leads to a definition of a document as a talking thing, whose strengths and weaknesses both arise from its relative immutability with respect to oral forms of communication. The relative immutability of documents has thus historically been important for establishing a record of transient events, or for preserving information whose precise linguistic form is of ritual or practical importance. Note though, that historically many societies have accorded greater authority to disciplined oral traditions as more reliable than parallel written ones.

With this caveat in mind, the following social aspects of information may be noted:

- *Social Value*: The information in documents as well as documents themselves are often valuable; the information because of the influence represented, and the document itself when it is believed to be a rare or unique and authentic representation of the information it contains.
- *Manifestation of authority*: Documents are often produced to provide a record that will be considered authoritative in the future, particularly with respect to government. Consider receipts, titles, and deeds as examples of proof of ownership, and passports or driver's licenses as proof of identity.
- *Conventional*: Documents inherit a key feature of language-based

communication in general: they are denoted as documents by convention. Virtually any medium can constitute a document provided the people involved can agree on the meaning represented. Hence cave drawings, hieroglyphics, scrolls of sheepskin, sheets of papyrus, ink on paper, magnetic tape and electronic files are all documents under certain accounts.

- *Manifestation of economic labour*: Historically, the effort required to produce a document has been significant, so only the most important documents were created. The Illuminated manuscript of the pre-Gutenberg era demonstrates the cost have become richer.
- *Manifestation of business processes*: Documents play many roles in the internal management of a business as well in the interfaces between businesses and their suppliers, employees, and customers. Current trends towards longer value chains and increased regulation increase the number of documents that must be generated and processed.
- *Instruments of Governance and Law*: The unchanging aspect of documents is crucial to the consistent communication of policy and administration of law to citizens. Documents that play such roles include constitutions, corporate annual reports and religious texts.
- *Analytical philosophical character*: The notion of document plays a role in political philosophy, as well as in the philosophy of law
- *Role in Religion*: Documents play a key role in religion, and constitute canonical content. Document-related terms such as dogma and doctrine have today acquired pejorative connotations primarily due to historical events associated with religious documents.
- *Cultural Significance*: Documents play a central role in art of all varieties. In the movie Office Space for instance, central plot elements are frustration with bureaucratic process involving the fictional "TPS reports" and a malfunctioning printer.
- *Metaphoric Significance*: Metaphors based on documents permeate our thinking, ranging from the obvious to the highly allegorical.

FUNCTIONAL CHARACTERISTICS

Documents also manifest several, more localized characteristics that determine how we use them in everyday life:

- *Manifest nature*: Information is physical, *i.e.* it always must exist in a tangible form, even when digital. IBM computer scientist Rolf Landauer is credited with this observation and working out its implications. By virtue of being realizations of chunks of information, documents are necessarily physical in all their forms.
- *Contextuality and Situatedness*: All communication takes place in a context, which includes at least the shared understanding of the

parties communicating. Explicit and implicit references to the context can convey a large amount of meaning by building on the shared understanding, but that meaning is lost to another party that does not share that context. For example, Shakespeare in the original would be incomprehensible to modern readers simply because of the evolution of language and spelling since the seventeenth century, and modern readers normally read modernized versions. Similarly, hypertext documents exist in a context which is lost if printed, leading to a different offline reading context.

- *Evolvability*: When we think of a document as a definitive source containing the best known information about a topic there is need to change that information as more is learned. This is frequently done by revising the document into a new version or edition. Typically, older versions are archived to facilitate understanding how the document has changed. In modern contexts, when technologies such as wikis or software source code are under discussion, this evolvability can require very sophisticated version control technologies.
- *Renderability*: Every abstract entity that is understood to be a document in some context can be rendered, often in more than one way. A rendition of a document refers to a particular physical or electronic representation of the information from the document. For example, a portable document format representation and a web page may contain the same information but have substantially different properties and appearances. We think of them as different renditions of the same document. We might similarly consider different translations of a document to be the same document although differences in language context and structure may make it impossible to express precisely the same meaning in both languages.
- *Affordances*: Documents in digital and physical forms manifest various "affordances". The affordances of a particular rendition of a document determine its uses. For example, paper has the affordances of allowing flipping and easy tactile manipulation, while digital forms are easier to edit.

CLASSICAL ROLES AND WORKFLOWS IN DOCUMENT PRODUCTION

There are a number of roles in which people are involved in the creation and distribution of traditional paper documents; some, but not all documents are processed by people acting in each role, each of which may be performed by an individual or a group. Books are a well known example of documents that require an extensive publication process, but many other documents undergo similar processes to at least some of those from book publication.

Each of these roles is considered to improve or add value to a document. These roles are generally understood as being clustered in various phases in the production of a classical document, including authorship, editing and prepress.

Roles and workflows in the production of modern digital documents are more variable and are discussed in the part on future documents:

- An author selects the content to be communicated and performs the initial organization and recording of the content. A document in this state is often called a manuscript.
- A reviewer reads the content and evaluates it with respect to the intended audience. Reviewers often recommend only the best documents to be published. Documented reviews are frequently published as guidelines for document consumers as well.
- An editor helps to organize and express the content so that the meaning is clear and understandable, and follows the conventions of the symbolic representation such as spelling and grammar.
- A publisher orchestrates the process of producing a document, often decides whether a document is worth the effort of publishing, and collects and disseminates the profits from sales of a produced document.
- A printer formats the document into a comfortable form such as a bound book. Printing can be a very complex and elaborate process, including
  - *Pagination:* function performed by an individual who takes on the tasks of organizing text, fonts, images, headings, footnotes, chapters and parts to accommodate the physical constraints of a printed page aesthetically.
  - *Pre–Press*: function performed by print shops in preparing paper documents for production.
  - *Imposition*: organizing desired pages on a larger media such that when folded and trimmed the pages will be upright and in order.
  - *Printing*: marking paper with ink or toner
  - Folding pages into parts
  - Binding pages together and covering
  - Trimming
  - Packaging
- A distributor manages inventory and physical distribution of printed documents to retailers.
- A retailer manages a local inventory and sales to consumers, and often is familiar with the content and can make appropriate recommendations.
- A librarian organizes, tracks borrowing of, and archives documents.

A publication process enables a consumer to purchase or borrow, read and learn from documents. Consumers are often the intended audience of the publication process.

DOCUMENT PRODUCTION TECHNOLOGY

Document production technology has evolved significantly through history. While a great deal can be said about ancient production technologies including papyrus, palm leaves, stone tablets and marking devices ranging from quills to chisels, the modern form of the document has evolved largely under the influence of printing technologies.

The Illuminated manuscript of Europe is a useful prototypical instance of the document at the end of its evolution before the widespread use of printing. The associated technology was largely a human one. Other cultures at this stage used other forms of pre-print era documents.

The history of printing can be traced as follows:

- Bronze Age civilizations made extensive use of seals for commercial and transactional purposes. The particular case of the signet ring was of particular importance, and is still in use in place of signatures in East Asian countries like Korea, where it is common for individuals to carry a seal.
- Chinese Woodblock printing was the first widespread technology that automated important parts of the document production process.

The Gutenberg Printing Press enabled the mass production of faithful copies of documents, and hence the widespread dissemination of information. The widespread access to information enabled fundamental changes to society in religion, government, law, business, and entertainment. Prior to the press the huge effort required to faithfully hand-copy severely limited the number of documents available, and hence access to the information contained therein. The effort to set type and prepare a document for reproduction was still high, but many high fidelity copies could be produced.The development of Lithography constituted the next great advance in document production technology and continues today to dominate the economic landscape of document production, an economic sector estimated to be of the order of $1 trillion. Lithography brought economies of scale and extremely high quality and low cost to documents.

The typewriter improved the accessibility of document production technologies and enabled it to enter mainstream workplaces. Carbon paper enabled a modest number of copies to be produced concurrently with the original. A brief era of photography-based technologies flourished in parallel with the age of typewriters. The Xerox Copier became a major milestone in document production by eliminating the typesetting effort required by a printing press. The Xerographic technology could produce durable and economical copies of a paper document easily and quickly. Modern digital printers from Xerox and other companies such as HP, Canon and Ricoh, can produce more than 240 black and white or 170 copies of a page each minute, and work with up to 6 colours and dry and wet inks. This technology supports a $100 billion market in digital printing, particularly in domains where lithography has clear limitations. Computers enabled information to be stored electronically in databases and electronic files on magnetic tapes, drums, and disks.

This led to a radical disruption of all document production technologies. Initially most of this information was printed onto paper by teletypes, but computer printers rapidly became faster and more sophisticated. Computers, by controlling lasers in xerography, micro-nozzles in inkjet systems, and tiny solenoids in mechanical systems, became capable of being serially embedded in the document production process. Computers are also critical to modern lithography.

A whole interaction style with computers was developed around the metaphor of working with documents and folders on a desktop, to the point that the word document is now commonly associated with the information stored in a computer file according to the metaphor. Today, electronic paper is viewed as one potential future evolutionary physical form of the prototypical document, as it can present the electronic document with the readability of printed paper.

DOCUMENT LIFE CYCLE MANAGEMENT TECHNOLOGY

Technology to manage documents has evolved in parallel with documents themselves. Of particular importance are practices concerning the preservation, archival, destruction and management of documents.

These constitute what is known as the "document life cycle":

- *Physical preservation*: Documents in both traditional physical forms and in digital physical forms such as magnetic media must be physically preserved. This aspect of document management deals with such issues as the aging of paper and obsolescence of magnetic media.
- *Storage*: This aspect includes management of scarce resources such as shelf space and disk space, and associated technologies such as optimal space utilization. Modern libraries such as the University of Nevada and the University of Michigan often use complex space-saving technologies such as robotic retrieval systems for stacks and moving bookshelves. In the digital realm, the entire discipline of compression technologies can be viewed as concerned with the storage of documents.
- *Cultural Preservation*: This function, traditionally ascribed to librarians involves the selection, arrangement and storage of documents in

safe places. The importance of this part of document life cycle management can be seen in the impact of historical events such as the destruction of books in ancient China and the burning of the library at Alexandria. Today, library and information science has evolved into an important academic discipline.

- *Bibliometrics*: This aspect of document management involves functions of indexing, generating statistics and taxonomies, and improving the usability of large collections of documents. The modern history of this management technology dates back to Melvil Dewey and the Dewey Decimal System. Today, the science of bibliometrics is largely concerned with managing the impact of electronic technologies. This aspect must also deal with ISBN numbers, Library of Congress data and other standards.
- *Digital Content Management*: The explosion of digital content has resulted in technologies to manage large collections of digital information generated by organizations. Such systems must manage access control and privileges, multiple electronic format, interface with printing infrastructures and enable collaborative work flows around documents.
- *Digital–Physical Interaction Management*: As long as both paper and digital documents continue to have value, the modern management technologies to manage their interaction will continue. Key to this management is the management of large scale and systematic scanning of physical documents.
- *Destruction*: With the increased cost of identity theft, corporate scandals and privacy concerns, the destruction of both paper and electronic documents has become increasingly important to manage. Technologies such as shredders play a role, as do verifiable processes of destruction of electronic documents to ensure compliance with privacy laws.
- *Security*: Shannon's information theory has led to an entire discipline that concerns itself with the security of documents, and associated technologies such as encryption, as well as more physical security features such as watermarks and making currency documents safe from counterfeiting.
- *Transportation*: The entire postal system, as well as modern courier systems, is largely built on the need to move documents physically from one location to the other.

THE DOCUMENT ECONOMY

The economics of the production and management of documents indirectly impacts every economic sector. While the total economic value of the document economy is hard to estimate, the economic sectors with business models directly dependent on documents include:

- *Document Authoring Technology*: This sector supports a huge variety of digital and physical production technologies, ranging from Microsoft Word to LaTeX to advanced layout software.
- *Education*: The production and processing of documents is so critical that entire educational disciplines have evolved around writing, editing, layout and design of documents. The information sciences are also part of the document economy.
- *Electronic Document Management*: Managing documents within organizations and in public and personal contexts supports a huge industry in content management systems, ranging from free public infrastructure such as wikipedia to proprietary enterprise applications such as Docushare and Documentum.
- *Physical Document Management*: Large manufacturing sectors producing everything from 3-ring binders to filing cabinets and office desks exist largely due to the need to process documents.
- *Media*: The paper industry exists to support the document economy.
- *Print equipment*: From lithography and xerography to pencils and crayons, an extraordinarily diverse set of equipment industries depend on documents.
- *Document Services*: In large organizations, the life of documents in the work flows and processes of daily activity represent an enormous locus of value addition and cost reduction, which has led to a burgeoning industry in managed document services, ranging from specialized niches to managed office printing.
- *Retail Production*: From large chains such as Kinko's in the United States to small copy shops and offset print shops, documents support a large production sector for the end user.
- *Publishing*: All publishing, ranging from offset-based newspaper and magazine printing, to highly customised modern publishing using publish-on-demand digital print technology, is part of the document economy. The publishing industry includes major sub-areas such as the writer's market, small, medium and large publishing houses, small and large distributors and a vast network of independent and chain bookstores, online retailers, a large used-documents market and subscription-based markets.
- *Document Transportation*: The international postal system, as well as the commercial package transportation systems represented by companies such as DHL and UPS have economic models based largely on the demand for document transportation.

FUTURE OF DOCUMENTS

Since the advent of the digital era, documents have been rapidly evolving, and may require fundamental reconcept-ualization. Efforts at this reconceptualization include Vannevar Bush's initial conceptualization of hypertext.

The impact of digital technology can be understood in terms of several key aspects:

- *Blurring the notion of document boundary*: Hypertext and Web content make it hard to determine what is being denoted by the term document. While the early days of the Web resulted in documents that mimicked their physical ancestors, Web content rapidly took on new characteristics. Reconceptualization of the notion of "boundary" is a key intellectual challenge.
- *Increasing structure and openness*: The document is going from an opaque container of information to a much more open, structured document. XML is underlying most document formats today. In the future, it will become even more queriable, with the actual elements of this document being tagged—*e.g.* HR-XML.
- *Dynamic nature*: Web analogs of traditional paper documents like a newspaper column have taken on a dynamic character due to the impact of technology enabling the addition of comments from readers. The document will increasingly become "virtual", bringing up-to-date information from various sources in one container—as such,it will be kept evergreen.
- *Paper and electronic are reconciling*: Paper has traditionally been a gap in document processing workflows. Technologies such as OCR, OMR, 2D Barcodes and Anoto pattern technology are helping get its content back into the electronic world. In the future however, Not only will that transition be seamless, but it will also be possible to track it while in the "physical" world through RFID and MemorySpot.
- *Hybrid automated/human authorship*: authorship workflows for digital documents have evolved to include the computer in a key role. Dynamic Web pages may be viewed as the joint output of a human author and a software system. Sophisticated examples of this phenomenon can be found in recent evolutions in paper documents as well. Variable data technology, for instance, allows creators of direct mail marketing documents to vary the content of every piece in a print run using technologies such as DesignMerge or Xmpie.
- *Prosumer workflows*: Content repositories such as Wikipedia radically alter traditional document production workflows by blurring roles such as author and editor.
- *Customizability*: Digital technology allows users to actively participate

in the construction of documents they see, realizing the postmodern notion of construction of meaning in an unexpectedly literal way.

- *Long Tail Economics*: Technologies such as blogs have allowed document production economics to operate with such radically cheap cost structures that single individuals can derive an income from a global audience with low capital expenses. This has led to an explosion of niche content.
- *Blurring of Documents and Interfaces*: Technologies such as Ajax or Apollo blur the distinction between documents and user interfaces to "intelligent" technologies, leading to a whole class of smart documents that can go beyond the passive nature of traditional documents.
- *Fluidity and Dynamic Microstructure*: Distinct from the impact of hypertext on the notion of document is the fluid potential of modern documents at the microlevel, which allows an enormous variety of word and sentence level dynamic phenonomenology.

DOCUMENT MANAGEMENT SYSTEM

A document management system is a computer system used to track and store electronic documents and/or images of paper documents. The term has some overlap with the concepts of content management systems. It is often viewed as a component of enterprise content management systems and related to digital asset management, document imaging, workflow systems and records management systems. Beginning in the 1980s, a number of vendors began developing systems to manage paper-based documents.

These systems managed paper documents, which included not only printed and published documents, but also photos, prints, etc. Later, a second style of system was developed, to manage electronic documents, *i.e.*, all those documents, or files, created on computers, and often stored on local user file systems.

The earliest electronic document management systems were either developed to manage proprietary file types, or a limited number of file formats. Many of these systems were later referred to as document imaging systems, because the main capabilities were capture, storage, indexing and retrieval of image file formats.

These systems enabled an organization to capture faxes and forms, save copies of the documents as images, and store the image files in the repository for security and quick retrieval. EDM systems evolved to where the system was able to manage any type of file format that could be stored on the network. The applications grew to encompass electronic documents, collaboration tools, security, and auditing capabilities.

COMPONENTS

Document management systems commonly provide storage, versioning, metadata, security, as well as indexing and retrieval capabilities.

Here is a description of these components:

- *Metadata*: Metadata is typically stored for each document. Metadata may, for example, include the date the document was stored and the identity of the user storing it. The DMS may also extract metadata from the document automatically or prompt the user to add metadata. Some systems also use optical character recognition on scanned images, or perform text extraction on electronic documents. The resulting extracted text can be used to assist users in locating documents by identifying probable keywords or providing for full text search capability, or can be used on its own. Extracted text can also be stored as a component of metadata, stored with the image, or separately as a source for searching document collections.
- *Integration*: Many document management systems attempt to integrate document management directly into other applications, so that users may retrieve existing documents directly from the document management system repository, make changes, and save the changed document back to the repository as a new version, all without leaving the application. Such integration is commonly available for office suites and e-mail or collaboration/groupware software. Integration often uses open standards such as ODMA, LDAP, WebDAV and SOAP to allow integration with other software and compliance with internal controls.
- *Capture*: Capture primarily involves accepting and processing images of paper documents from scanners or multifunction printers. Optical character recognition software is often used, whether integrated into the hardware or as stand-alone software, in order to convert digital images into machine readable text. Optical mark recognition software is sometimes used to extract values of check-boxes or bubbles. Capture may also involve accepting electronic documents and other computer-based files.
- *Indexing*: Track electronic documents. Indexing may be as simple as keeping track of unique document identifiers; but often it takes a more complex form, providing classification through the documents' metadata or even through word indexes extracted from the documents' contents. Indexing exists mainly to support retrieval. One area of critical importance for rapid retrieval is the creation of an index topology.
- *Storage*: Store electronic documents. Storage of the documents often includes management of those same documents; where they are

stored, for how long, migration of the documents from one storage media to another and eventual document destruction.

- *Retrieval*: Retrieve the electronic documents from the storage. Although the notion of retrieving a particular document is simple, retrieval in the electronic context can be quite complex and powerful. Simple retrieval of individual documents can be supported by allowing the user to specify the unique document identifier, and having the system use the basic index to retrieve the document. More flexible retrieval allows the user to specify partial search terms involving the document identifier and/or parts of the expected metadata. This would typically return a list of documents which match the user's search terms. Some systems provide the capability to specify a Boolean expression containing multiple keywords or example phrases expected to exist within the documents' contents. The retrieval for this kind of query may be supported by previously-built indexes, or may perform more time-consuming searches through the documents' contents to return a list of the potentially relevant documents.
- *Distribution*: A published document for distribution has to be in a format that can not be easily altered. As a common practice in law regulated industries, an original master copy of the document is usually never used for distribution other than archiving. If a document is to be distributed electronically in a regulatory environment, then the equipment tasking the job has to be quality endorsed AND validated. Similarly quality endorsed electronic distribution carriers have to be used. This approach applies to both of the systems by which the document is to be inter-exchanged, if the integrity of the document is highly in demand.
- *Security*: Document security is vital in many document management applications. Compliance requirements for certain documents can be quite complex depending on the type of documents. For instance, in the United States, the Health Insurance Portability and Accountability Act requirements dictate that medical documents have certain security requirements. Some document management systems have a rights management module that allows an administrator to give access to documents based on type to only certain people or groups of people. Document marking at the time of printing or PDF-creation is an essential element to preclude alteration or unintended use.
- *Workflow*: Workflow is a complex problem and some document management systems have a built-in workflow module. There are different types of workflow. Usage depends on the environment the electronic document management system is applied to. Manual

workflow requires a user to view the document and decide who to send it to. Rules-based workflow allows an administrator to create a rule that dictates the flow of the document through an organization: for instance, an invoice passes through an approval process and then is routed to the accounts payable department. Dynamic rules allow for branches to be created in a workflow process.

A simple example would be to enter an invoice amount and if the amount is lower than a certain set amount, it follows different routes through the organization. Advanced workflow mechanisms can manipulate content or signal external processes while these rules are in effect.

- *Collaboration*: Collaboration should be inherent in an EDMS. In its basic form, a collaborative EDMS should allow documents to be retrieved and worked on by an authorized user. Access should be blocked to other users while work is being performed on the document. Other advanced forms of collaboration allow multiple users to view and modify a document at the same time in a collaboration session. The resulting document should be viewable in its final shape, while also storing the markups done by each individual user during the collaboration session.
- *Versioning*: Versioning is a process by which documents are checked in or out of the document management system, allowing users to retrieve previous versions and to continue work from a selected point. Versioning is useful for documents that change over time and require updating, but it may be necessary to go back to or reference a previous copy.
- *Searching*: Finds documents and folders using template attributes or full text search. Documents can be searched using various attributes and document content
- *Publishing*: Publishing a document is sometimes tedious and involves the procedures of proofreading, peer or public reviewing, authorizing, printing and approving etc. Those steps ensure prudence and logic thinking. Any careless handling may result in the inaccuracy of the document and therefore mislead or upset its users and readers.

  In law regulated industries, some of the procedures have to be completed as evidenced by their corresponding signatures and the date(s) on which the document was signed. Refer to the ISO divisions of ICS 01.140.40 and 35.240.30 for further information. The published document should be in a format that is not easily altered without a specific knowledge or tools, and yet it is read-only or portable.

STANDARDIZATION

Many industry associations publish their own lists of particular document control standards that are used in their particular field. The following is the list of some of the relevant ISO documents. Divisions ICS 01.140.10 and 01.140.20.

The ISO has also published a series of standards regarding the technical documentation, covered by the division of 01.110:

- ISO 2709: 1996 Information and documentation—Format for information exchange
- ISO 15836: 2009 which replaces ISO 15836:2003 Information and documentation—The Dublin Core metadata element set
- ISO 15489: 2001 Information and documentation—Records management
- ISO 21127: 2006 Information and documentation—A reference ontology for the interchange of cultural heritage information
- ISO 23950: 1998 Information and documentation—Information retrieval—Application service definition and protocol specification.
- ISO/CD 10244 Document management—Business process/workflow baselining and analysis associated with EDMS technologies
- ISO 32000—portable document format

DOCUMENTATION

Documentation may refer to the process of providing evidence or to the communicable material used to provide such documentation. Documentation may also refer to tools aiming at identifying documents or to the field of study devoted to the study of documents and bibliographies.

Subfields of documentation include:

- Medical documentation
- Technical documentation
- Legal documentation
- Administrative documentation
- Historical documentation

Documentation In Computer Science:

The following are different types of documentations usually seen in the Computer Science field:

- Architectural and Design documentation.
- Technical Documentation.
- User Documentation.
- System Documentation.
- Marketing Documentation.

There are various types of Documentation Tools which are available for this purpose.Documentation understood as document is any communicable material used to explain some attributes of an object, system or procedure. It is often used to mean engineering documentation or software documentation, which is usually paper books or computer readable files that describe the structure and components, or on the other hand, operation, of a system/ product. A professional whose field and work is documentation used to be termed a documentalist. Normally, documentalists are trained or have a background in both a specific subject and in the field of documentation. A person who more or less exclusively writes technical documentation is called a technical writer. Technical writers are similarly trained or have a background in technical writing, along with some knowledge of the subject(s) they are documenting. Often, though, they collaborate with subject matter experts, such as engineers. Common types of computer hardware/software documentation include online help, FAQs, how-tos, and user guides.

The term RTFM is often used colloquially in regard to such documentation, especially to computer hardware and software user guides. A common type of software document frequently written by software engineers in the simulation industry is the SDF. While developing the software for a simulator, which can range from embedded avionics devices to 3D terrain databases by way of full motion control systems, the engineer keeps a notebook detailing the development lifecycle of the project. The notebook can contain a requirements part, an interface part detailing the communication interface of the software, a notes part to detail the proof of concept attempts to track what worked or didn't work in solving certain problems, and a testing part to detail how the software will be tested to prove conformance to the requirements of the contract.

The end result is a detailed description of how the software is designed, how to build and install the software on the target device, and any known weaknesses in the design of the software. This document will allow future developers and maintainers of the trainer to come up to speed on the software design in as short a time as possible and have a documented reference when modifying code or searching for bugs.

PRINCIPLES

While associated ISO standards are not easily available publicly, a guide from other sources for this topic may serve the purpose. David Berger has provided several principles of document writing, regarding the terms used, procedure numbering and even lengths of sentences, etc.

The following is a list of guides dealing with each specific field and type:

- Documentation in health care
- Thesis writing
- Papers for academic journal publishing

PROCEDURES AND TECHNIQUES

The procedures of documentation vary from one sector, or one type, to another. In general, these may involve document drafting, formatting, submitting, reviewing, approving, distributing, repositing and tracking, etc., and are convened by associated SOPs in a regulatory industry.

JOURNAL VOUCHER PREPARATION AND APPROVAL

INTRODUCTION

roper preparation and adequate support for Journal Vouchers (JV) is important to ensure JVs accurately record financial events and detailed audit trail documentation exists. Proper preparation and adequate support for JVs is the joint responsibility of Agency Office of the Chief Financial Officer (OCFO), and Centers' OCFO personnel. The accurate and timely preparation of financial statements and other financial reports is often dependent upon accurate, timely and fully supported JVs.

NASA Agency OCFO and each of the Centers shall take due care and diligence to fully comply with each of the following requirements:

- Internal controls;
- Use of JVs;
- Supporting documentation;
- Approval thresholds; and
- Management oversight and review.

Applicability. The requirements in this stage are applicable to all NASA organizational elements that prepare and approve JVs.

For the purposes of this NPR, a transaction is considered to be a journal voucher when:

- The General Ledger accounts to be debited and credited are selected and entered by the user;
- A transaction is corrected with a regular SAP document;
- Embedded system logic is not used to determine the general ledger accounts to be posted, or;
- When transactions meeting the criteria in 1.1.3.1.a to 1.1.3.1.c above are reversed or when a reversing document is a correction.

Automated distributions of summary amounts such as the distribution of payroll charges provided by the Department of Interior (DOI) based on the automated labour distribution information are not within the scope of this stage.

AGENCY REQUIREMENTS

Operational Controls. Operational internal controls shall be in place to ensure the proper recording of JVs. JVs may be prepared at the NASA Center level or at the Agency level. The Center CFO and the Director of the NASA Shared Services Center (NSSC) are responsible for developing center level operating procedures that ensure full compliance with the requirements of this stage.

General Requirements. All JVs shall be:

- Sequentially numbered in the Center's JV log and systematically numbered by the core financial system when posted by the reporting unit.
- Classified as a correction entry or a source entry based on user ID. Each SAP user has a duplicate user ID that starts with ER. These are to be used when recording transactions to identify those JVs and transactions that are correcting errors. Normal user IDs should be used on source JVs. Additional types of JVs may be added by the Agency OCFO in order to ensure greater management control and oversight of the JV process.
- Adequately documented to support the validity and amount of the JV transaction.
- Reviewed, and approved before posting at the appropriate level of management by the appropriate Agency or Center CFO or designee to ensure proper recording of entries at the posting account, appropriation, and fund levels.
- Annotated with the name, title, date, office symbol, and signature of both the preparer and the approver. In an electronic environment, the name, title, and office symbol may be represented by a user identification. A separate table shall be maintained to correlate user ID to identifying information.
- Maintained in sequential order in a central location in either hard copy, electronic form or both. The Center OCFO and the Agency OCFO must each maintain a summary log of all JVs that identifies the JV numbers and dollar amounts. The log must also reference the SAP document number that was recorded for the JV, the SAP document that was corrected and the source document information supporting the entry.

Segregation of Duties. In order to maintain the proper segregation of duties, the functions of preparation and approval of JVs must be performed by different individuals. Once the JV is prepared, the preparer submits the JV together with the supporting documentation to the approving official for approval. When the approver has approved and initialed the JV, the preparer enters the JV into the core financial system. The preparer must then give the approving official a copy of the system printout showing how the JV was posted. Centers must have adequate internal controls in place to ensure that

JVs are posted exactly as they were approved. This should be accomplished as part of the periodic monitoring and control processes.

ROLES AND RESPONSIBILITIES

Director for Financial Management, Agency OCFO shall:

- Review and, if appropriate, approve Center JVs exceeding $50 Million that are submitted by Center CFOs.
- Review and, if appropriate, discuss with the Agency DCFO and approve all prior period adjustment JVs.

Financial Management Division Branch Chief, Agency OCFO shall:

- As needed, request Agency level JVs and supporting documentation from the Center CFOs.
- Review the Agency level JVs and supporting documentation submitted by the Center CFOs for completeness and accuracy.

Center CFO shall:

- Together with the Center DCFO review and, if appropriate, approve Center JVs with dollar amounts greater than $25 Million and equal to or less than $50 Million
- Review Center JVs with amounts greater than $50 million and, if appropriate, forward to The Director for Financial Management, Agency OCFO for approval.
- Prepare Agency level JVs and supporting documentation as requested by the Financial Management Division Branch Chief, Agency OCFO.

Center Deputy Chief Financial Officer shall:

- Together with the Center CFO review and, if appropriate, recommend approval of Center JVs with dollar amounts greater than $25 Million and equal to or less than $50 Million.
- Together with the Center Reporting Branch Chief review and, if appropriate, approve Center JVs with dollar amounts greater than $10 Million and equal to or less than $25 Million.

Center Reporting Branch Chief shall:

- Together with the Center Reporting Branch Chief review and, if appropriate, recommend approval of Center JVs with dollar amounts greater than $10 Million and equal to or less than $25 Million.
- Review and, if appropriate, approve Center JV equal to or less than $10 Million.

USE OF JOURNAL VOUCHERS

JV Groupings. NASA has two primary types of JVs:

1. Correcting entries, and
2. Source entries.Correcting Entries.

Correcting entry JVs adjust for errors detected subsequent to posting including errors identified during the financial statement reporting and review process. This type of accounting entry includes specific amounts, accounts, and/or transactions related to the required correction. In some cases, correcting entries are required to adjust for errors on previously prepared JVs. In those instances, correcting entries should both reverse the incorrect entries and record the correct amount.

In some cases, both entries can be made with one JV properly documented by a single set of supporting documentation. Regardless of whether a single JV is prepared, or multiple JVs are prepared, the correcting JV shall include a copy of the original JV, documentation supporting the correct amount and a narrative explanation detailing the reason why the original entry is incorrect and why the correcting entry is necessaryAll error corrections shall be recorded in SAP using ER user IDs so they can be identified by the Agency OCFO on a NASA-wide basis.

This applies when transactional corrections or other document types are used for error correction. Where feasible, error correction JV transactions shall be linked to the original transactions that were corrected. In cases where corrections are processed through interfaces and an ER user ID cannot be used, the Center shall still employ the approval process and will log the transactions in a manner that will allow them to be identified and sent to the Agency OCFO on a monthly basis.JVs record those accounting entries that, due to system limitations or timing differences have not been otherwise recorded. By nature, source-entry JVs are usually summarized at the entity level by general ledger account.

The source-entry accounting transaction shall be supported by documentation for the summarized amounts and identify the location of the transaction-level supporting detail. These documents shall be recorded in SAP using normal user IDs. Source entry JVs generally are used for month-end closing and year-end processing and closing purposes. Source-entry JVs also may include postings of information provided through data calls, such as those required to record values for property, plant, and equipment recognition; if so, such JVs must be supported by documentation for the summarized amounts and identify the location of the transaction-level supporting detail. Presentation.

Both correcting and source entry JVs normally will be summarized amounts for which documentation is required. In these situations, the summarized accounting entry represents the amount to record the sum of the detailed transactions. In all such cases, the summarized accounting entry shall include documentation of the effect of the detailed transactions and identify the location of the transaction-level supporting detail. JV Reversal Transactions. When JVs are reversed, the transactions must be prepared, approved, recorded, and documented in accordance with all of the requirements applicable to the original JV except when the JVs are reversed automatically as part of the routine JV reversal process. In those instances, documentation and approval for the original JVs will be considered as the documentation and approval for the reversing entry.Sub-groupings. Both correcting and source entry JVs are further subdivided into audit-recommended JVs and customer-requested JVs. Audit-Recommended JVs. If, as a result of their audit, auditors recommend a JV adjustment be made, the auditors shall be asked to provide copies of the appropriate work papers or relevant information from the work papers to support the recommended JV adjustment.

The JV approving official shall perform an analysis of the recommendation using the auditors' work papers and other relevant information to determine if the recommended adjustments should be made. If the JV approving official identified determines that the auditors' recommended adjustments are required, a correcting JV shall be prepared. If the JV approving official determines that the audit recommended adjustments are not required, no adjustment shall be made. All auditor recommended adjustments must be approved by the Center CFO or DCFO and the Director Financial Management, Agency OCFO.

Any determination regarding JV preparation shall:

- Document why the adjustment is, or is not, required;
- Indicate how the JV approving official determined the audit recommendation should, or should not, be followed;
- Identify the audit recommendation serving as the basis for the actions taken;
- Include documentation of the decision to prepare or not prepare a JV, along with other pertinent information as the documentation for that voucher.

Customer-Requested JVs. When NASA personnel prepare proposed JVs to enter adjustments or corrections, the approving officials at NASA Centers or Headquarters must determine that they comply with this JV preparation guidance.

Evidence to support the adjustment must include, at a minimum, supporting documentation which has been reviewed and approved by the JV approving official and any related analysis performed by the JV approving official to ascertain that the adjustment is fully supported and in accordance with this JV preparation and approval guidance.

SUPPORTING DOCUMENTATION

Documentation. Proper documentation, in either hard copy, electronic form or both is necessary to support all JV entries. This documentation must be sufficient for the approving official and auditors to clearly understand the reason for preparing the JV and to be able to determine that it is proper and accurate. A request for a JV entry not supported by accurate or proper documentation shall be denied with a demand for additional information required to process the JV, along with any applicable authoritative guidance to support the need for the JV.

The supporting documentation, whenever practical, should be attached to a copy of the JV. In some cases, however, due to the large number of detailed transactions summarized in the voucher, it may not be practical to attach all of the documentation. In those cases, specific and detailed information summarizing the content and identifying the location of the supporting documentation shall be attached to the voucher.

The specific types of JV and the explanations of what is considered sufficient documentation. Note: Regardless of what method of documentation is used for any category of JV, *i.e.,* whether it is a detailed listing, a narrative explanation, or a calculation supporting the amount, the dollar amount(s) on the JV shall be clearly and readily identifiable in the supporting documentation.

Identified Errors and Reasonableness Checks/Timing Differences due to Monthly/Annual Closing. When the JV approving official has identified errors through analysis, reasonableness checks, quality control procedures, subsequent activity occurring after a period closes, or other means, a correcting JV shall be prepared. In the event an auditor identified an apparent error or omission and provided the documentation for the JV, the JV approving official will be a management official at the appropriate authorizing level, consistent with the entity internal control structure.

Evidence to support either an "authorized official" or "auditor identified" correcting JV shall include a detailed listing of identified errors, narrative explaining why the original entry is incorrect, why the correcting entry is necessary, a related analysis documenting the calculation of the correct amount, and the sources of the data used in the analysis. Reconciliation of Trial Balance and Budget Execution Reports.

When the JV approving official has determined during a reconciliation of data between two or more sources that a discrepancy exists, a correcting JV may be necessary. JV entries included in this category often are made to reconcile trial balances or other source data reported by NASA Headquarters or Centers to NASA's budget execution reports. Evidence to support this type of JV includes reference to specific documents, other source data, and a complete analysis that supports the correct amount.

If a JV is necessary, the voucher shall document why the discrepancy exists in the data, it shall contain evidence to support the proposed correction, and a description of the methodology used to validate the entries on the JV.Reversing Entries for Prior Reporting Period. When monthly or yearly accruals or correcting entries have been made for reporting purposes, they may need to be reversed in the following reporting period. The JV reversing entries shall include documentation regarding the original accrual or correcting entry and an explicit statement that the JV is a reversing entry. Data Call Entry.

Frequently, during the financial statement preparation process, source-entry information is provided by data calls where data are not recorded on a detailed transaction basis. For example, transactions at the detail levels from sources external to the OCFO may not be available in the core financial systems or information required from external Government agencies to prepare the financial statements are available only in summarized forms.

If this occurs, JVs shall be prepared to record the summarized data call amounts, so these amounts can be recorded in the general ledger trial balance. The data call entry shall be supported by documentation for the summarized amount and shall identify the source or location of the transaction-level supporting detail and/or information for the entry. Data call information, in most cases is not contained in the core financial systems and is provided by sources outside of the CFO's office.

Examples of an independent source include the NASA logistics data calls, environmental liability data calls, and accrual information from the Department of Labour and the Office of Personnel Management. Evidence to support the JV includes the transmission record of the data.

Examples of data call entries include:

- Property, plant and equipment;
- Operating materials and supplies;
- Environmental liabilities;
- Contingent liabilities; and
- Employee benefits data, Federal Employees Compensation Act data, and other information from other Federal sources.

Other Accruals. A number of typical month-end and year-end adjusting entries are made, and subsequently may be reversed at the beginning of the next period to accrue amounts for payroll, workers compensation, judgment fund liabilities, unfunded leave, and other transactions. The supporting documentation for these other accrual JVs shall include a narrative explaining the basis for the accrual, a worksheet documenting the calculation of the amounts being recorded, and the basis for any subsequent reversal.

Prior Period Adjustments. All JVs that adjust amounts reported in audited financial statements issued for a previous fiscal year, regardless of amount and type, must be approved by the Center CFO and the Director Financial Management, Agency OCFO.

APPROVAL THRESHOLDS

Journal Vouchers Prepared and Posted at the Center Level. Approval of the JV also constitutes acceptance of the supporting documentation. The organizational level within the Center or NSSC, at which JVs must be approved, varies by the dollar amount of the voucher as shown by the following table.

Table. Approval Thresholds for Center Generated JVs

JV Dollar Amount	JV Approving Official
0 to $10 Million	Center Reporting Branch Chief
Over $10 Million to $25 Million	Center Reporting Branch Chief and Center DCFO
Over $25 Million to $50 Million	Center DCFO and Center CFO
Over $50 Million	Center CFO and Director for Financial Management, Agency OCFO

Prior period adjustments - JVs that are adjusting beginning balances Center CFO and Director for Financial Management, Agency OCFO All JVs regardless of the type or amount that adjust amounts reported in audited financial statements issued for a previous fiscal year must be approved by the Director for Financial Management, Agency OCFO.

All auditor recommended adjustments must be approved by the Center CFO or DCFO and the Director for Financial Management, Agency OCFO. Within each of the foregoing thresholds, other approval thresholds with lower dollar values than those specified may be established to accommodate the organizational level of those preparing the JV.

The Center CFO shall designate in writing the approval threshold structure—dollar thresholds and position of approving officials within the Center. In the event that the approval authorities must be delegated to an individual other than the one identified, that delegation must also be documented in writing and signed by the Center CFO.

Journal Vouchers Posted at the Agency Level. The Agency OCFO, Financial Management Division, Data Analysis Branch Chief in coordination with the External Reporting Branch Chief will, as needed, request Centers CFOs submit JVs that will be posted at the Agency Level. These JVs must be submitted with all applicable supporting documentation and approvals

Upon receipt of the requested JV the FMD, Data Analysis Branch Chief in coordination with the External Reporting Branch Chief will review the supporting documentation for completeness and the JV for accuracy. When the JV is determined to be accurate and all required documentation is present the Branch Chiefs will forward the JV to the FMD Director or his/her designee for approval. If the JV is over $100 million, the FMD Director will discuss the JV with the Agency DCFO prior to posting in SAP.

MANAGEMENT OVERSIGHT AND REVIEW

Managerial Controls. Adequate managerial internal controls shall be maintained at each level of management to ensure proper oversight of JV preparation. The Center CFO's and the Director of the NSSC must ensure the validity and accuracy of the JVs processed as part of their normal monthly financial management monitoring process by ensuring that adequate documentation exists to support the JV entry before it is recorded.

All corrections made by the Competency Center or by the Agency OCFO on behalf of the Centers or Agency OCFO are subject to this process. The Competency Center and/or the Agency OCFO will only make corrections/adjustments once this documentation is received. Copies of the documentation of the corrections will be attached to the Service Request and originals maintained in the Centers' logs and records. Service requests shall be established for activities performed either by the Competency Center or the Agency OCFO.

COMMERCIAL PAYMENT VOUCHERS AND SUPPORTING DOCUMENTS

AN OVERVIEW

Purpose

This stage prescribes the policy for the preparation of commercial payment vouchers and the supporting documentation. It highlights the forms most often used for contracts, receiving reports, and vouchers. It provides guidance on their usage, certification, and distribution to the paying office.

Scope

A properly certified voucher is the authority for Disbursing Officers to make payments of government obligations. The certifying officer must review evidence sufficient to support a determination that the payment is proper. Preparation and certification of a payment voucher by the entitleme1nt office advises the disbursing office that the contractual conditions for payment have been met.

5

International Trade

International trade is the exchange of capital, goods, and services across international borders or territories. In most countries, such trade represents a significant share of gross domestic product (GDP). While international trade has been present throughout much of history, its economic, social, and political importance has been on the rise in recent centuries. Industrialization, advanced transportation, globalization, multinational corporations, and outsourcing are all having a major impact on the international trade system. Increasing international trade is crucial to the continuance of globalization. Without international trade, nations would be limited to the goods and services produced within their own borders.

International trade is, in principle, not different from domestic trade as the motivation and the behaviour of parties involved in a trade do not change fundamentally regardless of whether trade is across a border or not. The main difference is that international trade is typically more costly than domestic trade. The reason is that a border typically imposes additional costs such as tariffs, time costs due to border delays and costs associated with country differences such as language, the legal system or culture. Another difference between domestic and international trade is that factors of production such as capital and labour are typically more mobile within a country than across countries. Thus international trade is mostly restricted to trade in goods and services, and only to a lesser extent to trade in capital, labour or other factors of production.

Trade in goods and services can serve as a substitute for trade in factors of production. Instead of importing a factor of production, a country can import goods that make intensive use of that factor of production and thus embody it. An example is the import of labour-intensive goods by the United States from China. Instead of importing Chinese labour, the United States imports goods that were produced with Chinese labour. One report in 2010 suggested that international trade was increased when a country hosted a network of immigrants, but the trade effect was weakened when the immigrants became assimilated into their new country. International trade is also a branch of economics, which, together with international finance, forms the larger branch of international economics.

HISTORY

The history of international trade chronicles notable events that have affected the trade between various countries. In the era before the rise of the nation state, the term 'international' trade cannot be literally applied, but simply means trade over long distances; the sort of movement in goods which would represent international trade in the modern world.

MODELS

The following are noted models of international trade.

ADAM SMITH'S MODEL

Adam Smith displays trade taking place on the basis of countries exercising absolute advantage over one another.

RICARDIAN MODEL

The Ricardian model focuses on comparative advantage, which arises due to differences in technology or natural resources. The Ricardian model does not directly consider factor endowments, such as the relative amounts of labour and capital within a country.

The Ricardian model makes the following assumptions:

- Labour is the only primary input to production.
- The relative ratios of labour at which the production of one good can be traded off for another differ between countries and governments

HECKSCHER-OHLIN MODEL

In the early 1900s a theory of international trade was developed by two Swedish economists, Eli Heckscher and Bertil Ohlin. This theory has subsequently been known as the Heckscher-Ohlin model (H-O model). The results of the H-O model are that countries will produce and export goods that require resources (factors) which are relatively abundant and import goods that require resources which are in relative short supply.

In the Heckscher-Ohlin model the pattern of international trade is determined by differences in factor endowments. It predicts that countries will export those goods that make intensive use of locally abundant factors and will import goods that make intensive use of factors that are locally scarce. Empirical problems with the H-O model, such as the Leontief paradox, were noted in empirical tests by Wassily Leontief who found that the United States tended to export labour-intensive goods despite having an abundance of capital.

The H-O model makes the following core assumptions:

- Labour and capital flow freely between sectors
- The amount of labour and capital in two countries differ (difference in endowments)
- Technology is the same among countries (a long-term assumption)
- Tastes are the same.

Reality and Applicability of the Heckscher-Ohlin Model

In 1953, Wassily Leontief published a study in which he tested the validity of the Heckscher-Ohlin theory. The study showed that the U.S was more abundant in capital compared to other countries, therefore the U.S would export capital-intensive goods and import labour-intensive goods. Leontief found out that the U.S's exports were less capital intensive than its imports. After the appearance of Leontief's paradox, many researchers tried to save the Heckscher-Ohlin theory, either by new methods of measurement, or by new interpretations. Leamer emphasized that Leontief did not interpret H-O theory properly and claimed that with a right interpretation, the paradox did not occur. Brecher and Choudri found that, if Leamer was right, the American workers' consumption per head should be lower than the workers' world average consumption. Many textbook writers, including Krugman and Obstfeld and Bowen, Hollander and Viane, are negative about the validity of H-O model. After examining the long history of empirical research, Bowen, Hollander and Viane concluded: "Recent tests of the factor abundance theory [H-O theory and its developed form into many-commodity and many-factor case] that directly examine the H-O-V equations also indicate the rejection of the theory." In the specific factors model, labour mobility among industries is possible while capital is assumed to be immobile in the short run.

Thus, this model can be interpreted as a short-run version of the Heckscher-Ohlin model. The "specific factors" name refers to the assumption that in the short run, specific factors of production such as physical capital are not easily transferable between industries. The theory suggests that if there is an increase in the price of a good, the owners of the factor of production specific to that good will profit in real terms. Additionally, owners of opposing specific factors of production (*i.e.*, labour and capital) are likely to have opposing agendas when lobbying for controls over immigration of labour. Conversely, both owners of capital and labour profit in real terms from an increase in the capital endowment. This model is ideal for understanding income distribution but awkward for discussing the pattern of trade.

NEW TRADE THEORY

New Trade Theory tries to explain empirical elements of trade that comparative advantage-based models above have difficulty with. These include the fact that most trade is between countries with similar factor endowment and productivity levels, and the large amount of multinational production (*i.e.* foreign direct investment) that exists. New Trade theories are often based on assumptions such as monopolistic competition and increasing returns to scale.

One result of these theories is the home-market effect, which asserts that, if an industry tends to cluster in one location because of returns to scale and if that industry faces high transportation costs, the industry will be located in the country with most of its demand, in order to minimize cost. Although new trade theory can explain the growing trend of trade volumes of intermediate goods, Krugman's explanation depends too much on the strict assumption that all firms are symmetrical, meaning that they all have the same production coefficients.

Shiozawa, based on much more general model, succeeded in giving a new explanation on why the traded volume increases for intermediate goods when the transport cost decreases.

GRAVITY MODEL

The Gravity model of trade presents a more empirical analysis of trading patterns. The gravity model, in its basic form, predicts trade based on the distance between countries and the interaction of the countries' economic sizes. The model mimics the Newtonian law of gravity which also considers distance and physical size between two objects. The model has been proven to be empirically strong through econometric analysis.

RICARDIAN THEORY OF INTERNATIONAL TRADE (MODERN DEVELOPMENT)

The Ricardian theory of comparative advantage became a basic constituent of neo-classical trade theory. Any under-graduate course in trade theory includes a presentation of Ricardo's example of a two-commodity, two-country model.

A common representation of this model is made using an Edgeworth Box. This model has been expanded to many-country and many-commodity cases. Major general results were obtained by McKenzie and Jones, including his famous formula. It is a theorem about the possible trade pattern for N-country N-commodity cases.

Contemporary Theories

Ricardo's idea was even expanded to the case of continuum of goods by Dornbusch, Fischer, and Samuelson This formulation is employed for example by Matsuyama and others. These theories use a special property that is applicable only for the two-country case.

Neo-Ricardian Trade Theory

Inspired by Piero Sraffa, a new strand of trade theory emerged and was named neo-Ricardian trade theory. The main contributors include Ian Steedman (1941–) and Stanley Metcalfe (1946–). They have criticized neo-classical international trade theory, namely the Heckscher-Ohlin model on the basis that the notion of capital as primary factor has no method of measuring it before the determination of profit rate (thus trapped in a logical vicious circle). This was a second round of the Cambridge capital controversy, this time in the field of international trade. The merit of neo-Ricardian trade theory is that input goods are explicitly included. This is in accordance with Sraffa's idea that any commodity is a product made by means of commodities. The limitation of their theory is that the analysis is restricted to small-country cases.

Traded Intermediate Goods

Ricardian trade theory ordinarily assumes that the labour is the unique input. This is a great deficiency as trade theory, for intermediate goods occupy the major part of the world international trade. Yeats found that 30 per cent of world trade in manufacturing involves intermediate inputs. Bardhan and Jafee found that intermediate inputs occupy 37 to 38 per cent of U.S. imports for the years 1992 and 1997, whereas the per centage of intrafirm trade grew from 43 per cent in 1992 to 52 per cent in 1997. McKenzie and Jones emphasized the necessity to expand the Ricardian theory to the cases of traded inputs. In a famous comment McKenzie pointed that "A moment's consideration will convince one that Lancashire would be unlikely to produce cotton cloth if the cotton had to be grown in England." Paul Samuelson coined a term *Sraffa bonus* to name the gains from trade of inputs.

Ricardo-Sraffa Trade Theory

John Chipman observed in his survey that McKenzie stumbled upon the questions of intermediate products and discovered that "introduction of trade in intermediate product necessitates a fundamental alteration in classical analysis." It took many years until Y. Shiozawa succeeded in removing this deficiency. The Ricardian trade theory was now constructed in a form to include intermediate input trade for the most general case of many countries and many goods. This new theory is called Ricardo-Sraffa trade theory. Based on an idea of Takahiro Fujimoto, who is a specialist in automobile industry and a philosopher of the international competitiveness, Fujimoto and Shiozawa developed a discussion in which how the factories of the same multi-national firms compete between them across borders. International *intra-firm competition* reflects a really new aspect of international competition in the age of so-called global competition.

International Production Fragmentation Trade Theory

Fragmentation and International Trade Theory widens the scope for "application of Ricardian comparative advantage." In his chapter entitled *Li & Fung, Ltd.: An agent of global production,* Cheng used Li & Fong Ltd as a case study in the international production fragmentation trade theory through which producers in different countries are allocated a specialized slice or segment of the value chain of the global production.

Allocations are determined based on on "technical feasibility" and the ability to keep the lowest final price possible for each product. An example of fragmentation theory in international trade is Li & Fung's garment sector network with yarn purchased in South Korea, woven and dyed in Taiwan, the fabric cut in Bangladesh, pieces assembled in Thailand and the final product sold in the United States and Europe to major brands.

In 1995 Li & Fung Ltd purchased Inchcape Buying Services, an established British trading company and widely expanded production in Asia. Li & Fung supplies dozens of major retailers, including Wal-Mart Stores, Inc., branded as Walmart.

INTERNATIONAL BUSINESS

International business comprises all commercial transactions (private and governmental, sales, investments, logistics,and transportation) that take place between two or more regions, countries and nations beyond their political boundaries. Usually, private companies undertake such transactions for profit; governments undertake them for profit and for political reasons.

It refers to all those business activities which involve cross border transactions of goods, services, resources between two or more nations. Transaction of economic resources include capital, skills, people etc. for international production of physical goods and services such as finance, banking, insurance, construction etc.

A multinational enterprise (MNE) is a company that has a worldwide approach to markets and production or one with operations in more than a country. An MNE is often called multinational corporation (MNC) or transnational company (TNC). Well known MNCs include fast food companies such as McDonald's and Yum Brands, vehicle manufacturers such as General Motors, Ford Motor Company and Toyota, consumer electronics companies like Samsung, LG and Sony, and energy companies such as ExxonMobil, Shell and BP.

Most of the largest corporations operate in multiple national markets. Areas of study within this topic include differences in legal systems, political systems, economic policy, language, accounting standards, labour standards, living standards, environmental standards, local culture, corporate culture, foreign exchange market, tariffs, import and export regulations, trade agreements, climate, education and many more topics. Each of these factors requires significant changes in how individual business units operate from one country to the next.

PHYSICAL AND SOCIETAL FACTORS OF COMPETITIVE SOCIAL ENVIRONMENT

The conduct of international operations depends on companies' objectives and the means with which they carry them out.

The operations affect and are affected by the physical and societal factors and the competitive environment:

Operations:

- *Objectives*: Sales expansion, resource acquisition, risk minimization, Diversify their revenue stream.

Means:

- *Modes*: Importing and exporting, tourism and transportation, licensing and franchising, turnkey operations, management contracts, direct investment and portfolio investments.
- *Functions*: Marketing, global manufacturing and supply chain management, accounting, finance, human resources.
- *Overlaying Alternatives*: Choice of countries, organization and control mechanisms.

Physical and societal factors:

- Political policies and legal practices
- Cultural factors
- Economic forces
- Geographical influences

Competitive factors:

- Major advantage in price, marketing, innovation or other factors.
- Number and comparative capabilities of competitors.
- Competitive differences by country.
- Local taxes.

Risk:

- Strategic risk
- Operational risk
- Political risk
- Country risk
- Technological Risk
- Environmental Risk
- Economic Risk
- Financial risk
- Terrorism Risk

FACTORS THAT INFLUENCED THE GROWTH IN GLOBALIZATION

There has been growth in globalization in recent decades due to the following eight factors:

1. Technology is expanding, especially in transportation and communications.
2. Governments are removing international business restrictions.
3. Institutions provide services to ease the conduct of international business.
4. Consumers know about and want foreign goods and services.
5. Competition has become more global.
6. Political relationships have improved among some major economic powers.
7. Countries cooperate more on transnational issues.
8. Cross-national cooperation and agreements.

IMPORTANCE INTERNATIONAL BUSINESS EDUCATION

- Most companies are either international or compete with international companies.
- Modes of operation may differ from those used domestically.
- The best way of conducting business may differ by country.
- An understanding helps you make better career decisions.
- An understanding helps you decide what governmental policies to support.

Managers in international business must understand social science disciplines and how they affect all functional business fields.

Importance of Studying International Business

The International Business standards focuses on the following:

- Raising awareness of the interrelatedness of one country's political policies and economic practices on another;
- Learning to improve international business relations through appropriate communication strategies;
- Understanding the global business environment—that is, the interconnected-ness of cultural, political, legal, economic, and ethical systems;
- Exploring basic concepts underlying international finance, management, marketing, and trade relations; and
- Identifying forms of business ownership and international business opportunities.

By focusing on these, students will gain a better understanding Political economy. These are tools that would help future business people bridge the economical and political gap between countries. There is an increasing amount of demand for business people with an education in International Business. A survey conducted by Thomas Patrick from University of Notre Dame concluded that Bachelor's degree holders and Master's degree holders felt that the training received through education were very practical in the working environment.

Business people with an education in International Business also had a significantly higher chance of being sent abroad to work under the international operations of a firm. The following table provides descriptions of higher education in International Business and its benefits.

	Master's	Doctorate
Who is this degree for	People interested in management careers with multinational companies	People who are interested in academic or research careers
Common Career Paths (with approximate median annual salary)	• Chief executives ($167,000)* • General or operations managers ($95,000)*	• University business professors ($75,000)* • Economists ($91,000)*
Time to Completion	1–2 years full-time	3–5 years in addition to master's or other foundational coursework
Common Graduation Requirements	• Roughly 15-20 graduate level courses • Internship or study abroad programme • Foreign language requirement • Dissertation • Teaching requirement	Most (or all) of the master's degree requirements, plus: • At least 12 more graduate level courses • Ph.D. qualifier exams • Dissertation prospectus (proposal)
Prerequisites	Bachelor's degree and work experience, quantitative expertise	Bachelor's or master's degree in business or related field
Online Availability	Yes	Limited

MONOPOLISTIC COMPETITION IN INTERNATIONAL TRADE

Monopolistc competition models are used under the rubric of imperfect competition in International Economics. This model is a derivative of the monopolistic competition model that is part of basic economics. Here it is tailored to international trade.

SETTING UP THE MODEL

Monopolies are not often found in practice, the more usual market format is oligopoly: several firms, each of whom is big enough that a change in their price will affect the price of the other firms, but none with an unchallenged monopoly.

When looking at oligopolies the problem of *interdependence* arises. Interdependence means that the firms will, when setting their prices, consider the effect this price will have on the actions of both consumers and competitors. For their part, the competitors will consider their expectations of the firm's response to any action they may take in return.

Thus, there is a complex game with each side "trying to second guess each others' strategies." The Monopolistic Competition model is used because its simplicity allows the examination of one type of oligopoly while avoiding the issue of interdependence.

BENEFITS OF THE MODEL

The appeal of this model is not its closeness to the real world but its simplicity. What this model accomplishes most is that it shows us the benefits to trade presented by economies of scale.

ASSUMPTIONS OF THE MODEL

- Each firm is presumed to be able *differentiate its product* from that of its rivals. Cars are a good example here; they are very different, yet in direct competition with each other. This means there will be some customer loyalty, which allows for some flexibility for the firm to move to a higher price. In other words, not all of a firm's customers would leave for other products if the firm raised its prices.
- This model dismisses the issue of interdependence when a firm sets its price. The firm will act *as if it were a monopoly* regarding the price it sets, not considering the potential responses from its competitors. The justification is that there are numerous firms in the market, so each receives only scant attention from the others.

Background of the Model

- An industry consisting of a number of firms, each of which produces differentiated products. The firms are monopolists for their products, but depend somewhat of the number of reasonable alternatives available and the price of those alternatives. Each firm within the industry thus faces a demand that is effected by the price and prevalence of reasonable alternatives.

- Generally we expect a firm's sales to increase the stronger the total demand for the industry's product as a whole. Conversely, we expect the firm to sell less if there are a significant number of firms in the industry and/or the higher the firm's price in relation to those competitors. The demand equation for such a firm would be:

$$Q = S \times [1/n - b \times (P - P)]$$

- "Q" = the firm's sales. "S" is the total sales of the industry. "n" is the number of firms in the industry, "b" is a constant term representing the responsiveness of a firm's sales to its price. "P" is the price charged by the firm itself. "P" is the average price charged by its competitors.
- The intuition of this model is:
- If all firms charge the same price their respective market share will be 1/n. Firms charging more get less, firms charging less get more.
- (Note) Assume that lower prices will not bring new consumers into the market. In this model consumers can only be gained at the expense of other firms. This simplifies things, allowing a focus on the competition among firms and also allows the assumption that if S represents the market size, and the firms are charging the same price, the market share of each firm will be S/n.

INTERNATIONAL TRADE LAW

International trade law includes the appropriate rules and customs for handling trade between countries. However, it is also used in legal writings as trade between private sectors, which is not right. This branch of law is now an independent field of study as most governments has become part of the world trade, as members of the World Trade Organization (WTO). Since the transaction between private sectors of different countries is an important part of the WTO activities, this latter branch of law is now a very important part of the academic works and is under study in many universities across the world. International trade law should be distinguished from the broader field of international economic law.

The latter could be said to encompass not only WTO law, but also law governing the international monetary system and currency regulation, as well as the law of international development. The body of rules for transnational trade in the 21st century derives from medieval commercial laws called the *lex mercatoria* and *lex maritima* — respectively, "the law for merchants on land" and "the law for merchants on sea." Modern trade law (extending beyond bilateral treaties) began shortly after the Second World War, with the negotiation of a multilateral treaty to deal with trade in goods: the General Agreement on Tariffs and Trade (GATT). International trade law is based on theories of economic liberalism developed in Europe and later the United States from the 18th century onwards. International Trade Law is an aggregate of legal rules of "international legislation" and new lex mercatoria, regulating relations in international trade.

"International legislation" – international treaties and acts of international intergovernmental organizations regulating relations in international trade. lex mercatoria - "the law for merchants on land". Alok Narayan defines "lex mercatoria" as "any law relating to businesses" which was criticised by Professor Julius Stone. and lex maritima - "the law for merchants on sea.

WORLD TRADE ORGANIZATION

In 1995, the World Trade Organization, a formal international organization to regulate trade, was established. It is the most important development in the history of international trade law. The purposes and structure of the organization is governed by the *Agreement Establishing The World Trade Organization,* also known as the "Marrakesh Agreement". It does not specify the actual rules that govern international trade in specific areas.

These are found in separate treaties, annexed to the Marrakesh Agreement:

Scope of WTO:

- Provide framework for administration and implemen-tation of agreements;
- Forum for further negotiations;
- Trade policy review mechanism; and
- Promote greater coherence among members economics policies

Principles of the WTO:

- Principle of non-discrimination (most-favoured-nation treatment obligation and the national treatment obligation)
- Market access (reduction of tariff and non-tariff barriers to trade)
- Balancing trade liberalisation and other societal interests
- Harmonisation of national regulation (TRIPS agreement, TBT agreement, SPS agreement)

TRADE IN GOODS

The GATT has been the backbone of international trade law throughout most of the twentieth century. It contains rules relating to "unfair" trading practices — dumping and subsidies.

TRADE AND INTELLECTUAL PROPERTY

The World Trade Organisation Trade Related Intellectual Property Rights

(TRIPS) agreement required signatory nations to raise intellectual property rights (also known as intellectual monopoly privileges). This arguably has had a negative impact on access to essential medicines in some nations.

DISPUTE SETTLEMENT

Most prominent in the area of dispute settlement in international trade law is the WTO dispute settlement system. The WTO dispute settlement body is operational since 1995 and has been very active since then with 369 cases in the time between 1 January 1995 and 1 December 2007. Nearly a quarter of disputes reached an amicable solution, in other cases the parties to the dispute resorted to adjudication. The WTO dispute settlement body has exclusive and compulsory jurisdiction over disputes on WTO law.

INTERNATIONAL TRADE BARRIERS

TARIFF AND NON-TARIFF BARRIERS

Tariffs and Tariff Rate Quotas

Tariffs, which are taxes on imports of commodities into a country or region, are among the oldest forms of government intervention in economic activity. They are implemented for two clear economic purposes. First, they provide revenue for the government. Second, they improve economic returns to firms and suppliers of resources to domestic industry that face competition from foreign imports. Tariffs are widely used to protect domestic producers' incomes from foreign competition. This protection comes at an economic cost to domestic consumers who pay higher prices for import competing goods, and to the economy as a whole through the inefficient allocation of resources to the import competing domestic industry.

Therefore, since 1948, when average tariffs on manufactured goods exceeded 30 per cent in most developed economies, those economies have sought to reduce tariffs on manufactured goods through several rounds of negotiations under the General Agreement on Tariffs Trade (GATT). Only in the most recent Uruguay Round of negotiations were trade and tariff restrictions in agriculture addressed. In the past, and even under GATT, tariffs levied on some agricultural commodities by some countries have been very large. When coupled with other barriers to trade they have often constituted formidable barriers to market access from foreign producers. In fact, tariffs that are set high enough can block all trade and act just like import bans. Round of negotiations were trade and tariff restrictions in agriculture addressed.

In the past, and even under GATT, tariffs levied on some agricultural commodities by some countries have been very large. When coupled with other barriers to trade they have often constituted formidable barriers to market access from foreign producers. In fact, tariffs that are set high enough can block all trade and act just like import bans. Round of negotiations were trade and tariff restrictions in agriculture addressed. In the past, and even under GATT, tariffs levied on some agricultural commodities by some countries have been very large. When coupled with other barriers to trade they have often constituted formidable barriers to market access from foreign producers. In fact, tariffs that are set high enough can block all trade and act just like import bans.

Issues

In the Uruguay round of the GATT/WTO negotiations, members agreed to drop the use of import quotas and other non-tariff barriers in favour of tariff-rate quotas. Countries also agreed to gradually lower each tariff rate and raise the quantity to which the low tariff applied. Thus, over time, trade would be taxed at a lower rate and trade flows would increase. Given current U.S. commitments under the WTO on market access, options are limited for U.S. policy innovations in the 2002 Farm Bill vis a vis tariffs on agricultural imports from other countries.

Providing higher prices to domestic producers by increasing tariffs on agricultural imports is not permitted. In addition, particularly because the U.S. is a net exporter of many agricultural commodities, successive U.S. governments have generally taken a strong position within the WTO that tariff and TRQ barriers need to be reduced.

Non-Tariff Trade Barriers

Countries use many mechanisms to restrict imports. A critical objective of the Uruguay Round of GATT negotiations, shared by the U.S., was the elimination of non-tariff barriers to trade in agricultural commodities (including quotas) and, where necessary, to replace them with tariffs – a process called tarrification. Tarrification of agricultural commodities was largely achieved and viewed as a major success of the 1994 GATT agreement. Thus, if the U.S. honours its GATT commitments, the utilization of new non-tariff barriers to trade is not really an option for the 2002 Farm Bill.

Domestic Content Requirements

Governments have used domestic content regulations to restrict imports. The intent is usually to stimulate the development of domestic industries. Domestic content regulations typically specify the per centage of a product's total value that must be produced domestically in order for the product to be sold in the domestic market (Carbaugh).

Several developing countries have imposed domestic content requirements to foster agricultural, automobile, and textile production. They are normally used in conjunction with a policy of import substitution in which domestic production replaces imports. Domestic content requirements have not been as prevalent in agriculture as in some other industries, such as automobiles, but some agricultural examples illustrate their effects.

Australia used domestic content requirements to support leaf tobacco production. In order to pay a relatively low import duty on imported tobacco, Australian cigarette manufacturers were required to use 57 per cent domestic leaf tobacco. Member countries of trade agreements also use domestic content rules to ensure that non-members do not manipulate the agreements to circumvent tariffs.

For example, North American Free Trade Agreement (NAFTA) rules of origin provisions stipulate that all single-strength citrus juice must be made from 100 per cent NAFTA origin fresh citrus fruit. Again, as is the case with other trade barriers, it seems unlikely that introducing domestic content rules to enhance domestic demand for U.S. agricultural commodities is a viable option for the 2002 Farm Bill.

Import Licenses

Import licenses have proved to be effective mechanisms for restricting imports. Under an importlicensing scheme, importers of a commodity are required to obtain a license for each shipment they bring into the country. Without explicitly utilizing a quota mechanism, a country can simply restrict imports on any basis it chooses through its allocation of import licenses. Prior to the implementation of NAFTA, for example, Mexico required that wheat and other agricultural commodity imports be permitted only under license. Elimination of import licenses for agricultural commodities was a critical objective of the Uruguay Round of GATT negotiations and thus the use of this mechanism to protect U.S. agricultural producers is unlikely an option for the 2002 Farm Bill.

Import State Trading Enterprises

Import State Trading Enterprises (STEs) are government owned or sanctioned agencies that act as partial or pure single buyer importers of a commodity or set of commodities in world markets. They also often enjoy a partial or pure domestic monopoly over the sale of those commodities. Current important examples of import STEs in world agricultural commodity markets include the Japanese Food Agency (barley, rice, and wheat), South Korea's Livestock Products Marketing Organization, and China's National Cereals, Oil and Foodstuffs Import and Export Commission (COFCO). STEs can restrict imports in several ways.

First, they can impose a set of implicit import tariffs by purchasing imports at world prices and offering them for sale at much higher domestic prices. The difference between the purchase price and the domestic sales price simply represents a hidden tariff. Import STEs may also implement implicit general and targeted import quotas, or utilize complex and costly implicit import rules that make importing into the market unprofitable. Recently, in a submission to the current WTO negotiations, the United States targeted the trade restricting operations of import and export STEs as a primary concern.

A major problem with import STEs is that it is quite difficult to estimate the impacts of their operations on trade, because those operations lack transparency. STEs often refuse to provide the information needed to make such assessments, claiming that such disclosure is not required because they are quasi-private companies. In spite of these difficulties, the challenges provided by STEs will almost certainly continue to be addressed through bilateral and multilateral trade negotiations rather than in the context of domestic legislation through the 2002 Farm Bill.

Technical Barriers to Trade

All countries impose technical rules about packaging, product definitions, labeling, etc. In the context of international trade, such rules may also be used as non-tariff trade barriers. For example, imagine if Korea were to require that oranges sold in the country be less than two inches in diameter. Oranges grown in Korea happen to be much smaller than Navel oranges grown in California, so this type of "technical" rule would effectively ban the sales of California oranges and protect the market for Korean oranges. Such rules violate WTO provisions that require countries to treat imports a nd domestic products equivalently and not to advantage products from one source over another, even in indirect ways. Again, however, these issues will likely be dealt with through bilateral and multilateral trade negotiations rather than through domestic Farm Bill policy initiatives.

Exchange Rate Management Policies

Some countries may restrict agricultural imports through managing their exchange rates. To some degree, countries can and have used exchange rate policies to discourage imports and encourage exports of all commodities. The exchange rate between two countries' currencies is simply the price at which one currency trades for the other. For example, if one U.S. dollar can be used to purchase 100 Japanese yen (and vice versa), the exchange rate between the U.S. dollar and the Japanese yen is 100 yen per dollar. If the yen depreciates in value relative to the U.S. dollar, then a dollar is able to purchase more yen. A 10 per cent depreciation or devaluation of the yen, for example, would mean that the price of one U.S. dollar increased to 110 yen.

One effect of currency depreciation is to make all imports more expensive in the country itself. If, for example, the yen depreciates by 10 per cent from an initial value of 100 yen per dollar, and the price of a ton of U.S. beef on world markets is $2,000, then the price of that ton of beef in Japan would increase from 200,000 yen to 220,000 yen. A policy that deliberately lowers the exchange rate of a country's currency will, therefore, inhibit imports of agricultural commodities, as well as imports of all other commodities. Thus, countries that pursue deliberate policies of undervaluing their currency in international financial markets are not usually targeting agricultural imports.

Some countries have targeted specific types of imports through implementing multiple exchange rate policy under which importers were required to pay different exchange rates for foreign currency depending on the commodities they were importing. The objectives of such programmes have been to reduce balance of payments problems and to raise revenues for the government. Multiple exchange rate programmes were rare in the 1990s, and generally have not been utilized by developed economies.

Finally, exchange rate policies are usually not sector-specific. In the United States, they are clearly under the purview of the Federal Reserve Board and, as such, will not likely be a major issue for the 2002 Farm Bill. There have been many calls in recent congressional testimony, however, to offset the negative impacts caused by a strengthening US dollar with counter-cyclical payments to export dependent agricultural products.

Precautionary Principle, Sanitary and Phytosanitary Barriers to Trade

The precautionary principle, or foresight planning, has recently been frequently proposed as a justification for government restrictions on trade in the context of environmental and health concerns, often regardless of cost or scientific evidence. It was first proposed as a household management technique in the 1930s in Germany, and included elements of prevention, cost effectiveness, and ethical responsibility to maintain natural systems. In the context of managing environmental uncertainty, the principle enjoyed a resurgence of popularity during a meeting of the U.N. World Charter for Nature (of which the U.S. is only an observer) in 1982.

Its use was re-endorsed by the U.N. Convention on Bio-diversity in 1992, and again in Montreal, Canada in January 2000. The precautionary principle has been interpreted by some to mean that new chemicals and technologies should be considered dangerous until proven otherwise. It therefore requires those responsible for an activity or process to establish its harmlessness and to be liable if damage occurs. Most recent attempts to invoke the principle have cited the use of toxic substances, exploitation of natural resources, and environmental degradation. Concerns about species extinction, high rates of birth defects, learning deficiencies, cancer, climate change, ozone depletion, and contamination with toxic chemicals and nuclear materials have also been used to justify trade and other government restrictions on the basis of the precautionary principle.

Thus, countries seeking more open trading regimes have been concerned that the precautionary principle will simply be used to justify non-tariff trade barriers. For example, rigid adherence to the precautionary principle could lead to trade embargoes on products such as genetically modified oil seeds with little or no reliance on scientific analysis to justify market closure. Sometimes, restrictions on imports from certain places are fully consistent with protecting consumers, the environment, or agriculture from harmful diseases or pests that may accompany the imported product. The WTO Sanitary and Phytosanitary (SPS) provisions on technical trade rules specifically recognize that all countries feel a responsibility to secure their borders against the importation of unsafe products. Prior to 1994, however, such barriers were often simply used as excuses to keep out a product for which there was no real evidence of any problem.

These phony technical barriers were just an excuse to keep out competitive products. The current WTO agreement requires that whenever a technical barrier is challenged, a member country must show that the barrier has solid scientific justification and restricts trade as little as possible to achieve its scientific objectives. This requirement has resulted in a number of barriers being relaxed around the world. It should be emphasized that WTO rules do not require member countries to harmonize rules or adopt international standards — only that there must be some scientific basis for the rules that are adopted. Thus, any options for sanitary and phytosanitary initiatives considered in the 2002 Farm Bill must be based on sound science and they do not have to be harmonized with the initiatives of other countries.

INTERNATIONAL TRADE: RISKS AND RISK ASSESSMENT

INTERNATIONAL TRADE PRACTICES

All forms of business contain elements of risk, but when it comes to international trade, the risk profile enters a new dimension. Internationally, you seldom have common laws that can support the transaction, as would be the case within one country.

Instead, established trade practices and conventions are used to settle the undertakings made by the parties. The key to successful trade transactions, therefore, depends on a knowledge of these established practices and ensuring that the undertakings in the individual contract are in line with such practices. This is why it is crucial for the seller to have started with a correct risk assessment before finally entering into the transaction.

Sometimes, however, the circumstances in a particular case are so obvious that one hardly thinks of it as a risk assessment, whereas in other situations a thorough risk assessment needs to be done. The main sources for international trade practices are publications issued by the International Chamber of Commerce, which will be referred to many times throughout this book. In every new transaction one has to take it for granted that, from the outset, the parties will have different views about various aspects of the terms of payment. This is quite logical since the most important function of these terms for both seller and buyer is to minimize not only the risks involved, but also the cost of payment and of the financing of the transaction.

The negotiation process

The seller will always try to get terms that will maximize the outcome and minimize the risk. However, they must also be prepared to accommodate reasonable demands from the buyer in order to match other competitors and reach a deal that is acceptable to both parties, thereby also developing a good long-term business relationship. Should the seller be inflexible on this point, it could result in an adverse competitive situation with the potential risk of losing the deal. On the other hand, demands from the buyer that are too stringent can have the same result, or be resolved by means of a higher price or some other amendment to the final agreement.

The outcome of these negotiations will depend on past knowledge and experience, which is even more important if the buyer bases their request for tender on simplified or standar-dized terms of payment, usually to their own advantage. In many cases, such terms are adapted to conditions that are not optimal for the seller, compared with what the seller could have reached if they were individually negotiated. In such a case it is important to be able to argue and convince the buyer that there might be other solutions that can satisfy any reasonable demands, in order to find the optimal result for both parties. There is, however, another – and in some countries very common – way to bridge the gap between the parties, if the seller has to abstain from some demands in negotiations with the buyer.

The seller could approach a third party, often a credit insurance company, in order to reduce the commercial risk which could not be covered through the agreed terms of payment. Finally, it should be noted that the business practices which have been established over time in different countries or regions also create at least a common ground for both parties when starting their payment negotiations, ie choice of currency, form of payment and terms of financing.

Local banks, trade councils and the chambers of commerce in both the seller's and the buyer's country can draw on their experience and give impartial advice on local business practice regarding both the form of payment and the more specific terms of payment, while also taking the size, commodity and other aspects of the potential transaction into account. Such considerations can then be the starting point for negotiations between the parties.

Different forms of trade risk

There are always potential drawbacks in trying to categorize such a general concept as trade risks which could have so many different forms and shapes, but it also has great illustrational advantages, particularly when they also coincide with commonly used business expressions. Figure shows the main risk structure in international trade, which will affect both the seller's and the buyer's view of the terms of payment.

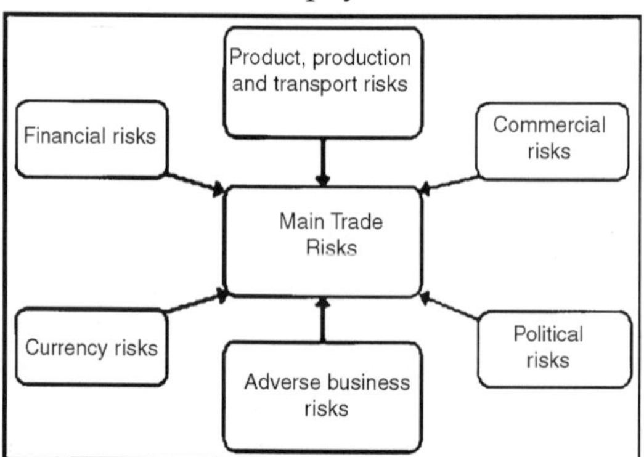

Fig. Different Forms of Risk in International Trade

Obviously, all these risks combined do not often occur in one and the same transaction. For example, a sale to a Norwegian customer in USD may be just a matter of a straight commercial risk on the buyer, whereas delivery of a tailor-made machine to Indonesia has to be risk assessed in quite another way. In quite general terms, the risk structure is directly linked to the obligations undertaken by the seller. This assessment can often be made relatively simple as a commercial risk only, but, in other cases, for example if the transaction also involves assembly, installation, testing or a maintenance responsibility, the assessment has to involve many other aspects as well.

The question of risk is to a large degree a subjective evaluation, but it is still important for both parties to have a good knowledge of these matters in order to carry out a proper and meaningful risk assessment. Only thereafter does the question arise about how to cover these risks through the terms of payment together with other limitations in the contract, if applicable, and together with separate credit risk insurance or guarantees, as the case may be. It should also be noted that most export credit insurance, taken by the seller as additional security, could be impaired or even invalid should the seller themselves not have fulfilled – or been able to fulfil – their obligations according to the contract.

This is another reason why it is so important that the obligations of the seller, according to the contract, are always directly related to those of the buyer. Otherwise the seller may end up in a risk situation that is worse than anticipated at the time of entering into the contract. When all the necessary evaluations have been done, the final decision as to whether the deal is secure enough to be entered into has to be taken. The worst that can happen is finding, after the contract has been signed, that it contains risks that the seller was unaware of at that time. It is then often too late to make changes.

Terms of delivery and terms of payment

The terms of delivery also have to be defined in order to determine when and where the seller has fulfilled the obligations to deliver according to the contract and what is needed in order to do so.

There is a clear connection between these two sets of terms insofar as payment is mostly related to the point at which the risk passes from the seller to the buyer as specified by the terms of delivery; it is to be made either at that particular time or at a specific time thereafter. This connection makes it necessary to outline some basic facts about the different terms of delivery. The standard rules of reference for the interpretation of the most commonly used trade terms in international trade are Incoterms 2000 issued by the International Chamber of Commerce Publication 560.

These rules are now generally recognized throughout the world, so any other unspecified trading terms, which may often have different meanings for companies in different countries, should be avoided. When agreed upon between the parties, these rules and their latest revisions must always be referred to in the sales contract and in all related documentation, for example CIF Hong Kong, Incoterms 2000. The basic purpose of these rules is to define how each Incoterm, as agreed in the sales contract, should be dealt with in terms of delivery, risks and costs, and specify the responsibility of the buyer and seller. For example, who should arrange and pay freight, other transport charges, insurance, duties and taxes?

These aspects are often referred to as the critical points in international trade, detailing at what point the risk is transferred from the seller to the buyer and how the costs involved should be split between the parties. There are presently 13 defined Incoterms, split into four groups, related to the seller's obligation to deliver the goods. Some Incoterms can be used only for maritime transport whereas others can be used for all modes of transport; similarly, some are more suitable than others for use in combination with terms of payment based on 'clean payments' in connection with open account trading, while others are used in combination with 'documentary payments'.

These four groups are:

1. *Group E*: Where the seller has to make the goods available at their premises. The only example is EXW – Ex Works, where the seller must place the goods at the disposal of the buyer at the seller's premises or another named place not cleared for export and not loaded on any collecting vehicle.
2. *Group F*: Where the seller must deliver the goods to a carrier appointed by the buyer. For example, FOB – Free on Board.
3. *Group C*: Where the seller themselves must contract for the carriage of the goods, but without assuming risk of loss of, or damage to, the goods or additional costs due to events occurring after shipment.

For example, CIF – Cost Insurance and Freight, where the seller delivers the goods when they pass the ship's rail in the port of shipment and must pay the costs and freight necessary to bring the goods to the named port of destination, but including also the procurement of insurance against the buyer's risk of loss of, or damage to, the goods during carriage.

4. *Group D*: Where the seller also has to bear all costs and risks required to deliver the goods to the place of destination. For example, DDP – Delivered Duty Paid where the seller must deliver the goods to the buyer, cleared for import, and not unloaded at the named place of destination.

When choosing the appropriate terms of delivery, deciding factors include:

- The transportation route, the buyer and the nature of the goods, including the mode of transport;
- Standard practice, if any, in the buyer's country or any regulation set by the authorities of that country to benefit their own transport or insurance industry;
- Procedures, where the seller should avoid terms of delivery, which are dependent on obtaining import licences or clearance of goods to countries they cannot properly judge;
- The competitive situation, where the buyer often suggests their preferred terms of delivery and the seller has to evaluate these terms in relation to the risks involved.

For a standard delivery between established trade partners, neighbouring countries or countries belonging to a common trading area, this question is often easily agreed upon as a matter of standard practice with only an adjustment related to the actual freight and insurance charges, often in connection with open account trading. In these cases, the Incoterms Groups E and F are often used, where the buyer takes the main responsibility for transport and risk of the purchased goods. However, in other cases and when the seller wants to have better control of the delivery process and be able to select transport and/or insurance, the delivery terms C and D are more frequently used.

PRODUCT RISKS

Product risks are risks that the seller automatically has to accept as an integral part of their commitment. First, it is a matter of the product itself, or the agreed delivery; for example, specified performance warranties or agreed maintenance or service obligations. There are many examples of how new and unexpected working conditions in the buyer's country have led to reduced performance of the delivered goods. It could be negligence concerning operating procedures or restrictions, careless treatment, lack of current maintenance, but also damage due to the climate or for environmental reasons. Matters of this nature may well lead to disputes between the parties after the contract has been signed and to increased cost for the delivery as a whole.

It is important for the seller to have the contract, and specifically the terms of payment, worded in such a way that any such changes, which are directly or indirectly due to the actions of the buyer or originating within their country, will automatically include compensation or corresponding changes in the seller's commitments. This can be either in economic terms or in originally agreed time limits, or both. It goes without saying that these risks become even more complicated when it comes to whole projects or larger and more complex contracts. These are often completed over longer periods and involve many more possible combinations of interrelated commitments between the commercial parties, not only between the seller and the buyer, but also often involving other parties in the buyer's country, both commercial and political.

Manufacturing risks

This risk appears all too frequently when the product is tailor-made or has unique specifications. In these cases there is often no other readily available buyer if the transaction cannot be completed, in which case the seller has to carry the cost of any necessary readjustment, if that is even an option. Risks of this nature occur as early as the product planning phase but may often be difficult to cover from that time owing to the special nature of these products. But they also involve specific risks for the buyer, who often has to enter into payment obligations at an early stage but without the security of the product itself until it has been delivered and installed. In order to safeguard the interests of both parties, the terms of payment are often divided into part-payments related to the production and delivery phases, in combination with separate guarantees, to cover the risks as they occur in different phases of the transaction.

Transport risks and cargo insurance

From a general risk perspective it is not only the product but also the physical movement of the goods from the seller to the buyer that has to be evaluated, based on aspects such as the nature of the product, size of delivery, the buyer and their country, and the actual transportation route. Most goods in international trade, apart from smaller and non-expensive deliveries, are covered by cargo insurance, providing cover against physical loss or damage whilst in transit, either by land, sea or air, or by a combination of these modes of transport. The cover under a cargo or marine cargo policy is almost always defined by standard policy wordings issued by the Institute of London Underwriters.

These are called Institute Cargo Clauses. While there are numerous clauses that will apply to different cargos, the widest cover is provided under

Institute Cargo Clauses A or with more restrictive cover under Institute Cargo Clauses B and Institute Cargo Clauses C. Cargo insurance is therefore normally provided through one of these Institute Cargo Clauses A, B or C, plus separate war clauses and strike clauses. The question of who should arrange the insurance is determined by the agreed terms of delivery, as defined by the Incoterms 2000 and described earlier. These terms also define the critical point during transport, where the risk is transferred from the seller to the buyer.

That can be any given point between a named place at the seller's location and a named place at the buyer's location. That specified critical point determines the seller's and the buyer's responsibility to arrange insurance, as required. However, there is another aspect of risk coverage that the seller has to be particularly aware of, and that is the potential risk of the buyer arranging insurance according to some of the terms of delivery. If such a term of delivery is chosen, for example FOB and the buyer fails to insure in a proper and agreed way, the goods may arrive at the destination in a damaged condition and without adequate insurance cover. If, at the same time, the terms of payment allow for payment after delivery, this risk de facto becomes a risk for the seller, who may end up with unpaid for, uninsured and damaged goods at the point of destination.

Such a situation is obviously a consequence of the seller agreeing to terms of payment that did not cover the actual commercial risk, but the insurance risk involved could, in most cases, have been eliminated by separate seller's interest contingency insurance. From the seller's perspective, there are basically three different ways to insure the cargo, either with an open insurance policy covering most or all shipments within the seller's basic trade as agreed in advance with the insurer, or with a specific insurance policy, covering specific shipments on an *ad hoc* basis or those which are outside the set criteria of the open policy.

The open policy is by far the most common in international trade, normally reviewed on an annual basis, and with a 30–60-day cancellation clause, should conditions deteriorate substantially. The open cover is the most cost-effective alternative, but it also has obvious administrative advantages and will automatically secure the actual coverage of all individual shipments under the policy. The third basic form of cargo insurance is seller's interest contingency insurance normally only offered as a complement to the open policy or as integral part of a specific policy, and on an undisclosed basis as far as the buyer is concerned. This insurance covers the risk that the goods may arrive at their destination in a damaged condition, resulting in the buyer's refusal to accept them or they may simply be unable or unwilling to pay for commercial or political reasons, including failure to produce a valid import licence. In such cases the insurance covers the physical loss of, or damage to, the goods, but it does not cover the credit risk on the buyer, which has to be covered through the terms of payment, in conjunction with any other arrangements. The seller should bear in mind that cargo insurance is a specialized business, where cover and conditions may vary according to the commodity or goods to be shipped, the transportation route and the mode of transport, which is a major reason why open policy cover is the most common in international trade. But normal risk management procedures will always apply: new and adverse conditions and/or additional risks must be reported or approved by the insurer, and the policy normally excludes loss or damage due to wilful misconduct or insufficient, unsuitable or inadequate packing or container stowage by the assured party.

Cargo insurance can be obtained directly from an insurance company or, very often today, directly through the transporting company or the forwarding agent handling the goods. In some countries it is also quite common to use independent cargo insurance brokers, who may be more able to select the most cost-efficient insurance package, based on specific conditions or the trade structure in each individual case. However, the seller should always ensure that the selected insurer has or is part of an established international network for dealing with claims and settlement procedures.

COMMERCIAL RISKS (PURCHASER RISKS)

Commercial risk, also called purchaser risk, is often defined as the risk of the buyer going into bankruptcy or being in any other way incapable of fulfilling the contractual obligations. One might first think of the buyer's payment obligations but it also covers all other obligations of the buyer, according to the contract, necessary for the seller to fulfil their obligations. How does the seller, therefore, evaluate the buyer's ability to fulfil their obligations?

In most industrialized countries within the Organization for Economic Co-operation and Development area, it is relatively easy to obtain a fair picture of potential buyers, either to study their published accounts or to ask for an independent business credit report, which is a more reliable way of dealing with customer risks. This will also give much broader information about the buyer and their business, and not simply some selected economic figures from which the seller often cannot draw any decisive conclusions.

Credit information

Export trade may be an important factor in the potential growth of business; however, the risks involved in carrying out international business can also be high. In little more than a decade, the world of commerce has changed dramatically. In this commercial environment, the global suppliers of credit information have become a vital source of knowledge and expertise, based on the great wealth of information that they maintain about consumers and how they behave, about businesses and how they perform, and about different markets and how they are changing. The more the seller understands their customers, the more they are able to respond to their individual needs and circumstances. Credit information suppliers help the seller use information to reach new customers and to build, nurture and maximize lasting customer relationships.

Credit information thus forms a vital part of establishing the structure of a potential export transaction and, in particular, the terms of payment to be used. In some cases the information can be provided instantly, inexpensively and in a standardized manner on the internet, but in other cases a more researched profile is required.

Each seller must have a policy for obtaining up-to-date information about the commercial risk structure in connection with any new potential buyer or business and with outstanding export receivables. How this is done may differ depending on the volume and structure of the exports, but it is recommended at least to review the business information systems offered by the larger providers and to choose an alternative that is optimal for the individual seller as to the services and costs involved.

The seller should, however, be aware that the contents and accuracy of the business information may vary, depending on the registered information available about the company. The contents can sometimes also be difficult to evaluate and questions always arise about how up to date it really is, particularly when dealing with customers outside the most advanced industrialized countries.

With buyers from non-OECD countries the matter becomes even more complicated. The information, if available, will be much more difficult to evaluate and it will be harder to assess how it has been produced and how it should be analysed. In these cases, the information probably has limited value anyway, because other risk factors, such as the political risk, may be greater – and terms of payment that reflect this combined risk have to be chosen. The seller may also be able to get assistance abroad through the export or trade council or similar institutions in their country, and/or from the commercial sections of embassies abroad, which can assist with market surveys and other studies in that country.

Even banks can participate by issuing introductory letters to their branches or correspondents, enabling the seller to obtain more up-to-date information about the local business conditions and form an opinion about the buyer and their business in connection with the contract negotiations.

ADVERSE BUSINESS RISKS

Adverse business risks include all business practices of a negative nature, which are not only common but also almost endemic in some parts of the world. This could have serious consequences for the individual transaction, but also for the general business and financial standing of the seller, as well as their moral reputation. We are, of course, referring to all sorts of corrupt practices that flourish in many countries, particularly in connection with larger contracts or projects: bribery, money laundering and a variety of facilitation payments:

- Bribery in general can broadly be defined as the receiving or offering of an undue reward by or to any holder of public office or a private employee designed to influence them in the exercise of their duty, and thus to incline them to act contrary to the known rules of honesty and integrity.

This quotation is taken from a UK government body, and even if it is not a legal definition, it gives an accurate description of the problem. If bribery is generally a technique to press the seller for undue rewards, money laundering often has the opposite purpose, which is to invite the seller to do a deal that may on the face of it seem very advantageous, but where the true intention is to disguise or conceal the actual origin of the money involved. It covers criminal activities, corruption and breaches of financial sanctions. It includes the handling, or aiding the handling, of assets, knowing that they are the result of crime, terrorism or illegal drug activities.

Criminal and terrorist organizations generate large sums of cash, which they need to channel into the banking, corporate and trade financial systems, and both banks and traders can innocently fall victim of such activity if not exercising due diligence. A frequently used technique is over-invoicing or inflated transactions, with or without payment to a third party, where the seller may be completely unaware that they could be part of a ruse to launder money.

The seller should also be particularly observant in the case of cash payments and be aware that new anti-money laundering regulations must be complied with for such payments in most countries. A reputable business adds respectability to any organization being used for laundering operations, and money launderers will try to use any business, directly through ownership, or indirectly by deceit.

Developing nations are particularly vulnerable to money launderers because they usually have poorly regulated financial systems. These provide the greatest opportunities to criminals. In general terms, a suspicious transaction is one that is outside the normal range of transactions from the seller's point of view, in particular in relation to new customers or where an old customer changes transaction structure in an unusual way.

It can include:

- Unusual payment settlements;
- Unusual transfer instructions;
- Secretiveness;
- Rapid movements in and out of accounts;
- Numerous transfers;
- Complicated accounts structures.

Bribery, money laundering and any other form of corrupt behaviour is bad for business; it distorts the normal trade patterns and gives unfair advantages to those involved in it. It is also extremely harmful for the countries themselves, owing to the damage it causes to the often fragile social fabric; it destroys the economy and is strongly counterproductive for trade and all forms of foreign investments into the country.

In the long run, such practices also prevent social and economic stability and development, and it has an especially negative impact on the most disadvantaged parts of the population. Even within the countries where these practices are frequent among individual public and private employees, it is almost always illegal, even if the countries lack the means and the resources to tackle these problems effectively.

The need for a strong policy

The World Bank and the OECD have put a great deal of resources into combating corruption worldwide, and in most countries corruption is now illegal even when committed overseas. The companies also have full responsibility for the wrongdoings of their employees abroad when acting for the company. As a consequence of the inclusion of anti-corruption laws, it is also incorporated in the procedures of all government departments, for example in the rules of the respective export credit agency. Any violation of the anti-corruption statement that the seller has to give when applying for such insurance could have serious implications for its validity. It is often not even the threat of prosecution that should most worry the seller.

There have been a number of cases in which companies were allegedly involved in corrupt behaviour, but where the true circumstances were not fully disclosed. The allegation could be damaging enough, sometimes based only on rumours emanating from economic groups or political factions within the society to stop or postpone a project or to favour another bidder. Such rumours, true or false, or involving either smaller facilitation payments or large-scale bribery to senior private or public officials, can drag on for years, with economic and detrimental consequences for the company, both overseas and at home. Every company involved in overseas trade or investments should have a clear anti-corruption policy that is implemented and clearly understood by all its employees, and supervised by the management in an appropriate way. Such a policy is also supported by local laws, which give both the company and its employees a much stronger moral and legal defence against every attempt to extort bribes from them or attempt to induce them into any other form of corrupt practice.

POLITICAL RISKS

Political risk or country risk is often defined as: 'the risk of a separate commercial transaction not being realized in a contractual way due to measures emanating from the government or authority of the buyer's own or any other foreign country'. No matter how reliable the buyer may be in fulfilling their obligations and paying in local currency, their obligations to the seller are nevertheless dependent on the current situation in their own country – or along the route of transport to that country.

However, in practice, it may be difficult to separate commercial and political risk because political decisions, or other similar acts by local authorities, also affect the local company and its capabilities of honouring the contract. For example, some countries may change taxes, import duties or currency regulations, often with immediate effect, which could undermine the basis for contracts already signed.

Other common measures include import restrictions or other regulations intended to promote local industry and to save foreign currency. Even with just the risks of such actions, they all have the same negative implications for the transaction and the buyer's possibility of fulfilling their part of the contract.

Seen from a broader perspective, political risk could be divided into different underlying causes, such as:

- Political stability;
- Social stability; and
- Economic stability.

Political stability is often seen as an important criterion of the real political risk. This stability indicates, in general terms, the likelihood or the probability of a country's involvement in, or being affected by, acts of terror, war or internal violence from groupings within the country or sanctions or blockades from other nations. The constant risk of rapid and unexpected change in economic policy or in the form of nationalization or similar measures as a consequence of political instability will have the same effect; they are all extremely damaging for any private commercial economic activity in the country.

Unfortunately, there are presently numerous examples of this political instability in many parts of the world. The social stability of a country is also of great importance, mainly on a long-term basis. However, the developments in many countries, not only developing countries, show all too well how unexpectedly and rapidly social instability can turn into violence or terrorist activity that can paralyse the country or its economy. Economic stability is equally important to maintain the confidence of a country and its economy. A weak infrastructure, dependence on single export or import commodities, a high debt burden and lack of raw materials are critical factors that, together with other developments, can easily change economic stability in a short time. Even currency restrictions and other more indirect currency regulations such as 'pegging' against other currencies, often USD, could have serious long-term economic consequences, as seen in many countries. The turbulent situation in many developing countries is a constant reminder of the fragility of economic stability in many countries around the world.

Other forms of political or similar risk

Apart from the real political risks already discussed, there are other measures taken by authorities in the buyer's home country that can affect the buyer and their ability or willingness to fulfil the transaction; for example, demands for product standards, new or changed energy or environmental requirements – measures that could have a genuine purpose or be put in place partly to act as trade barriers to promote sectors or important industries within the country. Irrespective of the purpose, such actions, often called 'non-tariff barriers', could have a negative impact on the signed transaction.

Other, more open measures are sometimes also implemented, often at short notice, as has been seen within the European Union, for example, where the objective has often been to prevent a rapid increase in imports from some emerging market countries, in order to protect the EU's own industry or allow more time to adapt to new trade patterns. But countries involved in the transit of goods have to be considered as well as countries related to subcontractors or suppliers of crucial components. In these cases, perhaps it is not the political risk as defined, but other measures that are more important; for example, the risk of labour market conflicts in the form of strikes or lockouts that could interrupt delivery of components needed for the timely execution of the agreed sales contract.

Not least, the risk involved in ordinary force majeure clauses should be mentioned, even if the background is not political but caused by other factors outside the control of the commercial parties themselves. When used by other parties, such clauses could, for example, release a subcontractor from their delivery obligations during the periods they are applicable, with corresponding effects for the seller. Even bank guarantees and other obligations in favour of the seller could be of limited value during such periods if, as is normally the case, they only cover commitments according to a contract, which may refer to such clauses.

The same goes for presentation of documents under a letter of credit, where the bank will not accept documents that have expired during such interruption of the bank's business. However, when used by the seller, such clauses could protect them against actions for breach of contract, where performance of their contractual obligations is prevented by incidents outside their control.

This is often referred to as 'frustration of contract' and a typical clause might say:

- The Company shall have no liability in respect of any failure or delay in fulfilling any of the Company's obligations to the extent that fulfilment thereof is prevented, frustrated, impeded and/or delayed or rendered uneconomic as a consequence of any fire, flood, earthquake, other natural disaster or Act of God, industrial dispute or other circumstances or event beyond the Company's reasonable control.

Currency risks

If payment is going to be made in a currency other than that in which the seller incurs their costs, a new currency risk will arise. In most cases, the seller's main costs will be in local currency, which automatically creates such a risk if invoicing in another currency. The size of that risk will depend on the currency and the outstanding period until payment. Since the introduction of the euro, invoicing in that currency has become increasingly common in European trade and also with sellers outside the euro zone. This development is likely to accelerate with additional countries joining the euro zone. Traditionally, however, the USD has been the preferred third-party currency.

This applies particularly to raw materials and certain commodities in general, and for many other services such as freight and insurance. It is also commonly used in countries where the United States maintains a strong economic or political influence.

Available statistics do not usually show currency distribution for international trade of goods and services, but it can generally be expected that exports invoiced in smaller trade currencies are diminishing in favour of the larger ones, and will probably continue to do so. Most exporters will therefore have to become accustomed to invoicing in foreign currency and to the management of currency risk exposure.

Assessment of currencies

Traditionally, currencies have been divided into groups of 'strong' and 'weak' currencies, and this view has affected the general conception of preferred trade currencies, even though the highest preference is often for the currency of the home country. Sterling, the yen, the Swiss franc and even the euro and maybe some others would probably be regarded as strong currencies, while others would be seen as neutral, weak or unstable. An evaluation such as this may perhaps have its justification in a longer perspective for currencies where the home countries have maintained economic and political stability over the years, together with a strong economy, low inflation and stable confidence in the future maintenance of this policy.

It should, however, be enough to look at the development of the USD, which has changed its value vis-à-vis other large currencies dramatically over the years to realize that such sweeping statements can have their risks. Furthermore, for most parties it is not the long-term currency development that is most interesting, but rather the shorter perspective, limited to the time-span during which current deals are paid. Then the situation can be reversed, for in that shorter perspective, a currency can have a development in complete contrast to its long-term trend. In the shorter perspective, other factors, real or expected, may be more important, such as interest rate changes, political news and larger price movements in base commodities, central bank currency interventions, statements and statistics.

All these factors, combined with subjective evaluations by millions of participants in the currency markets, will together constantly create new short-term trends. For those who want to follow short-term currency development, most banks and many other financial or currency institutions publicize information via the internet or e-mail on a regular basis – both retrospectively and actual, together with analysis and evaluations of future trends.

FINANCIAL RISKS

In practice, every international trade transaction contains an element of financial risk. Purchasing, production and shipment all place a financial burden on the transaction that forces the seller to determine how alternative terms of payment would affect liquidity during its different phases until payment – and how this should be financed. And, if the deal is not settled as intended, an additional financial risk occurs.

In the case of subcontractors, who do not share the risks of the transaction and are paid according to separate agreements, the risk increases accordingly and even more so should the seller have to offer a supplier credit for a shorter or longer period. When it comes to larger and more complex transactions, this financial risk aspect is even more obvious. One of the major problems for the seller could be to obtain bankable collateral for the increased need for finance and guarantees.

Even after production and delivery, the seller could still be financially exposed in the case of unforeseen events and delays until final payment. Sometimes the interaction between the seller and the buyer can make it difficult to establish the exact cause for the delay in payment and there are then fewer chances for the seller to refer to a specific breach of contract on the part of the buyer.

On the other hand, if the seller has paid enough attention when drafting the sales contract, including the terms of payment, then it is more likely that any reason for delays will be possible to determine according to the clauses of the contract. There could be numerous reasons for such delays, for example issuing a letter of credit too late, late changes in specification of the goods, late arrival of the vessel, congestion in port, changes in the transport route, to name a few. The real risk also tends to increase with longer and consequently more costly transport distances. Bureaucratic delays in many countries, as well as delays in the banking system, will have the same result – the final payment to the seller will not be made as anticipated according to the contract.

Apart from ordinary overdrafts during production and delivery, the need for finance is also determined by the amount of credit that the seller may have to offer as part of the deal. If so, the financial risk is increased in line with the prolonged commercial and/or political risk.

A careful risk assessment is the first important step to a successfully completed transaction because it is the basis for the seller's own strategy, and for the final decision on what is acceptable in the negotiations with the buyer in order to minimize the risks involved.

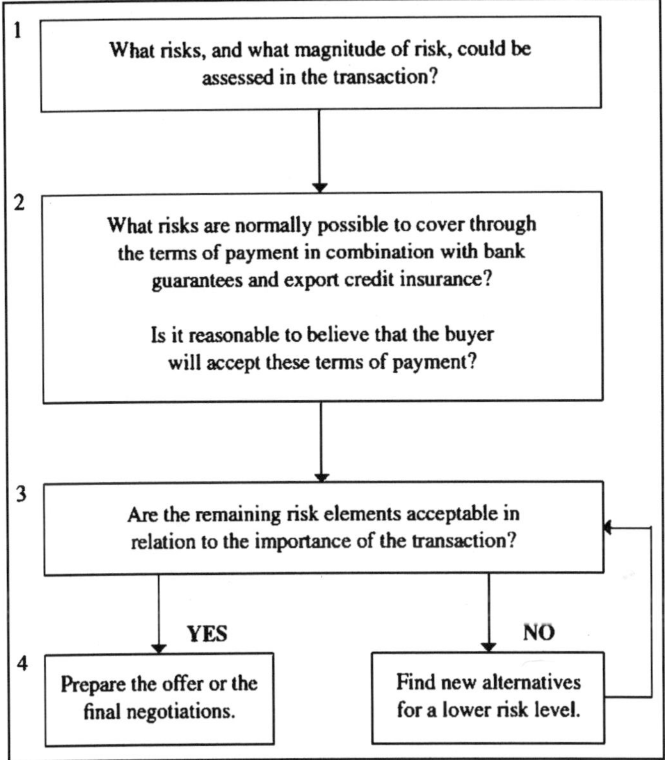

Fig. Risk Assessment – A Summary

Financial risk and cash management

Other forms of financial risk are more obvious but have to be underlined in this context; for example, if the seller misjudges the risks involved in the transaction and becomes exposed through terms of payment that do not cover the real risk situation, or mistakenly enters into the deal without proper risk protection.

It goes without saying that such miscalculations can have serious financial consequences, from delays in payment to loss of capital. The financial risks are generally intimately connected to the structure of the terms of payment. The safer they can be made, the more the financial risk will automatically be reduced, the timing of the payments will be more accurate and the liquidity aspect of the transaction better assessed – in fact, the very essence of cash management.

The safer the terms of payment the parties have agreed upon, the more costly they will normally be. And, if they contain bank security, such as a letter of credit or a bank guarantee, that will also reduce available credit limits within the buyer's own bank. However, the buyer is often not prepared to accept higher costs and the use of their own credit limits in order to satisfy what might be seen as excessive demands from the seller, involving methods of payments, which in their opinion, are not normal practice in their country or normally accepted by the company. It is then up to the seller to evaluate the transaction, including potential competition from other suppliers. Eventually, the seller may have to accept the terms of payment offered and try to cover the remaining risks in some other way or to find a compromise by offering compensation to the buyer for the increased bank charges and/or the additional costs incurred by the use of the buyer's existing credit limits.

BUSINESS AND SOCIAL NETWORKS IN INTERNATIONAL TRADE

Nations appear to trade too much with themselves and too little with each other. Jonathan Eaton and Samuel Kortum calculate that "zero gravity" would implya more than fivefold increase in world trade. Attempts to explain this "mystery of the missing trade" have increasingly focused on informal trade barriers, especially weak enforcement of international contracts (James Anderson and Douglas Marcouiller forthcoming) and inadequate information about international trading opportunities. Business and social networks that operate across national borders can help to overcome these kinds of informal trade barriers. For example, Saxenian shows that a transnational community of Indian engineers has facilitated outsourcing of software development from Silicon Valley to regions like Bangalore and Hyderabad.

Research can provide us with insight into *how* transnational networks overcome informal trade barriers, and at the same time can serve to document and even quantify the existence of these barriers. Determining the relative importance of contract enforcement versus informational barriers is especially important since they point to quite different areas of concern for policymakers. Whereas transnational networks have primarily been studied as means of overcoming informal trade barriers, much of the research on the impact of domestic networks on international trade has been motivated byte perception that they constitute informal trade barriers in themselves, with network members colluding to increase their market power by restricting foreign competition. There is also a new line of work that investigates the effect of domestic networks on the composition of international trade.

EXAMPLES AND DEFINITIONS

Empirical research into the impact of networks on international trade has tended to lead theorizing. Most of the empirical work surveyed concerns co ethnic networks and business groups with publicly recorded membership such as the Japanese *keiretsu*. Coethnic networks are communities of individuals or businesses that share a demographic attribute such as ethnicity or religion. Business groups are "sets of firms that are integrated neither completely nor barely at all", and where the lineages of the members can often be traced back to a founding family or small number of allied families. Typical mechanisms serving to integrate the firms include mutual stockholdings and frequent meetings of top executives.

This focus on coethnic networks and business groups is explained by observability rather than primacy of importance: census takers will not record the characteristic "former employee of IBM," yet the fact that many of the key decision makers in the hard disk drive industry shared this characteristic contributed to the rapid spread of popularity of Singapore as a site for FDI, according to industry observers. However ubiquitous networks maybe in the conduct of international trade little can be learned about their impact unless they're observable. In some contexts the keyset re of the networks studied below is that their members are engaged in repeated exchange that helps sustain cooperation/ collusion.

In other contexts the key feature is that network members have thorough knowledge of each others' characteristics, which helps them match with each other or refer each other to outside business opportunities. These key features roughly correspond to two definitions of economic networks used in the sociological literature. The first, based on Joel Podolny and Karen Page, defines an economic network as *a group of agents that pursue repeated, enduring exchange relations with one another*. The second, weaker definition is based on the work of Granovetter: a set of actors who know each others' relevant characteristics or can learn them through referral.

For some purposes these definitions are clearly too broad to be useful. Organized international spot markets do not exist for most traded goods (especially manufactures), so it is entirely possible that systematic micro surveys would reveal that even byte repeated exchange definition most international trade could be viewed as taking place through networks. Egan and Mody, for example, state of trade in bicycles and footwear, "Most U.S. buyers interviewed for this study preferred long-term, stable and direct relationships with both developed and developing country suppliers." This broad definition of the role of networks in international trade may provide insight in some contexts, which suggests that this network view of trade could provide a new way of thinking about the connection between trade and technology transfer. It clearly will not do, however, when evaluating the claim that networks overcome informal barriers to trade, because it admits networks that were created by trade. This internation-alization may have taken place generations ago, but in this case we will see that it is more accurate to say that these networks are sustained by the trade they're creating than to say that these networks were created by trade.

The concentration of empirical research on business groups and co ethnic networks has two unfortunate potential side effects. First, conclusions might be biased byte difficulty of entry into these networks relative to others. Second, the impression might be conveyed that networks are a vestigial or at least culture-bound phenomenon.

This impression would come from the beliefs that co ethnic or co-religious ties are of declining importance in commerce and that business groups are confined to less developed countries (the *grupos económicos* of Latin America or "business houses" of India) or East Asia (the *chaebol* of Korea or *keiretsu* of Japan). Though trends for coethnic networks and business groups need not apply to networks as a whole, we should nevertheless note that the former belief is at least debatable and the latter belief is incorrect: business groups are ubiquitous in the developed countries of continental Europe.

NETWORKS AND OPPORTUNISM

Enforcement of contracts in international trade presents a difficult problem. This part is concerned with how networks facilitate trade across polities by building, or substituting for, trust when contract enforcement is weak to non-existent. Regarding the overseas Chinese network, Maurray Weidenbaum and Samuel Hughes report, "If a business owner violates an agreement, he is blacklisted. This is far worse than being sued, because the entire Chinese network will refrain from doing business with the guilty party." This kind of description suggests that transnational networks deter opportunism in a modern setting, yet the bulk of the more analytical literature has focused on the distant past or extremely underdeveloped environments.

This focus is related to the exclusive reliance of this literature on the tools of theory and case study. An important future task should be collection of data for contemporary networks that facilitate statistical testing of hypotheses. The literature surveyed invariably uses the repeated exchange definition of networks. Its subject is always *trade Diasporas,* which are ethnic or religious groups with settlements at endpoints and transshipment points of a trade route.

According to the survey by Philip Curtin, trade Diasporas dominated cross-cultural trade in most parts of the world until the nineteenth century. Curtin uses the term "cross-cultural" because the term "international" is an anachronism for the period preceding the rise of the nation-state. To some extent trade Diasporas constituted polities in themselves, but their legal enforcement powers were very weak. Sellers often avoided this problem by traveling with their goods, but agency relations were also prevalent in many trade Diasporas. The use of agency's best documented by Curtin for Armenians and several West African trade Diasporas. Curtin asserts, "Within the [17th–18th century] Armenian community, contracts could be made on a handshake." How were trade Diasporas able to deter opportunistic behaviour and thereby sustain agency? One leading answer is given by Cohen: a trade Diaspora created trust by establishing a "moral community."

An advantage of Cohen's work is that he studies a trade Diaspora, the Hausa in West Africa, that is *contemporary* to the time in which he is writing, which allows him to observe the operation of the Diaspora directly rather than infer it from historical documents. The key actors in Cohen's account are landlord brokers resident in Ibadan, Nigeria, site of the main Hausa trading settlement. These landlord-brokers employed commission agents ("clients") to sell cattle or purchase kola nuts on behalf of dealers located elsewhere in the Diaspora.

Opportunistic behaviour byte landlord brokers vis-à-vis the dealers was limited byte fact that they fell under the authority of the chief of the Hausa quarter in Ibadan and by their tradition of accumulating wealth in the form of housing assets: "A landlord cannot sell his houses overnight and leave the community after embezzling the money of traders. On the other hand, when it is necessary, the Chief can put a great deal of pressure on a landlord in difficulties to sell some of his housing assets in order to meet his financial obligations to traders". No such mechanisms prevented cheating bit he clients of the landlord broker, however, so it is here where development of "moral community" is most crucial.

Cohen notes that the relationships between a landlord-broker and his clients constitute a network rather than a hierarchy within the larger network-polity of the Diaspora, not only because there is no binding means of dispute resolution, but also because "the line of demarcation [between landlords and clients] is not rigid but is continually crossed by men moving to the one category or to the other." He argues that theft was deterred by teeing the repeated economic exchange between a landlord-broker and his clients to building of pseudo-kin relations: "The landlord will tyro marry the client off to... the foster daughters of his wives, or the daughters of his own relatives or of his wives' relatives"; "The landlord can thus be seen as the centre of a network of kinship relations with his clients".

Of course this group endogamy was facilitated by the separate identity the Diaspora minority maintained within the host society. Cohen concludes that "the relationship which thus develops between landlord and client cannot be measured in material or contractual terms alone. It is a relation which cannot be completely reduced to economic or political relations. There is an inescapable moral bond as well." The other leading answer to the question of how trade diasporas were able to sustain agency relations is given by Greif: the threat of collective punishment of deviant agents ball merchants (principals) in the Diaspora substituted for trust. Formally, a repeated game equilibrium in which the strategy of each merchant in a coalition is to refuse forever to deal with an agent who cheats *any* merchant in the coalition sustains a lower efficiency wage premium than a repeated game equilibrium in which each merchant's strategy's to punish only an agent who cheats him.

The higher efficiency wage required to prevent the agent from cheating under a bilateral punishment strategy could be so high as to make agency relations unprofitable. Greif studies the Maghreb traders of the eleventh-century Mediterranean through their documents. Like Cohen in his discussion of landlord-brokers and clients, Greif emphasizes the "horizontal" or non-hierarchical nature of the Maghreb network: "One does not observe the existence of two separate 'classes'... an agents class and a merchants class... the Maghribi traders group was a homogeneous group of middle-class traders and each of them operated as a merchant and as an agent at the same time." He presents evidence for both the transmission of information regarding past conduct of agents throughout the network required byte coalition strategy and for the operation of collective punishment.

For example, when the creditors of Samhun ben Da'ud, a prominent trader from Tunisia, were not paid, he complained that"... their letters filled with condemnation had reached everyone." Regarding collective punishment, Greif reports the following example: "an agent who lived in Jerusalem, Abun ben Zedaka, was accused of embezzling the money of a Maghribi trader. When word of this accusation reached other Maghribi traders, merchants as far away as Sicily canceled their agency relations with him."

Since establishment of a moral community and collective punishment of cheaters are not mutually exclusive mechanisms for discouraging opportunistic behaviour among agents, it seems likely that both were used among the Hausa, Maghreb's, and other trade Diasporas. Indeed, Cohen mentions that the chief of the quarter could resort to "public scandalizing" of a landlord-broker whom he could not punish effectively in other ways. This was accomplished through a special meeting, held in front of the house of the accused man, to which many Hausa dealers who happened to be in the quarter would be invited, ensuring the spread of the scandal throughout the Diaspora. Similarly, kinship ties are not entirely absent from the analysis by Greif, who states that the Maghribi coalition was able to surmount the "endgame" problem because "an old agent would not cheat because he feared that he would be punished through the punishment imposed on his relatives.

Only moral responsibility of relatives was required to enable traders to base their relations upon a reputation mechanism despite the fact that each of them lived for a finite number of years." To some extent it may be that different theoretical perspectives of Cohen and Greif, rather than differences between the Hausa and Maghribi trade Diasporas, caused the former to emphasize moral community and the latter to emphasize collective punishment. On one very important point, however, the two authors are in complete agreement: both the Hausa and the Maghreb's maintained their separate identities *for economic reasons, i.e.,* to facilitate their participation in profitable trade. The efficiency consequences of using networks to solve the problem of opportunism in cross-cultural (or international) trade would seem to be straightforward.

It seems clear that there is net trade creation, which should yield the usual gains from improved allocation of resources, and that the network members themselves should capture a surplus from cooperation. In addition to the theoretical argument of Greif that principals within a repeated exchange network can playa lower wage to their agents, Cohen shows that the Hausa out-competed both the main rival West African ethnic group (the Yoruba) and Europeans in controlling the cattle and kola trades. Greif, however, raises the intriguing possibility that the use of networks to facilitate cross-cultural trade, while statically efficient, is actually dynamically inefficient.

In particular, because an agent from outside the group must be paid a higher wage, the growth of trade handled by a network is hindered by the reluctance of merchants following a "collectivist strategy" to initiate inter economy relations. This is not true for merchants following an "individualist strategy" of bilateral punishment. In my view this argument is not decisive for two reasons. First, the savings to the traders following a collectivist strategy from paying lower wages may finance greater investment and growth in the presence of imperfect capital markets. Second, the network may simply incorporate the trader from the other economy. The exclusiveness of even co ethnic networks can be exaggerated: Cohen notes that "it is possible for some non-Hausa... to become, in effect, Sabo Hausa [Hausa of the Quarter]"; and regarding the overseas Chinese, Constance Lever- Tracyet al. report that "those studied in Australia were proud of trusting relations they had built up with Anglophone Australians."

Of course the process of incorporation requires time and resources, but it may be cheaper in present discounted value terms than paying a higher wage forever. Indeed, part of what the greater savings of traders following a collectivist strategy might finance is precisely investment in cultivation of new network members. Whether or not networks create inefficiencies in expanding trade to new areas or cultures is thus an empirical question. Greif also argues that the use of networks to suppress opportunistic behaviour in international trade was dynamically inefficient in the sense that it hindered institutional innovation designed to accomplish the same purpose. He shows that during the twelfth century the Genoese, whom he identifies as following individualist strategies, "developed an extensive legal system for registration and enforcement of contracts" as well as bookkeeping innovations that made it easier to detect theft of goods being sent overseas. It certainly seems clear that the use of networks to substitute for formal-legal means of enforcing contracts will hinder the improvement of such means. Improvements in international contract enforcement and other formal-legal means of substituting for trust in international trade have continued to the present day. Two important examples are international commercial arbitration and letters of credit. International commercial arbitration offers a private means of dispute resolution; Laurence Craig, William Park, and Jan Paulsson are the standard reference for International Chamber of Commerce arbitration. Letters of credit allow the trading parties to shift some of their commercial credit risk to the issuing bank and allow the buyer to defer payment until the shipment passes quality inspection.

Such innovations have surely reduced the demand for networks as a means of deterring opportunistic behaviour in international trade and have contributed, along with technological innovations in communication and transport, to "the twilight of the trade diasporas" An important future direction for the literature on transnational networks and opportunism should be to move beyond trade diasporas and to integrate contemporary international trade law and institutions into the analysis as outside options that may influence how the networks operate.

NETWORKS AND OPPORTUNITIES

A more recent literature has emphasized that, in addition to being used to transmit information about past opportunistic business conduct, networks can be used to transmit information about current opportunities for profitable international trade (or investment). The literature surveyed almost always uses the "characteristics knowledge" definition of networks, since the keys knowing the agents' characteristics so as to be able to match them to opportunities.

Transnational networks can facilitate this matching through provision of market information, letting suppliers know that consumers in a particular country will be receptive to their products, or enlightening suppliers on how to adapt their products to consumer preferences in a given country.

Korean wig exports to the United States are an especially well-studied example:

- Korean wig importers' contribution to the Korean wig import business was far greater than their numbers. From these immigrant wig importers, South Korea wig manufacturers could obtain information on new styles and market trends. Since they were not able to develop new styles of their own (prominent U.S. hair designers continuously eloped innovative styles), South Korean wig manufacturers had to depend entirely on Korean immigrant wig importers for information on trends in U.S. wig fashion.

Within a given foreign market, transnational networks can also help producers of consumer goods to find appropriate distributors, assemblers to find the right component suppliers, and investors to find joint-venture partners.

Weidenbaum and Hughes write of the overseas Chinese:

- The members of the bamboo network operate in the interstices of the trading world. They make components, manufacture for others, and perform subassembly work. They are also heavily involved in wholesaling, financing, sourcing, and transporting.... The leading businessmen know each other personally and do deals together, with information spreading through an informal network rather than through more conven-tional channels.

The empirical analyses reviewed below have provided evidence for the trade-creating effects of immigrants and of business groups operating across national borders. Immigrants know the characteristics of many domestic buyers and sellers and carry this knowledge abroad. Foreign direct investment by one or more members of a domestic business group has the same effect. These empirical papers have not been guided by formal theory. The measures of network strength used are *ad hoc,* and the models predicting trade to which they're added are taken "off the shelf."

As a result it is hard to identify the extent to which the estimated coefficients tell us that transnational networks work through provision of market information and matching and referral services as opposed to other means. Readers should therefore keep in mind that all the results reported are open to alternative interpretations. We first consider studies of the impact on bilateral trade of immigrants. An immediate concern is that, rather than a network effect, any positive impact might simply reflect immigrant taste for goods from their countries of origin or the correlation of immigration with country characteristics that promote trade, such as proximity. David Gould allays both concerns by estimating separate equations for exports and imports and including country dummies in his study of the immigrant impact on U.S. bilateral trade with 47 trading partners during the period 1970–86.

His basic estimating framework is Jeffrey Bergstrand's formulation of the gravity equation, to which Gould adds a lagged dependent variable, the stock of immigrants in the United States from each partner, and measures of immigrant skill composition and length of staying the United States. The coefficients on the immigrant stock are positive and highly significant in both the export and import equations, but the coefficients on the immigrant skill composition and length of stay variables are insignificant. The implied long-run elasticity's indicate that a 10-per cent increase in immigrants to the United States will increase U.S. exports to the country of origin by 4.7 per cent and U.S. imports from the country of origin by 8.3 per cent.

A reasonable interpretation of the larger point estimate for the import elasticity's that it combines a taste effect and a network effect, while the export elasticity only reflects a network effect. Keith Head and John Ries essentially repeat Gould's exercise for Canada, investigating the impact of immigrants on Canadian bilateral imports and exports for 136 trading partners during the period 1980–92. Their constant elasticity specification using a lagged dependent variable is closest to that of Gould, the main differences being omission of country dummies and use of a Tobit specification to allow for the many observations of zero on Canadian bilateral exports and imports.

For two different measures of the immigrant stock the estimated coefficients are positive and significant in both the export and import equations. The implied long-run elasticity's for the preferred immigrant stock measure indicate that a 10-per cent increase in immigrants to Canada will increase Canadian exports to the country of origin by 1.3 per cent and Canadian imports from the country of origin by3.3 per cent. The fact that these elasticity's are much lower than those estimated by Gould could be due to the nature of Canadian compared to U.S. trade: Head and Ries point out that "Canada's main export categories, natural resources and United States-bound automotive goods, do not seem likely candidates for transactions cost reductions by immigrants." We turn next to studies of the trade creating effects of business groups operating across national borders. Both studies surveyed are concerned with whether foreign direct investment in manufacturing by assemblers in "vertical" *keiretsu* stimulates exports by other *keiretsu* members.

Having an assembler abroad whose characteristics they know could be helpful to suppliers looking for export opportunities. René Belderbos and Leo Sleuwaegen investigate the 1988 intensity of exports to the European Community (EC) of 86 Japanese firms classified in the electronics or precision machinery industries. They regress the log of the ratio of firm exports to the EC to total sales minus exports to the EC on various firm characteristics plus a dummy for whether the firm is a member of a vertical *keiretsu* for which the assembler operated one or more manufacturing plants in the EC. The *keiretsu* dummy's positive and significant in all specifications. Head and Ries examine total exports of 96 *keiretsu* suppliers in the automobile and electronics industries for the period 1966–90. They regress the log of firm exports on firm characteristics, counts of the firm's foreign distribution and manufacturing investments, and the count of foreign manufacturing investments byte assembler of the vertical *keiretsu* to which the supplier belongs.

The *keiretsu* assembler investment count is positive and highly significant. Rauch and Vitor Trindade (forthcoming) attempt a partial synthesis of the literatures surveyed in this section and the previous one by examining the trade-creating effects of what is, in all probability, the largest transnational network (or set of interlinked national networks) in the world: the overseas Chinese. On the one hand, the overseas Chinese can be seen as a latter day trade Diaspora that deters opportunistic behaviour in international transactions. On the other hand, the overseas Chinese can promote trade by providing market information and matching and referral services because they use co ethnic business societies to keep knowledge of network members' characteristics fresh:

- This networked organizational system also distinguishes ethnic Chinese business patterns from other "personality" methods of conducting business. These types of business patterns developed along with various institutional supports, like clan halls, regional place associations, and "umbrella" organizations such as the Chinese Benevolent Associations in both local and overseas communities. These institutions were primarily involved in maintaining the social "glue" necessary for normative relationships and practices to continue over time and space. The contemporary evolution of these types of institutions has led to new forms of organization, such as the Greater Chinese Entrepreneurs' Conferences, the Chinese Business Fairs, and a number of other international ethnic Chinese conferences devoted primarily to business connections and transactions.

Rauch and Trinidad try to distinguish the trust and business opportunity impacts of the overseas Chinese network on bilateral trade by estimating separate gravity equations for commodities that have "reference prices" and commodities that do not. A reference price is defined as a price that is quoted without mentioning a brand name or other producer identification. Commodities that possess reference prices are taken to be sufficiently homogeneous that if traders see the price differential between two countries' markets is large enough to cover customs and transport costs, they know it is profitable to ship the product.

Commodities that do not possess reference prices are taken to be sufficiently differentiated that prices cannot convey enough of the information relevant for international trade: buyers and sellers must be matched in characteristics space, and hence the thicker information that can be provided byte overseas Chinese network is much more important than for international trade in homogeneous commodities. In contrast, moral community or the threat of collective sanctions should deter equally shipments of rotting fruit or stockings with runs. The same lack of distinction between commodities with and commodities without reference prices should hold for other forms of opportunistic behaviour such as failure to pay for a shipment one has received.

Rauch and Trinidad thus argue that an economically and statistically greater impact of the overseas Chinese network on bilateral trade in commodities without reference prices than in commodities with them establishes a presumption that this network has a quantitatively important effect by matching traders with business opportunities, in addition to its effect through building or substituting for trust. Rauch and Trinidad adapt Jeffrey Frankel's formulation of the gravity equation and begin with his sample of 63 countries. They have data on ethnic Chinese population shares for 57 and 59 of these countries circa 1980 and 1990, respectively, and estimate equations for the log of bilateral trade (sum of exports and imports) for each year separately. The strength of the overseas Chinese network for any two trading partners is measured byte product of their ethnic Chinese population shares, which gives the probability that, if we select an individual at random from each country, both will be ethnic Chinese. The gravity equation estimates to compute the per centage increases in bilateral trade attributable to the overseas Chinese network, evaluating all variables at their mean values. As we would expect, the network impact is much larger for trade between countries with ethnic Chinese population shares at the levels prevailing in Southeast Asia than for all other country pairs.

The per centage increases in bilateral trade attributable to direct and indirect colonial ties are also provided as a standard for comparison, where an indirect colonial tie exists between two countries that had the same colonial power. The integration of commercial interests that prevailed during colonial periods should have established a common business language or lingua franca and a set of business contacts, facilitating the search by producers for the right distributors, by assemblers for the right suppliers, and so on. The differences across commodity groups reported in table are all statistically significant, and confirm that the increase in bilateral trade attributable to the overseas Chinese network is larger for differentiated than for homogeneous products.

We see that the impact on bilateral trade of both the overseas Chinese network and direct and indirect colonial ties is lower in 1990 than in 1980 for both the homogeneous and the differentiated commodity groups. This could reflect strengthening of international contract enforcement mechanisms and improvements in communications technology, or it could reflect weakening of ethnic bonds and direct colonial ties and the spread of English as a common business language. Countering these (possible) trends are two tendencies that should increase rather than decrease the importance of networks for international trade.

First, the information intensity of trade is increasing: Rauch finds that differentiated products have increased their share of world trade from 56.5 per cent in 1970 to 67.1 per cent in 1990, and it seems likely that product differentiation itself is becoming ever finer. Second, supply of the other transnational networks covered by studies in this section is increasing: a rising flow of migrants, especially from poor to rich countries, has resulted in the foreign-born accounting for a growing share of the population of most rich countries, and business groups are increasingly spread across national borders. The implications for economic efficiency of transnational networks that provide information about profitable trading opportunities can be evaluated using the model of Rauch and Alessandra Casella. In their model production takes place as follows: producers match pair wise, and if the match is acceptable an internationally immobile resource ("labour") is employed to realize the productive opportunity. Domestic matching is characterized by complete information—every producer knows the type of every other—while international matching is hampered by incomplete information: because producers' types are not observable to foreigners, matching is effectively random. However, each producer has access only to the labour in his own country, so domestic matches must employ domestic labour, while international matches can employ labour in whichever country it is cheaper. International matches can thus serve to transfer labour demand (producer services) from the country where labour is scarce to where it is abundant, yielding the standard gains from trade. insurance, the delivery terms C and D are more frequently used.

Rauch and Casella model a transnational network as extending to the international market the complete information that prevails for non-members only in the domestic market: each network member knows the types of all other network members in both countries. This facilitates the transfer of labour demand and increases the extent to which the countries' factor endowment ratios can differ without ruling out achievement of full efficiency. In this respect the network acts like an improvement in the matching technology between countries. The network differs from such an improvement, however, in that it only reduces informational barriers for a subset of producers, so that distributive effects between network member and non-member producers can arise. Rauch and Casella find that in equilibrium where full efficiency's not achieved the network may cause aggregate profits of producers who are not members to fall even though world wages and world profits as a whole increase. Moreover, although the network must (weakly) increase the value of world output in a two-country model, Rauch and Casella show that this need not be true if there is more than one international market so that the network does not necessarily link the countries with the largest difference in factor endowment ratios: they demonstrate that in a three-country model a network can have an effect analogous to harmful "trade diversion."

NETWORKS AS MARKET STRUCTURE

Whereas transnational networks can help to overcome informal barriers to international trade, domestic networks can create informal barriers by facilitating collusion to restrict the market access of foreign firms. The dominant strand of the literature surveyed in this section investigates whether *keiretsu* act this way. The repeated exchange definition of networks is always used in this work.

A new line of research covered at the end of this section moves away from investigation of the relationship between networks and informal trade barriers to examine how the market structure created by domestic business groups influences the *composition* of trade. Studies of whether *keiretsu* act as barriers to imports (especially from the United States) are surveyed by Lawrence and Gary Saxon house. Two influential papers are K. C. Fung and Lawrence. Fung examines U.S. net exports to Japan for 22 industries in 1980.

In various specifications he consistently finds a negative, highly statistically significant, but quantitatively small effect of either the per centage of industry sales or the per centage of industry employment accounted for by *keiretsu*-affiliated companies. Collusion by *keiretsu* members to restrict imports is certainly not the only possible explanation for this result, and Lawrence is especially concerned about the alternative explanation that efficiency gains realized by *keiretsu* reduce the competitiveness of imports. He reasons that the latter explanation should imply that *keiretsu* increase industry exports as well as reduce imports. He examines the ratio of imports to Japanese domestic demand and the ratio of Japanese exports to total world exports for 37 industries in 1985.

The per centage of industry sales accounted for by *keiretsu*-affiliated firms is negatively and significantly related to import penetration, consistent with the findings of Fung, and is insignificantly related to the Japanese world export share. The *keiretsu* impact on imports found by Lawrence is quantitatively large, unlike that found beefing; setting the *keiretsu* sales per centage to zero would roughly double the average import share. When Lawrence splits the *keiretsu* variable into the per centage of industry sales accounted for by firms affiliated with "horizontal" versus vertical keiretsu, both are still negatively associated with import share but the vertical *keiretsu* variable has a positive and weakly significant effect on export share. If vertical *keiretsu* do indeed reduce imports and increase exports because of efficiency gains, it is most likely because the long-term supply relationships that exist within these repeated exchange networks encourage relationship specific investments. Barbara Spencer and LarryQiu model relationship specific investments by *keiretsu* suppliers in a paper designed to shed light on the United States-Japan auto parts dispute. In their model *keiretsu* auto parts suppliers make no verifiable investments that create rents for the *keiretsu* assembler, perhaps by reducing assembly costs by improving the "fit" with other *keiretsu* parts. Payments to the suppliers cannot be based on their investments and instead the assembler engages in simultaneous Nash bargaining over price with each supplier, where if bargaining breaks down the supplier does not produce and the assembler purchases a "generic" part, which could be produced by a U.S. supplier. Note that the equilibrium price exclusive of the rent to the assembler could exceed the price of the generic part.

Spencer and Qiu use their model to show how a number of equilibrium *keiretsu* behaviours could yield a false impression of collusion to restrict U.S. market access. First, under the reasonable assumption that the rents to the assembler generated by relationship specific investments are unobservable outside the *keiretsu*, it could appear that the assembler is sourcing parts from within the *keiretsu* even though prices are higher than those charged by outside suppliers. Second, if relationship-specific investments are more valuable to the assembler for parts with higher cost shares, imports could be restricted to lower value parts. Third, a reduction in trade barriers or prices charged by U.S. auto parts suppliers could lead to an expansion of Japanese auto production without any corresponding rise in imports by improving the bargaining power of the assembler with *keiretsu* suppliers. Moreover, as shown by Qiu and Spencer (forthcoming), a policy that directly requires an increase in the U.S. content of Japanese autos could paradoxically reduce the value of U.S. auto parts exports to Japan by reducing Japanese auto output due to lost benefits from relationship-specific investment. Suppose for the sake of argument that the model of Spencer and Qiu captures the true state of affairs regarding vertical *keiretsu.*

The question of whether vertical *keiretsu* or similarly organized business groups in other countries act as trade barriers then comes down to whether more efficient foreign suppliers can become members of the network. This is another version of the unanswered empirical question that arose in connection with evaluation of Greif's claim of dynamic inefficiency in the ability of transnational networks to overcome trade barriers. The work surveyed so far, in its focus on whether business groups (specifically, *keiretsu*) are "efficient or exclusionist," has nothing to say about the numbers or sizes of business groups, which could be important features of domestic market structure that influence foreign trade. In a series of papers and a book manuscript, Robert Feenstra, GaryHamilton, and coauthors have explored the implications for international trade of the differences between the size distributions and average "internalization" of Korean versus Taiwanese business groups.

Figures show the size and internalization of the 44 largest business groups (known as chaebol) in Korea in 1989 and the eighty largest business groups in Taiwan in 1994 for which data on internal transactions are available. The vertical axis measures internalization by the ratio of sales to other firms in each group to total group sales. The points labeled "without retail" exclude the purchases from other firms within the group of group trading companies and all other group firms within the wholesale and retail sector. We see that in Korea there exist five very large business groups, the smallest of which is larger than the largest business group in Taiwan.

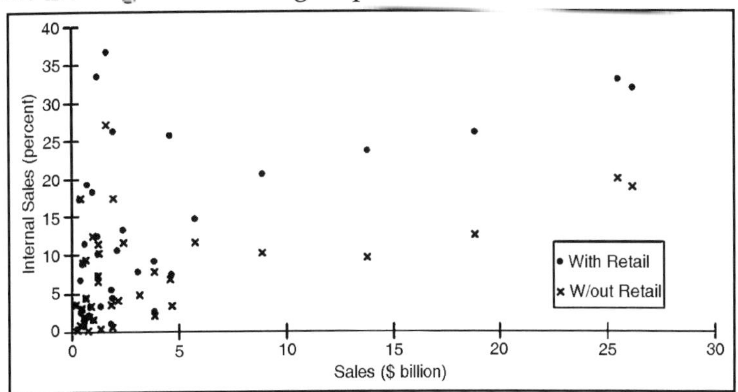

Fig. Korean Business Group.

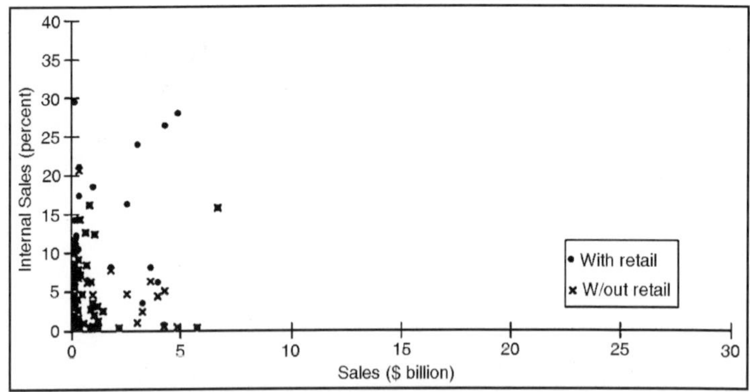

Fig. Tiawanese Business Group.

The weighted average internal sales ratios, with and without retail, respectively, are 22.1 and 12.2 per cent for the Korean sample versus 9.5 and 4.5 per cent for the Taiwanese sample. With their large size and high internalization the Korean groups are well suited to realization of economies of scale through long production runs of standardized products, whereas Taiwanese groups are better suited to serving niche markets by changing product design to meet the demands of overseas customers. Feenstra, Tzu-Han Yang, and Hamilton thus predict that U.S. imports from Taiwan will display greater within-industry product variety than U.S. imports from Korea.

This prediction is generally confirmed for the periods 1978–82 and 1983–88 in that the U.S. expenditure share within a five digit SIC industry on country varieties that are *not* supplied by *both* countries tends to be greater for Taiwan than Korea, except in a few intermediate goods industries where some of the largest and most internalized Taiwanese business groups are located. Feenstra, Yang, and Hamilton also find for these two periods that within intermediate goods industries the United States tended to import higher-priced varieties from Taiwan than from Korea, whereas the opposite was true within final goods industries. Taking price as a proxy for quality, they interpret these results as supporting the hypothesis of Dani Rodrik that, if reputations for quality tend to spill over to all exporters from a given country, large business groups will be better able to internalize this externality and hence have a greater incentive to produce high-quality goods.

Feenstra, Deng-Shing Huang, and Hamilton and Feenstra, Hamilton, and Huang develop a theoretical model of multiple business groups. They offset the complexity of dealing with many rather than one business group by dispensing with the view of business groups as networks and instead modeling them as hierarchies: each business group is a centrally organized set of firms that maximizes joint profits. The two papers begin with a model in which there is monopolistic competition in supply of both intermediate and final goods. This generates an incentive for business groups (vertically integrated firms) to form and eliminate the markups on intermediate goods in internal group transactions, each group trading off increased collective profits against a fixed "governance cost" for the group as a whole. For most parameter values the papers find two stable equilibrium: a low concentration equilibrium with a large number of low-internalization groups that sell to outsiders at low markups, and a high-concentration equilibrium with a small number of high-internalization groups that sell to outsiders at high markups. The intuition for the existence of multiple stable equilibrium is as follows. Start in the low-concentration equilibrium and artificially raise markups charged to outsiders for intermediate goods. This creates an incentive for existing groups to expand and incorporate more product varieties, but the market can only support a smaller number of these larger groups, the result being greater concentration that validates the higher markups.

Feenstra and Hamilton (forthcoming) argue that cultural and historical factors pushed Taiwan towards the low-concentration and Korea towards the high-concentration equilibrium. Due to the existence of low markups and greater product variety, consumer welfare is greater in the low-concentration (Taiwan) equilibrium. Whereas the literature surveyed in this section has a lot to say about the efficiency consequences of business groups, it is virtually silent on the question of whether business groups will become more or less important for international trade. Many writers on business groups in a context other than international trade take the functionalist position that they're responses to various "market imperfections," and that these market imperfections will ultimately vanish with economic development, taking business groups along with them.

The fate of business groups is, of course, bound up with the fate of the network form of organization in general, which at one time was widely believed to be a transitional stage on the way to the centrally administered multidivisional firm but now seems to be gaining ground against that hierarchical form. Entering this debate would take us well beyond the scope of this survey. For example, past investments by *keiretsu* suppliers to adapt their products to the specifications of assemblers in the home country could give them an advantage even over equally knowledgeable competing suppliers when the assembler establishes facilities abroad, providing an alternative explanation for the trade-creating effect of such foreign direct investment.

Similarly, the East Asian business groups might be solving problems of weak contract enforcement or lack of information regarding business opportunities in a purely domestic context. Taken as a whole, the international trade literature on business groups also needs to outgrow its exclusive focus on East Asia. Not only does this convey the misleading impression that business groups are not important for international trade elsewhere, but it may lead to biased inferences about the typical impact of business groups on trade. Another important step for this literature is micro-level studies of the openness of business groups to membership by foreign firms or of how business groups engage in importing and exporting. With firm-level empirical studies proliferating in the international trade field, there is less and less excuse for treating business groups as empirical (though not theoretical) black boxes. In particular, a great deal of insight into the questions of whether business groups exclude imports or how they provide variety and quality in exports could be had by studying the trading companies that are at the center of many groups.

NETWORK INTERMEDIARIES

Suppose that a firm looking for foreign buyers or sellers does not belong to an appropriate network. Conventional search is an option, but often a poor one if what the firm is searching for is not sufficiently homogeneous to have an informative price. An alternative is to engage a network intermediary, *i.e.*, an agent who sells access to and use of his network, typically for a commission on the value of the transactions realized. These intermediaries go byte names agent, broker, trader, etc., but not all actors so labeled should be considered network intermediaries.

Network intermediaries are distinguished by what Yung Rhee and Christine Soulier call their "deep knowledge" of the capabilities and preferences of the sellers or buyers in their networks:

- As highlighted in our Hong Kong survey, the most important resource that ETCs (export trading companies) have is their deep knowledge about external markets/buyers and local production capabilities/producers. Without such information, ETCs can hardly be effective in matching potential overseas buyers to local producers... the effectiveness of Japanese, Korean, and Hong Kong GTCs (general trading companies) has been based on the depth of their product-market knowledge and of the supplier-buyer network.

The networks to which these intermediaries sell access may consist of densely interconnected firms, such as business groups, or of firms that do virtually no business with each other, so that if one removed the intermediary they would not constitute a network at all. Descriptions of the activities of the former type of intermediaries suggest that thyme e crucial to both the ability of small, low-internalization business groups to provide product variety and the ability of large, high internalization business groups to realize economies of scale in the production of standardized goods. Of trading companies for groups of fashion shoe producers in Taiwan, You-tien Hsing writes, "A typical shoe trading company usually had 12–15 partner manufacturers.

To offset limited demand for each order, trading companies coordinated and allocated orders in accordance with the specialty of individual factories." Describing the large, general trading companies at the heart of many *keiretsu*, the *sogo shosha* of Japan, M. Y. Yoshino and Thomas Lifson state, "the *sogo shosha*'s uniqueness lies in its capacity to provide essential links between stages in a product system for a client firm." Studies of network intermediaries that sell access to unconnected firms have mainly concerned buyers who provide less developed country manufacturers with access to sets of developed country retailers. The principal interest of these studies is in how such network intermediaries translate the preferences of retailers into product designs and models and provide other technical assistance to the (low-tech) manufacturers.

The apparent importance of belonging to these transnational business and social networks does not prove that network intermediation is undersupplied, however, because the costs of establishing each of these transnational networks were sunk for purposes other than creating trade: it could be that the costs of setting up new network intermediaries would outweigh the benefits of the additional trade they would create. A crucial input to any evaluation of the case for market failure in provision of network intermediation is knowledge of the determinants of supply: how do actors become network intermediaries?

The literature is virtually silent on this question, but there exist many suggestive anecdotes: a former mergers and acquisitions officer for Chase Manhattan in Hong Kong who now matches leisure-related, California-based businesses with Asian partners; an industrial engineering consultant who had designed factory layouts throughout Asia who now matches U.S. toy designers with Chinese toy manufacturers; a leader of Daewoo's team of machine installation specialists and production line experts assigned to Bangladesh who subsequently opened a firm "engaged exclusively with the import and export trade of Bangladesh's new garment factories".

Such anecdotes, and intuition, suggest that actors become network intermediaries by accumulating "deep knowledge" of buyers and sellers through working with them in a non-intermediary capacity, then selling access to those with whom they formerly worked when this becomes more profitable. At the very least, it seems unlikely that this process will supply intermediaries whose networks span many industries. Realization of business opportunities often requires coordination across several industries, however. An entrepreneur seeking many component s to assemble into a final product for which he has a buyer, for example, could employ many specialized intermediaries, but this is likely to be cumbersome.

More importantly, the components need to be matched not only to the client but to each other, so only diversified intermediary could put together an attractive package. If diversified network intermediaries are not generated as a by-product of non-intermediary activity could an adequate supply result from more planned accumulation of contacts by actors who have already dedicated them to intermediation? There is good reason to believe that this kind of investment will fall short of the socially optimal level, because the intermediary may not be able to garner a large enough share of the surplus he creates for his clients to recover his investment. The fact that the intermediary needs deep knowledge of the members of his network in order to know which is the best match for his client means that the quality of service he provides his client is inherently non-contractible. In the absence of an enforceable contract based on payment for surplus created the intermediary must rely on his bargaining power, but this is limited because the specificity of each match leaves the intermediary with poor alternative transactions if bargaining breaks down. In addition to this contracting problem, there is a difficulty if one needs to be actually involved in the production process in order to acquire deep knowledge.

It is one thing to leave a career in production to become an intermediary when the opportunity to earn a better living presents itself, and quite another to participate in production with the plan of augmenting the network to which one will sell access as an intermediary, given the risk that by the time one has learned enough, markets or technology will have changed so as to destroy the synergy with one's existing network. The case for undersupply of network intermediation thus appears to be strongest for large diversified intermediaries. Some governments have evidently come to the same conclusion:

Rauch describes how the aforementioned *sogo shosha* and their imitators, the general trading companies (GTCs) of Korea and the foreign trade companies (FTCs) of Turkey, all benefited from implicit or explicit government subsidies during their start-up years, after which they became viable without subsidies.

This evidence that government policy can be used, in effect, to promote the formation of transnational networks is intriguing, but failed attempts to establish general trading companies in Taiwan and the United States make it clear that much further theoretical and empirical research is required before reliable policy recommendations can be formulated.

LEARNING IN NETWORKS

Economists have often modeled international technology transfer as an arm's-length phenomenon. Firms are not *taught* the new technology. Rather they engage in purposive imitative activity on their own, employ machinery and equipment that embodies foreign knowledge, license the new technology, and so on.

However, it is difficult to learn new technology through these mechanisms. There is a growing body of evidence that for less developed country(LDC) firms in particular a major and perhaps predominant source of technology transfer (and transfer of managerial know-how) is instruction by developed country buyers: producers seeking cheaper suppliers of inputs and distributors seeking cheaper suppliers of final goods.

Pack and John Page state:

- The motivation of the purchasers is to obtain still lower-cost, better quality products from major suppliers whose products account for a significant per centage of profits. To achieve this they're willing to transmit tacit and occasionally proprietary knowledge from their other OECD suppliers. Such transfers of knowledge are more likely to characterize simpler production sectors such as clothing and footwear or more generally those older technologies that are not hedged by restrictions adopted to increase appro-priability, such as patents and trade secrets.

These buyer– seller relationships are long-term and thus fit our repeated exchange definition of networks. One example of such evidence is a study by Egan and Mody , who surveyed U.S. buyers operating in LDCs, including "manufacturers, retailers, importers, buyers' agents, and joint venture partners".

They found:

- Buyers also render long-term benefits to suppliers in the form of information on production technology. This occurs principally through various forms of in-plant training. The buyer may send international experts to train local workers and supervisors .
- Buyers may also arrange short-term worker training in a developed country plant.

Rhee, Bruce Ross-Larson, and Garry Pursell surveyed Korean exporters of manufactures.

Their findings were similar to those of Egan and Mody:

- The relations between Korean firms and the foreign buyers went far beyond the negotiation and fulfillment of contracts. Almost half the firms said they had directly benefited from the technical information foreign buyers provided: through visits to their plants by engineers or other technical staff of the foreign buyers, through visits by their engineering staff to the foreign buyers

The Rhee, Ross-Larson, and Pursell survey was conducted in 1975. More recently Korea and the other advanced East Asian countries have played the role for LDCs that foreign buyers used to play for them. The role of Korea in developing garment exports from Bangladesh is an especially interesting case that is studied in Rhee. This case is part of the broader phenomenon of "triangle manufacturing" in East Asia: countries such as Korea and Taiwan continue to accept and fulfill the orders of developed country buyers for labour-intensive goods, but have "outsourced" the actual production to countries with lower wages. This process of learning foreign technology can be thought of as taking place within international production networks or "global commodity chains". This theoretical framework predicts that once LDC firms are incorporated into the "bottoms" of the chains, their learning will continue by movement up the chains. There are two types of chains: "producer driven" and "buyer-driven," which are illustrated in figure .

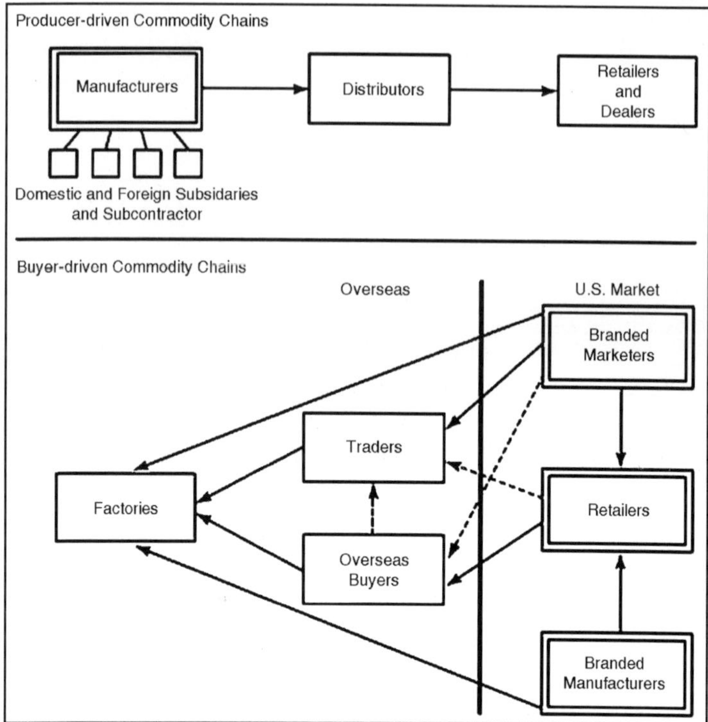

In the former, large manufacturers play the central roles in coordinating the production networks. Producer-driven chains are typical in capital- and technology-intensive industries such as automobiles, aircraft, semiconductors, and heavy machinery . In the latter, large retailers, branded marketers, and branded manufacturers play the coordinating roles.

Buyer driven commodity chains are typical in labour-intensive, consumer goods industries such as garments, footwear, toys, house wares, and consumer electronics. Profitability is highest at the tops of the chains where barriers to entry are greatest: scale and technology in producer driven chains, design and marketing expertise in buyer-driven chains. In buyer-driven commodity chains, one mode through which learning is predicted to continue is *organizational succession*: from assembler to original equipment manufacturer (OEM) to original brand-name manufacturer (OBM), which is from more subordinate, competitive, and low-profit positions to more controlling, oligopolistic, high-profit positions.

In the apparel industry, Gereffi finds that LDC firms that have parts provided to them for assembly learn how to find on their own the parts needed to make the product according to the design specified by the buyer (and may then subcontract the assembly); firms that have reached this level learn how to design and sell their own merchandise, becoming branded manufacturers (and may then subcontract the production, becoming branded marketers). Additional study's needed to determine whether this pattern of learning is common in other consumer goods industries, and what kind of learning modes might be present in producer-driven commodity chains.

REVIEW OF MAIN THEMES AND ISSUES FOR FUTURE RESEARCH

Numerous statistical and case studies provide evidence that transnational business and social networks promote international trade by alleviating problems of contract enforcement and providing information about trading opportunities. Some studies established a large quantitative importance for these network effects. Developments in the demand for networks will probably tend to reduce this quantitative importance in the future, while trends in the supply of networks will probably tend to increase it. On the demand side, institutional developments such as international commercial arbitration and letters of credit and technological improvements in communication reduce the need for networks, although this effect is offset by the increased share of differentiated products in international trade.

On the supply side, increased migration and increased foreign direct investment are extending ever more domestic networks across international borders. Perhaps the biggest unknown is the impact of e-commerce on the importance of networks for international trade. Certainly the use of search engines is likely to reduce the demand for networks, but this effect could be limited if, as it is said, the internet disseminates information but not understanding. New technology could interact with networks in surprising ways: for example, e-mail probably retards the decay of established networks. The efficiency implications of transnational networks would appear to be straightforward: they improve the allocation of resources by creating trade, and they generate surplus from cooperation for their members. Closer theoretical examination, however, raises three caveats.

First, less desirable network members may choose to enter the anonymous international market where their characteristics are not known, harming non-members even though the existence of a transnational network still increases world output in the aggregate. Second, a transnational network can have an effect analogous to harmful trade diversion if it links the "wrong" countries. Third, organization of international trade through networks may hinder its growth if transnational networks tend to be closed to new members. This last caveat is an especially important topic for empirical research because the openness of networks is also the key to whether otherwise efficiency-enhancing *domestic* networks *impede* international trade. As little as we know about the ability of existing transnational (or domestic) networks to incorporate new members, we know even less about how entirely new transnational networks are formed. This survey has discussed how domestic networks, when spread across international boundaries by migration or foreign direct investment, promote trade, and also how trade can help to maintain transnational networks once they're established, but nothing has been said about if and how trade *creates* transnational networks. An important question for future research is whether formation of new business and social networks can help us understand apparent hysteretic effects in bilateral trade, such as those found by Barry Eichengreen and Douglas Irwin.

INTERNATIONAL TRADE POLICY

UNDERSTANDING THE TRADE POLICY

Trade policy is a collection of rules and regulations which pertain to trade. Every nation has some form of trade policy in place, with public officials formulating the policy which they think would be most appropriate for their country. The purpose of trade policy is to help a nation's international trade run more smoothly, by setting clear standards and goals which can be understood by potential trading partners. In many regions, groups of nations work together to create mutually beneficial trade policies. Things like import and export taxes, tariffs, inspection regulations, and quotas can all be part of a nation's trade policy. Some nations attempt to protect their local industries with trade policies which place a heavy burden on importers, allowing domestic producers of goods and services to get ahead in the market with lower prices or more availability.

Others eschew trade barriers, promoting free trade, in which domestic producers are given no special treatment, and international producers are free to bring in their products. Safety is sometimes an issue in trade policy. Different nations have different regulations about product safety, and when goods are imported into a country with stiff standards, representatives of that nation may demand the right to inspect the goods, to confirm that they conform with the product safety standards which have been laid out.

Security is also an issue, with nations wanting to protect themselves from potential threats while maintaining good foreign relations with frequent trading partners. When nations trade with each other regularly, they often establish trade agreements. Trade agreements smooth the way for trading, spelling out the desires of both sides to create a stronger, more effective trading relationship.

Many trade agreements are designed to accommodate a desire for free trade, with signatories to such agreements making certain concessions to each other to establish a good trading relationship. Regular meetings may also be held to discuss changes in the financial climate, and to make adjustments to trade policy accordingly. For lay people, understanding trade policy can get quite complex.

The relevant rules, regulations, agreements, and treaties are often scattered across numerous government documents and departments, from State Departments which handle foreign policy to economic departments which deal with the nuts and bolts of things like converting currency. Often, the best resource for information is documents pertaining to specific trade agreements, such as the North American Free Trade Agreement. These documents spell out the trade policy of the nations involved in one convenient location, although the language used can become very complex.

BALANCE OF TRADE

Trade balance is the difference between a country's imports and exports. When a country's imports surpass its exports over a period of time, it is called a trade deficit. A country's balance of trade is its largest component when it comes to payments. The value of balance of trade is expressed in domestic currency and is denoted by the symbol, 'NX'.

Understanding Trade Balance

Trade balance is a reflection of a country's international market and its domestic consumption. A country's balance of trade comprises a major segment of balance of payments.

This is an effective mechanism to quantify a country's overall economic transactions with the rest of the world. It also affects the country's overall GDP for that particular period. What happens when a country's exports exceed the total imports during a given period? Then, the balance of trade is termed as trade surplus or favourable balance of trade.

Composition of Trade Balance

For a given country, trade balance comprises those products that a country trades on with other countries.

Factors that affect trade balance are:

- *Demand and Supply*: The demand and supply trend defines the cost of domestic products to be sold in the international market.
- *Domestic Business*: Sound, domestic policies are required to boost production and international trade. Some countries like the US provide subsidies to local manufacturers for exported goods and services.
- *Trade Agreements*: Bilateral agreements govern international trade and define the products and their prices in the global context.
- *External Pressures*: Many countries export items that face heavy competition in international market. This results in market segmentation and low pricing. Countries that are mostly oil exporters or IT hubs tend to generate favourable trade balance due

to less competition in the international market. External pressures also work in the form of trade bans. These bans are enforced by either individual countries or international organizations such as the WTO or IMF.

- *Exchange Rate*: For nations with low exchange rate values, balance of trade tends to remain unfavourable.

Proactive market policies are required to ensure that a country's trade balance remains favourable. A sound trade balance represents an important benchmark as it reflects economic stability between nations. It fortifies trade ties with other countries and generates immense possibilities to stem job losses, inflation and unemployment.

Economic impact

Conditions where Trade Imbalances may be Problematic

Those who ignore the effects of long run trade deficits may be confusing David Ricardo's principle of comparative advantage with Adam Smith's principle of absolute advantage, specifically ignoring the latter. The economist Paul Craig Roberts notes that the comparative advantage principles developed by David Ricardo do not hold where the factors of production are internationally mobile. Global labour arbitrage, a phenomenon described by economist Stephen S. Roach, where one country exploits the cheap labour of another, would be a case of absolute advantage that is not mutually beneficial. Since the stagflation of the 1970s, the U.S. economy has been characterized by slower GDP growth.

In 1985, the U.S. began its growing trade deficit with China. Over the long run, nations with trade surpluses tend also to have a savings surplus. The U.S. generally has lower savings rates than its trading partners which tend to have trade surpluses. Germany, France, Japan, and Canada have maintained higher savings rates than the U.S. over the long run. Few economists believe that GDP and employment can be dragged down by an over-large deficit over the long run. Others believe that trade deficits are good for the economy. The opportunity cost of a forgone tax base may outweigh perceived gains, especially where artificial currency pegs and manipulations are present to distort trade.

Wealth-producing primary sector jobs in the U.S. such as those in manufacturing and computer software have often been replaced by much lower paying wealth-consuming jobs such those in retail and government in the service sector when the economy recovered from recessions. Some economists contend that the U.S. is borrowing to fund consumption of imports while accumulating unsustainable amounts of debt. In 2006, the primary economic concerns centered around: high national debt, high non-bank corporate debt, high mortgage debt, high financial institution debt, high unfunded Medicare liability, high unfunded Social Security liability, high external debt and a serious deterioration in the United States net international investment position, high trade deficits, and a rise in illegal immigration. These issues have raised concerns among economists and unfunded liabilities were mentioned as a serious problem facing the United States in the President's 2006 State of the Union address.

On June 26, 2009, Jeff Immelt, the CEO of General Electric, called for the U.S. to increase its manufacturing base employment to 20 per cent of the workforce, commenting that the U.S. has outsourced too much in some areas and can no longer rely on the financial sector and consumer spending to drive demand.

Conditions where Trade Imbalances may Not be Problematic

Small trade deficits are generally not considered to be harmful to either the importing or exporting economy. However, when a national trade imbalance expands beyond prudence, adjustments tend to occur. While unsustainable imbalances may persist for long periods, the distortions likely to be caused by large flows of wealth out of one economy and into another tend to become intolerable. In simple terms, trade deficits are paid for out of foreign exchange reserves, and may continue until such reserves are depleted. At such a point, the importer can no longer continue to purchase more than is sold abroad.

This is likely to have exchange rate implications: a sharp loss of value in the deficit economy's exchange rate with the surplus economy's currency will change the relative price of tradable goods, and facilitate a return to balance or an over-shooting into surplus the other direction. More complexly, an economy may be unable to export enough goods to pay for its imports, but is able to find funds elsewhere.

Service exports, for example, are more than sufficient to pay for Hong Kong's domestic goods export shortfall. In poorer countries, foreign aid may fill the gap while in rapidly developing economies a capital account surplus often off-sets a current-account deficit. Finally, there are some economies where transfers from nationals working abroad contribute significantly to paying for imports. The Philippines, Bangladesh and Mexico are examples of transfer-rich economies.

Adam Smith on Trade Deficits

"In the foregoing part of this chapter I have endeavoured to show, even upon the principles of the commercial system, how unnecessary it is to lay extraordinary restraints upon the importation of goods from those countries with which the balance of trade is supposed to be disadvantageous. Nothing, however, can be more absurd than this whole doctrine of the balance of trade, upon which, not only these restraints, but almost all the other regulations of commerce are founded. When two places trade with one another, this [absurd] doctrine supposes that, if the balance be even, neither of them either loses or gains; but if it leans in any degree to one side, that one of them loses and the other gains in proportion to its declension from the exact equilibrium."

Milton Friedman on Trade Deficits

In the 1980s, Milton Friedman, the Nobel Prize-winning economist and father of Monetarism, contended that some of the concerns of trade deficits are unfair criticisms in an attempt to push macroeconomic policies favourable to exporting industries. Prof. Friedman argued that trade deficits are not necessarily important as high exports raise the value of the currency, reducing aforementioned exports, and vise versa for imports, thus naturally removing trade deficits not due to investment.

Milton Friedman's son, David D. Friedman, shares this view and cites the comparative advantage concepts of David Ricardo. In the late 1970s and early 1980s, the U.S. had experienced high inflation and Friedman's policy positions tended to defend the stronger dollar at that time. He stated his belief that these trade deficits were not necessarily harmful to the economy at the time since the currency comes back to the country. However, it may be in one form or another including the possible tradeoff of foreign control of assets. In his view, the "worst case scenario" of the currency never returning to the country of origin was actually the best possible outcome: the country actually purchased its goods by exchanging them for pieces of cheaply-made paper.

As Friedman put it, this would be the same result as if the exporting country burned the dollars it earned, never returning it to market circulation. This position is a more refined version of the theorem first discovered by David Hume. Hume argued that England could not permanently gain from exports, because hoarding gold would make gold more plentiful in England; therefore, the prices of English goods would rise, making them less attractive exports and making foreign goods more attractive imports.

In this way, countries' trade balances would balance out. Friedman believed that deficits would be corrected by free markets as floating currency rates rise or fall with time to encourage or discourage imports in favour of the exports, reversing again in favour of imports as the currency gains strength. In the real world, a potential difficulty is that currency markets are far from a free market, with government and central banks being major players, and this is unlikely to change within the foreseeable future.

Nevertheless, recent developments have shown that the global economy is undergoing a fundamental shift. For many years, the U.S. has borrowed and bought while in general, the rest of the world has lent and sold. However, as Friedman predicted, this paradigm appears to be changing. As of October 2007, the U.S. dollar weakened against the euro, British pound, and many other currencies. For instance, the euro hit $1.42 in October 2007, the strongest it has been since its birth in 1999. Against this backdrop, American exporters are finding quite favourable overseas markets for their products and U.S. consumers are responding to their general housing slowdown by slowing their spending.

Furthermore, China, the Middle East, central Europe and Africa are absorbing more of the world's imports which in the end may result in a world economy that is more evenly balanced. All of this could well add up to a major readjustment of the U.S. trade deficit, which as a per centage of GDP, began in 1991. Friedman and other economists have pointed out that a large trade deficit signals that the country's currency is strong and desirable.

To Friedman, a trade deficit simply meant that consumers had opportunity to purchase and enjoy more goods at lower prices; conversely, a trade surplus implied that a country was exporting goods its own citizens did not get to consume or enjoy, while paying high prices for the goods they actually received. Friedman contended that the structure of the balance of payments was misleading. In an interview with Charlie Rose, he stated that "on the books" the US is a net borrower of funds, using those funds to pay for goods and services. He essentially claimed that the foreign assets were not carried on the books at their higher, truer value. Friedman presented his analysis of the balance of trade in Free to Choose, widely considered his most significant popular work.

Frédéric Bastiat on the Fallacy of Trade Deficits

The 19th century economist and philosopher Frédéric Bastiat expressed the idea that trade deficits actually were a manifestation of profit, rather than a loss. He proposed as an example to suppose that he, a Frenchman, exported French wine and imported British coal, turning a profit. He supposed he was in France, and sent a cask of wine which was worth 50 francs to England. The customhouse would record an export of 50 francs. If, in England, the wine sold for 70 francs, which he then used to buy coal, which he imported into France, and was found to be worth 90 francs in France, he would have made a profit of 40 francs. But the customhouse would say that the value of imports exceeded that of exports and was trade deficit against the ledger of France. By reductio ad absurdum, Bastiat argued that the national trade deficit was an indicator of a successful economy, rather than a failing one. Bastiat predicted that a successful, growing economy would result in greater trade deficits, and an unsuccessful, shrinking economy would result in lower trade deficits. This was later, in the 20th century, affirmed by economist Milton Friedman.

Warren Buffett on Trade Deficits

The successful American businessman and investor Warren Buffett was quoted in the Associated Press as saying "The U.S trade deficit is a bigger threat to the domestic economy than either the federal budget deficit or consumer debt and could lead to political turmoil... Right now, the rest of the world owns $3 trillion more of us than we own of them." Buffett has proposed a tool called Import Certificates as a solution to the United States' problem and ensure balanced trade.

John Maynard Keynes on the Balance of Trade

In the last few years of his life, John Maynard Keynes was much preoccupied with the question of balance in international trade. He was the leader of the British delegation to the United Nations Monetary and Financial Conference in 1944 that established the Bretton Woods system of international currency management. He was the principal author of a proposal — the so-called Keynes Plan — for an International Clearing Union. The two governing principles of the plan were that the problem of settling outstanding balances should be solved by 'creating' additional 'international money', and that debtor and creditor should be treated almost alike as disturbers of equilibrium.

In the event, though, the plans were rejected, in part because "American opinion was naturally reluctant to accept the principal of equality of treatment so novel in debtor-creditor relationships". His view, supported by many economists and commentators at the time, was that creditor nations may be just as responsible as debtor nations for disequilibrium in exchanges and that both should be under an obligation to bring trade back into a state of balance. Failure for them to do so could have serious consequences. In the words of Geoffrey Crowther, then editor of The Economist, "If the economic relationships between nations are not, by one means or another, brought fairly close to balance, then there is no set of financial arrangements that can rescue the world from the impoverishing results of chaos."

These ideas were informed by events prior to the Great Depression when — in the opinion of Keynes and others — international lending, primarily by the U.S., exceeded the capacity of sound investment and so got diverted into non-productive and speculative uses, which in turn invited default and a sudden stop to the process of lending. Influenced by Keynes, economics texts in the immediate post-war period put a significant emphasis on balance in trade. For example, the second edition of the popular introductory textbook, An Outline of Money, devoted the last three of its ten chapters to questions of foreign exchange management and in particular the 'problem of balance'.

However, in more recent years, since the end of the Bretton Woods system in 1971, with the increasing influence of Monetarist schools of thought in the 1980s, and particularly in the face of large sustained trade imbalances, these concerns — and particularly concerns about the destabilising effects of large trade surpluses — have largely disappeared from mainstream economics discourse and Keynes' insights have slipped from view. They are receiving some attention again in the wake of the Financial crisis of 2007–2010.

Physical balance of trade

Monetary balance of trade is different from physical balance of trade. Developed countries usually import a lot of primary raw materials from developing countries at low prices.

Often, these materials are then converted into finished products, and a significant amount of value is added. Although for instance the EU has a balanced monetary balance of trade, its physical trade balance is negative, meaning that a lot less material is exported than imported. For this reason, activists talk about the issue of ecological debt which implies a sort of predatory economic system. The nature of the trade balance statistics is such that is conceals distorted material flow.

TARIFF

A tariff is a tax placed on imported goods. Each country has separate tariff regulations. The five main types of tariffs include revenue, ad valorem, specific, prohibitive and protective. A revenue tariff increases government funds. For example, countries that do not grow bananas may create a tariff on importing bananas.

The government would then make money from businesses that import bananas. An ad valorem tariff means that the tariff applies to a per centage of the import's value such as a set number of cents on every dollar of value. A specific tariff, on the other hand, means that the tariff is not concerned with the estimated value of the imported goods, but rather is based on specific amount of the goods. A specific tariff may apply to the number of goods imported or to the weight, volume or other measurement of the goods. A prohibitive tariff is one that is such as high cost that it keeps the item from being imported. A protective tariff is used to raise the price of imported goods as a protective measure against the competition from foreign markets. A higher tariff allows a local company to compete with foreign competition. Protective tariffs can be advantageous as they can help foster the local economy, but sometimes they can also make the price of the item so expensive that companies must charge more. For example, when gas prices become too high, industries such as the trucking industry may have to charge retailers more for delivering products.

The retail industry then has to mark up their items to allow for their increased transportation costs in order to make the same profit they once did. The end result is that consumers pay more for the goods. When no tariff or other restrictions are placed on imported goods, it is called free trade. Some people consider free trade to allow increased economic growth potential. Others counter that the removal of tariffs to permit free trade only makes the economy have to depend on global markets rather than increase the stability of domestic markets.

Kinds of Tariff

There are various types of tariffs:

- An ad valorem tariff is a set per centage of the value of the good that is being imported. Sometimes these are problematic, as when the international price of a good falls, so does the tariff, and domestic industries become more vulnerable to competition. Conversely, when the price of a good rises on the international market so does the tariff, but a country is often less interested in protection when the price is high.

They also face the problem of inappropriate transfer pricing where a company declares a value for goods being traded which differs from the market price, aimed at reducing overall taxes due.

- A specific tariff, is a tariff of a specific amount of money that does not vary with the price of the good. These tariffs are vulnerable to changes in the market or inflation unless updated periodically.
- A revenue tariff is a set of rates designed primarily to raise money for the government. A tariff on coffee imports imposed by countries where coffee cannot be grown, for example raises a steady flow of revenue.
- A prohibitive tariff is one so high that nearly no one imports any of that item.
- A protective tariff is intended to artificially inflate prices of imports and protect domestic industries from foreign competition especially from competitors whose host nations allow them to operate under conditions that are illegal in the protected nation, or who subsidize their exports.
- An environmental tariff, similar to a 'protective' tariff, is also known as a 'green' tariff or 'eco-tariff', and is placed on products being imported from, and also being sent to countries with substandard environmental pollution controls.
- A retaliatory tariff is one placed against a country who already charges tariffs against the country charging the retaliatory tariff. These are usually used in an attempt to get other tariffs rescinded.

Tariffs, in the 20th century, are set by a Tariff Commission based on terms of reference obtained from the government or local authority and suo motu studies of industry structure. Tax, tariff and trade rules in modern times are usually set together because of their common impact on industrial policy, investment policy, and agricultural policy.

A trade bloc is a group of allied countries agreeing to minimize or eliminate tariffs and other barriers against trade with each other, and possibly to impose protective tariffs on imports from outside the bloc. A customs union has a common external tariff, and, according to an agreed formula, the participating countries share the revenues from tariffs on goods entering the customs union. If a country's major industries lose to foreign competition, the loss of jobs and tax revenue can severely impair parts of that country's economy and increase poverty. If a nation's standard of living or industrial regulations are too great, it is impossible for domestic industries to survive unprotected trade with inferior nations without compromising them; this compromise consists of a global race to the bottom. Protective tariffs have historically been used as a measure against this possibility. However, protective tariffs have disadvantages as well.

The most notable is that they prevent the price of the good subject to the tariff from undercutting local competition, disadvantaging consumers of that good or manufacturers who use that good to produce something else: for example a tariff on food can increase poverty, while a tariff on steel can make automobile manufacture less competitive. They can also backfire if countries whose trade is disadvantaged by the tariff impose tariffs of their own, resulting in a trade war and, according to free trade theorists, disadvantaging both sides.

CUSTOMS WAR

A Customs war which is also known as a toll war or tariff war is a kind of economical variance flanked by two or extra states. In regulate to anxiety one of the states, the extra raises taxes or tariffs for a number of the products of that state. The latter state may also increase the tariffs. One of the latest toll wars happened in 1920's and 1930's between the Weimar Republic and Poland. The earlier state, led by Gustav Stresemann wanted to force Poland by creating an economic crisis to give up its territory and increased the tolls for coal and steel products developed there. As a reprisal, the Poles increased toll rates for many German products. This led to fast development of the port of Gdynia, which was the only way Poland could export its goods to Western Europe without having to transport them through Germany.

In September 1922 the Fordney-McCumber Tariff was signed by President Warren Harding. In the end, the tariff law raised the average American ad valorem tariff rate to 38 per cent. Trading partners complained immediately. Those injured by World War I said that, without access by their exports to the American market, they would not be able to make payments to America on war loans. But others saw that this tariff increase would have broader deleterious effects. Democratic Representative Cordell Hall said, "Our foreign markets depend both on the efficiency of our production and the tariffs of countries in which we would sell. Our own [high] tariffs are an important factor in each.

They injure the former and invite the latter." Five years after the passage of the tariff, American trading partners had raised their own tariffs by a significant degree. France raised its tariffs on automobiles from 45 per cent to 100 per cent, Spain raised tariffs on American goods by 40 per cent, and

Germany and Italy raised tariffs on wheat.. One can argue that the spiral of increasing tariffs was one of the main causes of the Great Depression. To avoid customs wars which are considered harmful to the world's economy, the World Trade Organization was created.

FREE TRADE

Free trade is a system in which goods, capital, and labour flow freely between nations, without barriers which could hinder the trade process. Many nations have free trade agreements, and several international organizations promote free trade between their members. There are a number of arguments both for and against this practice, from a range of economists, politicians, industries, and social scientists. A number of barriers to trade are struck down in a free trade agreement. Taxes, tariffs, and import quotas are all eliminated, as are subsidies, tax breaks, and other forms of support to domestic producers. Restrictions on the flow of currency are also lifted, as are regulations which could be considered a barrier to free trade.

Put simply, free trade enables foreign companies to trade just as efficiently, easily, and effectively as domestic producers The idea behind free trade is that it will lower prices for goods and services by promoting competition. Domestic producers will not longer be able to rely on government subsidies and other forms of assistance, including quotas which essentially force citizens to buy from domestic producers, while foreign companies can make inroads on new markets when barriers to trade are lifted. In addition to reducing prices, free trade is also supposed to encourage innovation, since competition between companies sparks a need to come up with innovative products and solutions to capture market share. Free trade can also foster international cooperation, by encouraging nations to freely exchange goods and citizens. Agreements between trading partners can also promote educational advantages, such as sending engineers to train with people in the top of the engineering field in one nation, or sending agriculture experts to rural areas to teach people about new farming techniques and food safety practices. Opponents of free trade often argue that it hurts domestic producers by opening up competition to companies which operate in nations with less stringent labour laws. In the European Union, for example, there are specific rules about working hours, fair rates of pay, working conditions, and so forth, which drive up the cost of production for companies which operate in the European Union. By contrast, labour laws in many developing nations like Honduras are much more lax, allowing companies to produce products at low cost, because they have low overhead costs.

Free trade has also raised concerns about product safety among some consumer advocates. A series of scandals in the early 21st century involving tainted food products from China highlighted the issue of purchasing goods from countries with inefficient or incomplete regulatory systems. Other people have suggested that free trade encourages companies to relocate, because when barriers to foreign trade are lifted, domestic companies have no reason not to move operations overseas to take advantage of cheaper labour, inexpensive supplies, and lax regulatory systems.

Skin of free trade

Free trade implies the following features:

- Trade of goods without taxes or other trade barriers.
- Trade in services without taxes or other trade barriers.
- The absence of "trade-distorting" policies that give some firms, households, or factors of production an advantage over others.
- Free access to markets.
- Free access to market information.
- Inability of firms to distort markets through government-imposed monopoly or oligopoly power.
- The free movement of labour between and within countries.
- The free movement of capital between and within countries.

Current status of Free Trade

Most countries in the world are members of the World Trade Organization, which limits in certain ways but does not eliminate tariffs and other trade barriers. Most countries are also members of regional free trade areas which lower trade barriers among participating countries. Most countries prohibit foreign airlines from cabotage and foreign landing rights are generally restricted, but open skies agreements have become more common. Notable contemporary trade barriers include ongoing tariffs, import quotas, sanctions and embargoes, currency manipulation of the Chinese yuan with respect to the U.S. dollar, agricultural subsidies in developed countries, and buy American laws.

Economics of free trade

Economic Models

Two simple ways to understand the potential benefits of free trade are through David Ricardo's theory of comparative advantage and by analyzing the impact of a tariff or import quota. A simple economic analysis using the law of supply and demand and the economic effects of a tax can be used to show the theoretical benefits of free trade.

Trade Diversion

According to mainstream economic theory, global free trade is a net benefit to society, but the selective application of free trade agreements to some countries and tariffs on others can sometimes lead to economic inefficiency through the process of trade diversion. It is economically efficient for a good to be produced by the country which is the lowest cost producer, but this will not always take place if a high cost producer has a free trade agreement while the low cost producer faces a high tariff. Applying free trade to the high cost producer can lead to trade diversion and a net economic loss. This is why many economists place such high importance on negotiations for global tariff reductions, such as the Doha Round.

Opinion of Economists

The literature analysing the economics of free trade is extremely rich with extensive work having been done on the theoretical and empirical effects. Though it creates winners and losers, the broad consensus among members of the economics profession in the U.S. is that free trade is a large and unambiguous net gain for society. In a 2006 survey of American economists, "87.5 per cent agree that the U.S. should eliminate remaining tariffs and other barriers to trade" and "90.1 per cent disagree with the suggestion that the U.S. should restrict employers from outsourcing work to foreign countries." Quoting Harvard economics professor N. Gregory Mankiw, "Few propositions command as much consensus among professional economists as that open world trade increases economic growth and raises living standards."

Nonetheless, quoting Prof. Peter Soderbaum of Malardalen University, Sweden, "This neo-classical trade theory focuses on one dimension, *i.e.*, the price at which a commodity can be delivered and is extremely narrow in cutting off a large number of other considerations about impacts on employment in different parts of the world, about environmental impacts and on culture." Most free traders would agree that there are winners and losers from free trade, but argue that this is not a reason to argue against free trade, because free trade is supposed to bring overall gain due to idea that the winners have gained enough to make up for the losses of the losers and then some.

Chang argues otherwise, saying that the economy could shrink as a result, and that some people being worse off due to trade displacement without recourse to welfare assistance to find a better job is not acceptable. In an assessment of the literature on the theory and empirical research relating to the benefits of free trade, Sonali Deraniyagala and Ben Fine found that much of the work was flawed, and concluded that the extent to which free trade benefits economic development is unknown. Theoretical arguments are largely dependent upon specific empirical assumptions which may or may not hold true. In the empirical literature, many studies suggest the relationship is ambiguous, and the data and econometrics underlying a set of empirical papers showing positive results have been critiqued.

The best of these papers use a simplified model, and the worst involve the regression of an index of economic performance on an index of openness to trade, with a mix of these two approaches common. In some cases, Deraniyagala and Fine claim, these indexes of openness actually reflect trade volume rather than policy orientation. They also observe that it is difficult to disentangle the effects of reverse causality and numerous exogenous variables. In Kicking Away the Ladder, Ha-Joon Chang reviews the history of free trade policies and economic growth, and notes that many of the now-industrialized countries had significant barriers to trade throughout their history.

Protectionism under the auspices of the infant industry argument was first pursued by Alexander Hamilton in the 1790s in opposition to the admonition of Adam Smith, who advised that the United States focus on agriculture, where it had a comparative advantage. In the 1840s Friedrich List, known as the father of the infant industry argument, advocated the infant industry argument for Germany. Chang's research shows that the United States and Britain, sometimes considered to be the homes of free trade policy, were aggressive protectionists. Britain did end its protectionism when it achieved technological superiority in the late 1850s with the repeal of the Corn Laws, but tariffs on manufactured products had returned to 23 per cent by 1950.

The United States maintained weighted average tariffs on manufactured products of approximately 40-50 per cent up until the 1950s, augmented by the natural protectionism of high transportation costs in the 19th century. The most consistent practitioners of free trade have been Switzerland, the Netherlands, and to a lesser degree Belgium. Chang describes the export-oriented industrialization policies of the Asian Tigers as "far more sophisticated and fine-tuned than their historical equivalents".

Opposition

The relative costs, benefits and beneficiaries of free trade are debated by academics, governments and interest groups. A number of arguments for and against in the ongoing public debate can be seen in the free trade debate article. Arguments for protectionism fall into the economic category or the moral category; a general argument against free trade is that it is colonialism or imperialism in disguise. The moral category is wide, including concerns of income inequality, environmental degradation, supporting child labour and sweatshops, race to the bottom, wage slavery, accentuating poverty in poor countries, harming national defence, and forcing cultural change. Free trade is often opposed by domestic industries that would have their profits and market share reduced by lower prices for imported goods. For example, if United States tariffs on imported sugar were reduced, U.S. sugar producers would receive lower prices and profits, while U.S. sugar consumers would spend less for the same amount of sugar because of those same lower prices.

The economic theory of David Ricardo holds that consumers would necessarily gain more than producers would lose. Since each of those few domestic sugar producers would lose a lot while each of a great number of consumers would gain only a little, domestic producers are more likely to mobilize against the lifting of tariffs. More generally, producers often favour domestic subsidies and tariffs on imports in their home countries, while objecting to subsidies and tariffs in their export markets. Socialists frequently oppose free trade on the ground that it allows maximum exploitation of workers by capital.

For example, Karl Marx wrote in The Communist Manifesto, "The bourgeoisie... has set up that single, unconscionable freedom — Free Trade. In one word, for exploitation, veiled by religious and political illusions, it has substituted naked, shameless, direct, brutal exploitation." Nonetheless, Marx favoured free trade solely because he felt that it would hasten the social revolution. To those who oppose socialism, this becomes an argument against free trade. "Free trade" is opposed by many anti-globalization groups, based on their assertion that free trade agreements generally do not increase the economic freedom of the poor or the working class, and frequently make them poorer.

Where the foreign supplier allows de facto exploitation of labour, domestic free-labour is unfairly forced to compete with the foreign exploited labour, and thus the domestic "working class would gradually be forced down to the level of helotry." To this extent, free trade is seen as nothing more than an end-run around laws that protect individual liberty, such as the Thirteenth Amendment to the United States Constitution. In this regard, protective trade policies are seen, not so much as protecting domestic producers, but rather, as protecting liberty itself. This argument actually comports with the economic analysis of Free Trade to the extent that "slavery and perfect competition equilibria are Pareto optimal."

Thus, while admitting that some gain in efficiency might be realized in the short-term by implementation of free trade policies, the long-term question of the cost of that efficiency in terms of loss of liberty remains. It is important to distinguish between arguments against free trade theory, and free trade agreements as applied. Some opponents of NAFTA see the agreement as being materially harmful to the common people, but some of the arguments are actually against the particulars of government-managed trade, rather than against free trade *per se*.

For example, it is argued that it would be wrong to let subsidized corn from the U.S. into Mexico freely under NAFTA at prices well below production cost because of its ruinous effects to Mexican farmers. Of course, such subsidies violate free trade theory, so this argument is not actually against the principle of free trade, but rather its selective implementation. Latin America performed poorly since tariff cuts in 1980s and 1990s, compared to protectionist China and Southeast Asia. According to Samuelson, it is wrong to assume a necessary surplus of winnings over losings. The paper, "Will inventions A or B lower or raise the new market-clearing real wage rates that sustain high-to-full employment" condemned "economists' over-simple complacency about globalization" and said that workers don't always win. Some economists try to emphasize that trade barriers should exist to help poor nations build domestic industries and give rich nations time to retrain workers.

Colonialism

It has long been argued that free trade is a form of colonialism or imperialism, a position taken by various proponents of economic nationalism and the school of mercantilism. In the 19th century these criticized British calls for free trade as cover for British Empire, notably in the works of American Henry Clay, architect of the American System and by German American economist Friedrich List. More recently, Ecuadorian President Rafael Correa has denounced the "sophistry of free trade" in an introduction he wrote for a book titled The Hidden Face of Free Trade Accords, written in part by Correa's current Energy Minister Alberto Acosta. Citing as his source the book Kicking Away the Ladder, written by Ha-Joon Chang, Correa identified the difference between an "American system" opposed to a "British System" of free trade. The latter, he says, was explicitly viewed by the Americans as "part of the British imperialist system." According to Correa, Chang showed that it was Treasury Secretary Alexander Hamilton, and not Friedrich List, who was the first to present a systematic argument defending industrial protectionism.

TRADE PACT

A trade pact is a wide ranging tax, tariff and trade pact that often includes investment guarantees. The most common trade pacts are of the preferential and free trade types are concluded in order to reduce tariffs, quotas and other trade restrictions on items traded between the signatories.

Definition of Trade Pact

An agreement between countries that seeks to increase the level of free trade. This is done by creating special tax, tariff and trade regulations that can reduce barriers. A trade pact can also come with a guarantee of an investment in one country by another, such as foreign direct investment. It is a form of economic integration.

Classification of trade pacts

By Number and Type of Signatories

A trade agreement is classified as bilateral when signed between two sides, where each side could be a country, a trade bloc or an informal group of countries. A trade agreement signed between more than two sides is classified as multilateral.

By Sophistication

There are a variety of trade agreements; with some being quite complex, while others are less intensive.

The resulting level of economic integration depends on the specific type of trade pacts and policies adopted by the trade bloc:

- Separate
  - Trade and Investment Framework Agreement
  - Bilateral Investment Treaty
  - *Preferential Trade Arrangement:* Limited scope and depth of tariffs reduction between the customs territories.
    1. *Free Trade Agreement Establishing a Free Trade Area:* Extensive reduction or elimination of tariffs on substantially all trade allowing for the free movement of goods and in more advanced agreements also reduction of restrictions on investment and establishment allowing for the free movement of capital and free movement of services
    2. *Common Market:* FTA with significantly reduced or eliminated restrictions on the freedom of movement of all factors of production, including free movement of labour and of enterprise; and coordination in economic policy
  - Currency union - sharing the same currency
- Composite
  - *Customs Union:* FTA with common external tariffs of all signatories in respect to non-signatory countries
    1. *Customs and Monetary Union:* Customs union with Currency union
    2. *Economic Union:* Customs union with Common market
    3. *Economic and Monetary Union:* Economic union with Currency Union
    4. *Fiscal Union:* Common coordination of substantial parts of the fiscal policies

Special Agreements

- World Trade Organization treaty
  - Agreements in the WTO framework
- The now defunct Multilateral Agreement on Investment

By the World Trade Organization

Typically the benefits and obligations of the trade agreements apply only to their signatories. In the framework of the World Trade Organization a different agreement types are concluded, whose terms apply to all WTO members on the so-called most-favoured basis, which means that benefitial terms agreed bilaterally with one trading partner will apply also to the rest of the WTO members.

All agreements concluded outside of the WTO framework are called preferential by the WTO. According to WTO rules these agreements are subject to certain requirements such as notification to the WTO and general reciprocity where unilateral preferences are allowed only under exceptional circumstances and as temporary measure.

The trade agreements called preferential by the WTO are also known as regional, despite not necessarily concluded by countries within a certain region. There are currently 205 agreements in force as of July 2007. Over 300 have been reported to the WTO. The number of FTA has increased significantly over the last decade. Between 1948 to 1994, the General Agreement on Tariffs and Trade, the predecessor to the WTO, received 124 notifications. Since 1995 over 300 trade agreements have been enacted.

The WTO is further classifying these agreements in the following types:

- Goods covering:
  - Basic preferential trade agreement
  - Free trade agreement
  - Customs union
- Services covering:
  - Economic Integration Agreement - any agreement, including a PTA, that covers services

Reaction

Trade pacts are frequently politically contentious since they may change economic customs and deepen interdependence with trade partners. Increasing efficiency through "free trade" is a common goal. For the most part, governments are supportive of further trade agreements. There have been however some concerns expressed by the WTO. According to Pascal Lamy, Director-General of the WTO, the proliferation of RTA "...is breeding concern — concern about incoherence, confusion, exponential increase of costs for business, unpredictability and even unfairness in trade relations." The position of the WTO is that while the typical trade agreements are useful to a degree, it is much more beneficial to focus on global agreements in the WTO framework such as the negotiations of the current Doha round.

The anti-globalization movement opposes such agreements almost by definition, but some groups normally allied within that movement, *e.g.* green parties, seek fair trade or safe trade provisions that moderate what they perceive to be the ill effects of globalization.

6

International Trade and Export Finance

FINANCE ALTERNATIVES

To be able to give or to arrange finance as part of an export transaction is increasingly important, both as a sales argument and to meet competition from other suppliers. This applies particularly in the case of heavier capital goods or whole projects, where finance is often an integrated part of the package, but it may also apply to raw materials, consumer goods and lighter capital goods for shorter periods.

The length of credit is often divided into short term, medium term and long term, even though such classifications are arbitrary and dependent on the purpose. Short-term credits are normally for periods up to one year, even though the typical manufacturing exporter would normally trade on short-term credits of 60 or 90 days, perhaps up to a maximum of 180 days.

Periods between one and two years may be described as both short and medium term depending on the purpose, whereas periods from two up to five years are medium term and periods above that are long-term credits. In general, the buyer often prefers to split the payment for capital goods into separate installments over longer periods, perhaps with the intention of matching the payments against the income generated from the purchased goods.

In such cases, the seller may have to offer these longer credit terms in order to be competitive. The credit period is usually calculated from the time of shipment of the goods, or some average date in case of several deliveries. However, in practice, payment is seldom made at that early stage and some form of credit is therefore included in most transactions. The seller may prefer to refinance such credits through ordinary bank credit facilities, especially for shorter periods and smaller amounts.

However, in other cases the financing has to be arranged in some other way, which can also affect the structure of the transaction. Another aspect of trade finance involves ways of obtaining security that will enable the seller to extend such credits, often directly through the terms of payment, or in combination with separate credit insurance. Such risk coverage and the terms under which such policies can be issued have a strong influence on how export credits can be structured, but they also affect the terms of payment and other conditions related to the transaction, particularly for longer periods. Figure provides a summary of the most frequently used techniques for financing or refinancing of international trade and the following text will be structured accordingly.

Of the alternatives, only one or two may be of interest in each case, depending on the particular area of business or trade cycle of the transaction, that is, the period from the time when the first costs are incurred for ordering raw material or other goods, until shipment and final payment from the buyer.

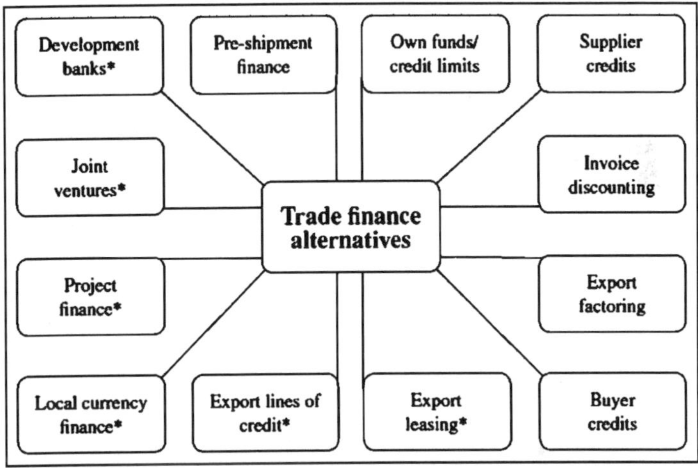

Fig. Summary of Trade Finance Alternatives.

However, the trade cycle also covers the time from when the first risks have to be incurred, for example agreements with other suppliers or simply the need to change internal procedures or preparations for the new production. This trade cycle can be relatively similar for most products within one and the same company, depending on the area of business, or it can be unique for every transaction. The character of the trade cycle will also differ between most suppliers and will determine the structure of the terms of payment, as well as the method of dealing with different trade finance alternatives.

PRE-SHIPMENT FINANCE

The expressions 'pre-export finance' and 'pre-shipment finance' are defined as the temporary working capital requirement needed for the fulfilment of one or several specific export transactions. This covers the cash flow related to costs of raw material and other goods, labour, equipment and overheads, until final payment – or until the earlier stage where receivables or debt instruments are received from the buyer, which can be refinanced. The period before delivery is often the most difficult part of the export transaction, particularly when trading on an open account basis. In that stage of the transaction the seller has only a sales contract, not a bill of exchange or other debt instruments related to the trade, nor any of the shipping documents that come with the actual delivery; for example, copies of the bill of lading and the invoice, showing that delivery has taken place and that a trade debt has been created.

For ordinary day-to-day transactions, the most frequent method of arranging pre-delivery finance requirements is through existing or additional bank credit limits, without involving the specific sales contract and/or the additional security, if any, created by the method of payment. However, when a business expands, or, in the case of individual larger or more complex transactions, when existing limits are fully used or needed elsewhere in the ordinary business, it is important to know how to find the additional means to finance the new transaction until payment is made or until documents can be produced, which are necessary for the refinancing. In some cases the sales contract itself can be used for creating that additional finance during the pre-delivery period, for example when a third party covers the buyer's payment obligations.

The difficulty of arranging pre-shipping finance in connection with open account trading is a major reason for the present development by SWIFT of a new SWIFTnet Trade Services Utility, a central data information database, which will increase the transparency of the transaction and reduce the uncertainty for the participating bank, enabling them to expand their pre-shipment finance. The existence of an L/C or a payment guarantee in favour of the seller could strongly facilitate the pre-shipment finance requirements in many ways.

The advantages of having the L/C made transferable are also obvious; it will automatically transfer not only the financial cash flow but also security from the seller to the suppliers, who might use the transferred L/C for their own pre-shipment arrangements. Many banks also extend special export loans on the basis of the L/C to a certain per centage of its value, with or without the L/C and its future proceeds pledged to the bank. Both the per centage and the collateral will most certainly vary depending on the many aspects to be considered by the bank, for example the issuing bank, the size and maturity of the L/C, its terms and conditions, the nature of the goods and, perhaps equally important, the knowledge and experience of the seller.

The advantages of an L/C as a pre-shipment finance instrument also applies to a payment guarantee issued by the buyer's bank in favour of the seller, but perhaps not to the same degree. The payment guarantee is more like a credit risk umbrella covering the general payment obligations of the buyer according to the contract. But it does not contain a mechanism, such as an L/C, where the issuing bank automatically has to pay, irrespective of the buyer's consent, when certain specified terms and conditions are met. Even though it is thereby less precise than an L/C, most banks will nevertheless regard such a guarantee as an important instrument for increasing the seller's credit limits. In a mutually advantageous business negotiation and when the commercial parties know each other well, the buyer may even be willing to make further concessions in the payment structure to accommodate the seller and their need for additional pre-delivery finance.

In fact, the buyer has already done so indirectly by agreeing to an L/C as a method of payment in the first place, or by having it made transferable. However, if agreeing to support the seller's pre-delivery cash flow, this could also be done through insertion of a so-called 'red clause' in its terms, even if such clauses are now relatively rare in international commercial trade. A red clause allows the seller to make use of an agreed part of the value of the L/C before delivering the documents, sometimes earmarked for payment only for some specific purpose. By inserting such clauses in the L/C, this pre-delivery part-payment will, in fact, become an advance payment.

However, such advance payments are otherwise mainly used only as part of an overall part-payment structure, with the larger part being payable at shipment and with one part up-front and often one part also as a deferred payment; this type of split is often used in contracts containing more than just delivery obligations, such as installation or maintenance and over a longer period. Even if any form of advance payment has to be secured by a conditional bank guarantee in favour of the buyer, and thus issued under the seller's existing credit limits, it is still to their advantage both from a cash-flow and a collateral perspective. Such a guarantee cannot be drawn upon as long as the seller fulfils the contractual obligations and therefore involves no additional risk; for that reason it may be issued with other, less stringent security requirements from the issuing bank, compared with ordinary lending.

WORKING CAPITAL INSURANCE/GUARANTEES

When dealing with pre-shipment finance, one also has to look at the sales contract between the commercial parties and how that could be used as a financial tool. Both private market insurers and export credit agencies may offer pre-delivery cover even if structured differently and with different requirements on the status of the buyer or on the terms of payment. Such cover can be issued in the form of an insurance policy to the exporter or directly as a guarantee to an authorized lending institution, thereby enabling the seller to obtain a loan to finance their export of goods and services.

This can then be used for the following purposes:

- Purchase of finished products for export;
- Cost of raw materials, equipment, supplies, labour and overheads to produce goods and/or provide services for export;

- Work in progress and finished export goods;
- Support standby L/Cs or other arrangements serving as contract or payment guarantees;
- Finance of open account or term receivables.

With such a working capital or pre-shipment guarantee, the seller would be able to increase their borrowing capacity considerably in comparison with normal lending criteria. Such insurance/guarantee may cover up to 90 per cent of the loan amount and with a maturity to match the underlying cash-flow requirements, typically from six months up to a few years. The existence of separate credit insurance will increase the security of the transaction and will have a strong influence on the bank's decision on additional finance.

This interaction between the seller, the insurer and the bank may be the key for securing additional pre-finance needed for the transaction. This procedure also gives the seller feedback on the terms on which the insurer and/or the bank may be willing to participate and what might be required from the seller and from the terms of the sales contract. Having achieved that, the seller will have secured the support needed from these institutions, covering both the risks involved and the cash needed as pre-shipment finance.

SUPPLIER CREDITS

Supplier credits are the most commonly used method of trade finance, mainly for shorter periods but to a lesser degree also for medium-term periods. Its structure is determined by the time-span of the credit, its size, the buyer's country and the method of payment agreed in the sales contract – details that determine not only the seller's risk exposure but also the structure required by the financial institution, should the credit have to be refinanced at a later stage. The possibility of the seller agreeing to a supplier credit is determined by how it can be refinanced, either through existing bank limits for smaller amounts and shorter periods, or by separate discounting or refinancing of the finance instrument that becomes available at shipment or shortly thereafter. The credit terms that can be offered by the seller are also important as a sales argument and as a competitive advantage – or at least as a means of being on an equal footing with competitors.

Sometimes the terms of such short credits can be made particularly advantageous for the buyer as part of the offer, even if the seller compensates themselves in another part of the contract. The problem for the buyer is that it is not easy to see if the price has been increased because of the favourable credit terms, and if so, by how much. There is also a risk that the seller may overcompensate for the risks in their credit offer if the buyer is unfamiliar or if the seller cannot evaluate the commercial risk correctly. The buyer, on the other hand, may ask for a quotation to include both cash against delivery and a supplier credit alternative in order to be able to make a fair comparison.

The buyer may even start the negotiations based on cash against delivery or short-term open account terms to allow for new and longer credit negotiations, when the price discussions are more or less concluded. It will then be more difficult for the seller to add the credit costs to the price and these will have to be part of a separate negotiation in which the buyer again tries to get the best solution – or arranges the finance elsewhere or, in the worst case, chooses another supplier altogether.

Irrespective of how the negotiations proceed, there are some general questions that the seller must evaluate before offering a supplier credit, such as:

- To what degree is the requested credit changing the commercial and/or the political risk involved in the transaction?
- Can the buyer be expected to take any open credit costs?
- Should the financial costs be included in the original price offer or should the seller be proactive by keeping the credit terms open as a separate question to be discussed with the buyer?
- How can such credit be refinanced?
- In the case of foreign currency invoicing, how should the currency risk be evaluated and covered?

In cases of shorter periods and smaller amounts, these questions are easily dealt with, but in other cases they might be one of the major aspects of the transaction.

SHORT-TERM SUPPLIER CREDITS

The most common form of short-term supplier credits is in combination with open account payment terms; that is, the contract is based on a future payment transfer, and the invoice specifies the date when payment must be received at the seller's account. However, the seller has no other security for the buyer's payment obligations. Sometimes, particularly for periods over 3–6 months, even short-term credits are arranged through a bill of exchange to be accepted by the buyer at delivery, thereby replacing the open credit with a documented debt instrument, payable at a specified later date. The seller may nevertheless also enclose a bill of exchange with the invoice even when trading on open account and on shorter payment terms showing the delivery date together with a fixed maturity date.

This could have value even if the bill is not accepted by the buyer because it connects the sales contract with the delivery and the buyer's corresponding payment obligations. This is the same procedure as used in connection with documentary collections, payable at presentation. The seller should also evaluate whether it would be beneficial to offer both cash against delivery terms and short-term credit on favourable terms as alternatives; however, if choosing the latter, then it will be conditional upon the buyer's acceptance of a bill of exchange when presented together with the invoice.

A short, well-documented supplier credit could have advantages for both parties, compared to open account payment terms, for the following reasons:

- It could be an additional advantage from a sales perspective;
- The buyer can use the credit for improved cash-flow management, perhaps at more favourable terms, but with the strict obligation to pay at maturity – with the risk for noting and protest of the accepted bill if not paid;
- The seller has the advantage of an accepted finance document that is easier to refinance at an earlier stage, if needed;
- The seller can plan liquidity more exactly at the outset, knowing that payment on maturity is highly likely; and
- The seller may wholly or partly include interest in the bill of exchange, compared with a later overdue interest.

The difference between open account payment terms and the accepted bill of exchange is also greater than one might first expect. With open account terms, the buyer has a stronger case for negotiating with the seller prior to payment, should it be considered that the delivery was not in accordance with the agreement. It could be anything from time of delivery to shortcomings in the quality or quantity of the goods – the main point is that the buyer may refuse to pay until the matter is resolved. However, by accepting the bill of exchange at or about the time of shipment, the buyer has an unconditional obligation to pay, irrespective of any real or alleged shortcomings discovered later in the delivery.

If the claim is correct, the buyer will probably get compensation; however, the bill must be paid at maturity, irrespective of the ongoing discussions with the seller. When documentary collection is used as the method of payment together with supplier credits, the documents will be released against acceptance of a bill of exchange with a fixed maturity. The documents are exchanged against the bill, normally without any further security for the seller. But, if the supplier credit is given as part of an L/C, the banks involved will determine the procedure and will also check the accuracy of the documents. Upon approval, the bill of exchange will be accepted and can then easily be discounted by the seller on favourable terms, mostly without recourse.

MEDIUM- AND LONG-TERM SUPPLIER CREDITS

Supplier credits of two years or more are usually arranged in connection with the sale of machinery, vehicles, equipment or other capital goods, and with credit documentation that tends to be more complex than for shorter periods. In these cases separate financial documentation is often used, with or without supplementary bills of exchange – or promissory notes with the same but more summarized wording compared to a complete loan agreement. When bills of exchange or promissory notes are refinanced externally, the seller often has a prearranged facility from a bank or financial institution, specifying the details, including the security required for such refinancing to take place. In any case, the seller is likely to have such refinancing agreed as part of the transaction, with all preconditions in place before delivery.

With longer supplier credits, two questions are important for both commercial parties to agree upon:

1. The choice of currency; and
2. The choice of fixed or floating interest rate.

The choice of currency need not be the same as the invoicing currency, even if that is normally the case. However, if the parties agree to a separate financing currency, they also have to agree at what future date the change from invoicing to financing currency will take place. The outcome may be a 'neutral' third-party currency, often USD, which also has good liquidity over longer periods and, therefore, is possible to hedge at reasonable terms. However, if the currency of the credit is not the buyer's home currency, then the buyer takes the currency risk, or the hedging cost, until final maturity. A bank guarantee as well as a currency transfer guarantee from the central bank may sometimes be required in order to make the notes acceptable for refinancing.

The choice of fixed or floating interest in a medium- or long-term supplier credit is primarily a choice of the buyer, if a fixed rate alternative can be obtained through the refinancing bank. That is most likely in the larger trade currencies, either as direct refinancing or through interest swaps, which are separate contracts with the bank, exchanging floating for fixed interest rate under a fixed period of time. Such contracts in the larger trade currencies can be obtained at reasonable rates for very long periods.

REFINANCING OF SUPPLIER CREDITS

In one way or the other, the exporter has to finance or refinance the supplier credit extended to the buyer, and some of these methods have been mentioned.

As a summary, some of the most used forms of refinancing supplier credits on short or medium term periods are:

- Bank loans and trade finance limits;
- Invoice finance facilities;
- Export factoring;
- Forfaiting;
- Structured export finance.

They are therefore more frequently used in connection with buyer credits but it is important to keep in mind that these forms of finance can also be used in connection with refinancing of supplier credits with longer maturities.

BANK LOANS AND TRADE FINANCE LIMITS

The most common method of refinancing short-term supplier credits is simply by using the seller's existing bank credit limits, often the current account and its overdraft facility, based on general collateral pledged to the bank in the form of fixed or floating charges on the company's assets.

This refinancing is then done at a floating interest rate determined by the lender as for any other domestic loans, but based on the prime or base rate of the country, set by the central bank. This form of domestic bank finance is mainly used to finance ordinary trade transactions based on open account payment terms, and since they represent the major part of international trade, the banks are also the main refinancing source of this shorter end of trade finance.

If the transaction is made in foreign currency, the seller may choose to take a separate loan in the same currency in order to refinance the supplier credit, but also in order to cover the currency risk involved. Such a loan could also have beneficial interest advantages if the currency in question has a lower interest rate than the domestic currency. The currency loan will then immediately be changed into local currency at the spot rate and repaid by the incoming payment from the buyer.

The cost for such a currency loan as compared to a domestic base or prime rate loan will be based on the following factors:

- The bank's refinancing costs, which are generally based n the interbank money market rates in that currency and for that period;
- The bank's interest margin as determined by the amount, customer relationship and market competition;
- The cost for any currency hedge.

Apart from these basic forms of general bank finance, banks also offer different forms of trade-related loans based on the individual transaction, normally connected to documentary collection and letters of credit, where if necessary the documents and the corresponding flow of money can also be pledged to the bank as additional security.

In connection with documentary collection, the banks may give advance payment against documents under collection to a certain per centage of their value often under a separate and more favourable trade-finance limit, to be used for self-liquidating trade transactions. The accepted short-term trade bill of exchange, normally three to six months, may also be discounted under the same limit. In case of a letter of credit payable by acceptance, some banks may offer export loans up to a per centage of its value, available from the time of its opening.

At the time of presentation of documents, the advising bank or the issuing bank will accept the bill of exchange, which can then almost automatically be discounted and the net proceeds paid to the seller. There are additional finance alternatives offered by both banks and finance companies, which become available after delivery and even in connection with open account trading, covering the short-term credit of normally 30–90 days included in most trade transactions.

At that time, the seller has fulfilled their delivery obligations and a payment obligation on behalf of the buyer has been created, evidenced by the seller's invoice. It is true that the buyer may have objections to how the delivery has been executed, but unless that is the case, it should be possible to refinance that invoice in one way or the other in order to generate immediate cash for the seller, less interest and fees involved in the refinancing.

The main distinction between the following two main areas:

1. Confidential factoring, where the finance is a transaction between the seller and the bank/finance company, of which the buyer is not aware.
2. Notified factoring, where the buyer is fully informed about the finance transaction, normally through an assignment on each invoice and where the seller is offered not just finance but also a range of other services.

The parties offering these services are either banks or bank-owned finance companies, which receive most of their business through referrals within the group, larger and independent finance or factoring companies, or smaller niche players concentrating on certain segments only. Since pure invoice discounting or other invoice finance facilities are a quite straightforward service offered by both banks and their finance companies but also by a number of other financial institutions, the term 'provider' is generally used in that section, whereas 'factoring company', or factor as it is commonly known, is used in the area of export factoring.

However, there are probably few areas within international trade finance where both terminology and procedures differ so much as to how such refinance is carried out in practice in all its different forms. The segmentation into invoice discounting and factoring may therefore not always be valid in all countries, but it nevertheless has a pedagogical advantage which will enable the reader to understand the concepts and make use of them to their advantage according to their individual circumstances.

INVOICE DISCOUNTING

Invoice discounting can briefly be described as the provision of finance of a bulk of receivables, mostly but not always secured by an earmarked floating charge or a specific debenture. Invoice discounting is a confidential facility; it is also mostly a pure lending facility where the title to the invoice and the right to the proceeds remain with the seller. It gives cash payment of a certain per centage of a bulk of receivables, and invoice discounting is therefore mostly used when the seller already has an internal system in place for effective credit control. Invoice discounting can accommodate most of the seller's invoices based on open account payment terms on a rolling basis; however, as it is confidential, the buyer is unaware of the facility and the seller is responsible for sales ledger administration and later collecting procedures, should that be necessary.

Some providers integrate invoice discounting with other services, such as credit information, credit insurance and debt collection, in order to make this combination more competitive at a reasonable cost. Even if these 'packages' are constructed somewhat differently, this combined service has even more similarities with factoring, seen from the seller's point of view. It is important to remember that there is no typical invoice discounting or invoice finance facility since they differ not only between countries but also between providers in one and the same country.

However, the main features of an ordinary invoice discounting facility used for trade finance purposes may include the following aspects:

- The buyer is unaware of the arrangements between the seller and the provider.
- The provider may arrange the opening of a separate bank account in the name of the seller, where all trade payments must be paid. This account, along with the invoices, could be, but is not necessarily, pledged to the provider as security.
- The seller is required to send copies of invoices to the provider to be included under the facility, in order for them to keep the pool of eligible invoices constantly updated. New invoices are included, and paid invoices, together with unpaid and long overdue invoices, are deleted.
- The provider will make the facility available to the seller at an agreed per centage of the underlying invoices in the 'pool'.
- The provider will send the seller regular statements in order for the seller to check against the export invoice ledger, and the seller will be obliged to send to the provider copies of that sales ledger at intervals for control purposes.

Invoice discounting is suitable for most companies and is particularly useful for smaller and rapidly growing companies whose balance sheets would not be sufficiently strong to allow for the volume of ordinary credit limits they may need for their expanding business. Such facilities mostly cover both domestic and export transactions in order to reach administrative advantages and critical mass, with foreign buyers mainly from developed and neighbouring countries where open account payment terms are normally practised. Invoice discounting is a 'with recourse' form of lending up to a certain level of the face value of the invoices, often 70–80 per cent, based on a risk assessment and mostly secured by either a general pledge on all the company's assets or a specific and unsecured debenture covering invoices not already pledged. The finance per centage offered is not only based on the invoices themselves, but also on their average distribution regarding amounts, buyers and countries. As it is a confidential facility based on invoices only, the general credit standing of the seller is most important, as is their experience and track record, and the aggregate of all these criteria will determine the per centage lending value and the cost structure.

In most cases, invoice discounting could be used as an ordinary overdraft facility at the seller's discretion, set by the volume of the underlying eligible invoices, forming a pool of available borrowing under the facility at any time. As the value of the pool of invoices fluctuates, more or less money will be available. In case of maximum utilization in conjunction with reduced total invoice value, or in case of non-payment when the invoice will be deleted from the pool, the seller may even have to repay money in order to keep the agreed per centage.

Invoice discounting can instantly release liquidity at a high per centage of the underlying receivables and because of the nature of the facility it can also be made relatively cost-effective, especially when covering both domestic and export sales, hence its popularity in many countries. Many providers also offer these facilities via the internet, which facilitates the practical day-to-day handling for both parties and gives the seller an instant picture of usage and availability at any time. The cost depends on the services involved, but the facility is often charged for by means of a flat fee related to the agreed total limit and an interest rate for actual usage which is normally higher than a normal overdraft facility, together with additional handling charges, based on volume and work involved.

EXPORT FACTORING

Factoring is a special form of short-term finance where a finance company purchases the seller's receivables and assumes the credit risk, either with or without recourse to the seller. Factoring is still mainly used in the industrialized countries and within trading areas with a relatively similar structure of harmonized laws, rules and procedures. It is generally more complex, involving not only finance but also additional services, and in many countries it is therefore used more selectively and often for larger individual amounts compared to invoice discounting finance.

In its original form, the seller entering into a factoring agreement sells the receivables to the factor, mostly also relieving themselves of the credit control and debt collection functions, which are assumed by the factor against a fee. In such a case, the factor also gains the title to the invoice and the right to the proceeds, and takes future decisions, if any, regarding collection and other measures, including the legal work in the event of non-payment. The seller will display a notification on the factored invoices, informing the buyer that the invoice has been transferred to the named factor, together with instructions on how payment is to be made directly to them in order to discharge their payment obligation. The seller also sends copies of the invoices and the shipping documents to the factor, but often the factor issues the invoices themselves upon instruction from the seller. The factor starts with a credit assessment of the seller and the general structure of their trade and previous export experience, followed by an assessment of the different buyers, including any insurance cover, in order to establish individual lending limits on the buyers and a total credit limit for the seller.

Factoring could have the following advantages for the seller:

- A better risk performance than for other finance alternatives through the credit information services included;
- More punctual payments from the buyers, as the seller is pre-notified of the sale of the invoices to the factor;
- The borrowing value of the invoices could be higher than through bank lending, thereby increasing the seller's total liquidity;
- The seller can use additional administrative systems to reduce workload.

Export factoring is mostly in the form of 'with recourse factoring' with up to 90 per cent of invoice value, with the provision that if the buyer fails to pay the invoice after a set period of time, the factor will be repaid by the seller. In some cases export factoring can be provided as 'non-recourse factoring', where the factor stands the risk in the event of bankruptcy or liquidation of the buyer. In these cases the seller will never be requested to repay the discounted invoice to the factor and can then remove the invoice from the receivables in the balance sheet. However, they may have to pay interest for the agreed waiting period after the due date, normally 60–90 days, as specified in the factoring agreement. Most such non-recourse factoring is either based on very good corporate names with little risk or secured by separate credit insurance or similar security.

It is often said that export factoring is more expensive than similar bank services, but such a comparison could be somewhat misleading as the services are difficult to compare. In most cases factoring does lead to considerably more punctual payments, better control of outstanding receivables and less administrative workload for the company. The factoring services are generally more efficient with regard to slow payers and in these cases the use of a factor can have an effect – and the seller avoids straining the business relationship. Apart from the interest charged, a flat service fee is also charged on every invoice factored, the size of which depends on workload and services included, numbers of factors involved and the total factoring turnover.

The seller should therefore complete a cost/revenue valuation in relation to the services offered – and needed – compared with other alternatives, for example invoice discounting finance. In practice, there are in principle two basic forms of export factoring, either the so-called 'two-factor export factoring', where the seller's domestic factoring company uses local correspondents in the buyer's country within a chain of cooperating factors, or 'direct export factoring', without a local factor being involved. However, some major international companies, originally within the area of credit insurance, have now expanded their services into the credit risk management area, thereby offering services relatively similar to those of the factors within their own organization through a network of branches around the world.

They can then offer in-house combinations of purchase of invoices, credit information, credit insurance and debt collection in competition with established factoring companies. Figure shows the two-factor alternative, in which the seller's factoring company cooperates with a domestic factor in the buyer's country. The use of domestic factors or branches of an international organization will often increase the overall cost structure, but has the advantage of a local presence, together with knowledge of the buyers and the local procedures for collecting money according to local law and common practice, including debt recovery, and is therefore mostly used for larger amounts.

FORFAITING

In many countries the refinancing of medium- or long-term supplier credits is handled by the commercial banks, either together or in competition with separate export banks specializing in export finance. The medium- and long-term finance market also includes the special forfaiting institutions, which have a long history in financing international trade. They are mainly located in the larger financial centres such as London and New York, but do not have the same importance today owing to increased competition from commercial and international banks. Forfaiting basically means the surrender of an unconditional future right to make a trade-related claim through accepted and freely negotiable bills or notes, in return for the receipt of prompt payment.

Forfaiting, whether through specialized departments within the banks or through a few traditional and still independent forfaiting houses, is a special type of discounting of trade-related and mostly fixed-term-interest bills of exchange with different maturity dates, without recourse to the seller. When it comes to risk evaluation of both individual buyers and countries, the forfaiters are well placed in trading these negotiable financial instruments, by spreading the risks through risk participation and distribution through domestic and international credit risk insurers, using reinsurance and syndication techniques.

Forfaiting risks are generally based on security in the form of first-class corporate risks, acceptable land risks, bank guarantees, standby L/Cs, undertakings from ministries of finance in the case of sovereign buyers, with or without currency transfer guarantees from a central bank. The diversity of the operations, often with specialization in different countries or areas together with existing exposure and limits, may therefore create different risk evaluations and credit decisions among these institutions. If a deal is acceptable, the forfaiting house will issue a firm or a conditional facility letter to the seller, specifying the terms and conditions for discounting and the interest level to be applied.

Forfeiting may normally require larger transactions to be cost-effective, but today this form of finance is often done as non-recourse invoice discounting by the commercial banks. However, the procedure is quite simple in both cases; at receipt of the bills or notes according to the terms in the facility letter, the net amount is paid to the seller without recourse.

BUYER CREDITS

Buyer credits are given directly to the buyer or the buyer's bank in connection with the export transaction, but not directly by the seller. This enables the seller to receive cash payment at delivery and/or at different stages of construction or installation, while at the same time a longer-term credit is extended to the buyer.

Buyer credits are normally used for larger individual transactions, particularly when the transaction involves more than just delivery of goods or covers a longer contract period, and often also when the delivery is tailor-made to the specifications of the buyer. Buyer credits may be given in two different forms, either directly to the buyer's bank for further on-lending to the buyer, or directly to the buyer, then mostly covered by a guarantee from the buyer's bank.

However, since this difference is relatively small from the perspective of the seller, we shall deal with both these forms as bank-to-buyer credits below. When exporting to industrialized countries, but also to many emerging market countries, buyer credits are usually arranged on pure market terms. However, outside these countries it is seldom possible to finance transactions of this nature on longer terms on the open market; they need to be backed by additional security, mostly in the form of export credit insurance. The seller should then coordinate the commercial negotiations with the buyer and with both the chosen bank and the insurer so that the contract and the corresponding loan agreement can be developed in parallel during the negotiating process.

One of the important aspects of buyer credits is how they relate to the underlying contract. Financial credits are principally unrelated to the obligations between the commercial parties, and that also applies to buyer credits when the buyer normally has to approve the delivery in connection with entering into the loan. The outstanding contractual risk at that time, if any, for the due fulfilment of the seller's obligations is then normally covered outside the loan agreement by a separate performance guarantee in favour of the buyer, in order to keep the commercial contract and the financial credit separate while protecting the buyer at the same time. Should that procedure not be suitable, the loan may contain recourse clauses towards the seller until the obligations of the seller are approved by the buyer, but that involves a corresponding credit risk on the seller which the lending bank has to approve. The loan agreement and its final wording have to be approved by all parties – the buyer, the seller, the banks and the credit insurer, if applicable.

It is normally based on the same principles as an ordinary international loan agreement, but also including the relevant parties to the commercial contract, in order for the two agreements to harmonize during the disbursement period. Thereafter, they should be seen as two totally separate agreements.

NORMAL TERMS AND CONDITIONS IN BUYER CREDITS

Buyer credits can be arranged in almost any way and on terms decided between the parties, as long as it is done on market terms without government support. However, when such support is needed, the credit terms must also comply with the Consensus rules. The exported goods should then qualify for credit periods of at least two years, with 15 per cent of the contract value as advance payment and a maximum of 85 per cent credit, with disbursement, repayment and interest structure according to Consensus rules. However, for buyer credits, the minimum contract value is normally much higher compared to ordinary supplier credits, since this type of financing is mainly applied to larger and often tailor-made transactions, which are more difficult and costly to arrange.

Buyer credits may be given in most trade currencies, at both floating and fixed-term rates. Officially supported rates may also be given, particularly on a fixed-term basis, even if the market rates often can be as competitive, particularly in a low-interest environment. Other finance techniques are also available to offer competitive fixed market rates for long-term credits and larger amounts through the international money or capital markets. If possible, offers can also be made to provide the loan, or part of it, in the buyer's local currency. The loan agreement in a buyer credit contains the same standard clauses as in every other international loan, such as conditions precedent, default clauses and applicable law, along with legal opinions regarding both the loan and the sales contract, showing that they are compatible, legally enforceable and duly executed. It must contain confirmation of receipt of the stipulated advance payments, but other relevant details of the commercial contract must also be included. The disbursement clauses also have to be properly documented.

THE INTERNATIONAL MONEY MARKET

Apart from purely domestic finance, based on prime or base interest rates fixed by the central banks, the market commonly used for the refinancing of trade finance is the international and unregulated money market or markets, operating within financial centres in different time zones. These markets trade in short-term currency loans and deposits, whereas the expression 'capital markets' refers to long-term periods, usually only for larger amounts and with fixed interest, for example through bonds and other long-term instruments.

Often the term 'Euro currency' is used for deposits traded on these markets, referring to funds that are held by a bank or other party outside the home country of the specific currency, but it now has nothing to do with Europe as such, even if that was where originally a major part of these funds were held. 'Eurodollar' is thus now a general reference regardless of location, for example to USD held outside the United States, and 'Euroyen' is a reference to JPY held anywhere outside Japan; the same goes for any other Euro currency. The money markets are not physical marketplaces but a general description of the trade itself, carried out in different currencies between numerous lenders and borrowers.

The major banks, both domestically and internationally, play a central role through their internal interbank deposit trading, which is crucial for both liquidity and stable market conditions – in the same way as banks operate in the currency market. For short-term loans and deposits in different currencies, this interbank money market is often referred to as the name of the financial centres where the main banks are operating; for example, the London Interbank Market, where the corresponding interest rates are referred to as London Interbank Offered Rates.

London is by far the largest money marketplace, not only in the European time zone, and is also the financial centre to which many commercial contracts or agreements worldwide are referred regarding interest rates for most trade currencies, even though other financial centres in different time zones are also often used to specify the interest rate for the main international currencies. There are also a number of financial centres where interbank money market rates are quoted in the local currency, for example TIBOR which stands for Tokyo Interbank Offered Rates, the free and unregulated money market rates for the Euroyen, which are published daily by the Japanese Bankers Association.

These constantly fluctuating money market rates are often different from the domestic base or prime rates in the same currency, which are regulated by the domestic central bank and mostly changed only at intervals in order to regulate economic activity within the country.

This difference between domestic and free money market interest rates could be quite significant in times of credit crunches or turmoil on the money markets and these unregulated rates are therefore the best indicator of the real cost of short-term money in that currency. When it comes to the euro currency itself, European banks have established an interbank reference rate called EURIBOR, which is the benchmark rate of the interbank euro money market that has emerged since 1999, sponsored by among others the European Banking Federation. EURIBOR is the rate at which euro interbank term deposits are offered between prime European and international banks, computed and published on the Reuter screen.

During the day, an interbank reference rate is fixed in most currencies, to be used as the reference rate in, for example, contracts and loan agreements. Most such rates are published daily by central banks or bank associations through different online information systems or separate web pages, usually at 11.00 am local time, for periods up to a year. They are also quoted in the newspapers as the established short-term international interest rates for the most common currencies. However, as the market interest rates change continuously during the day, more accurate information is also available, either through the banks' own internet-based information systems or through direct contact with their trading departments. For participants actively trading directly in the market, there are also specialized online systems available, with almost identical and instantly updated currency and money market information.

Therefore, when referring to floating interest rates in trade finance, these are often based on these interest rate fixings, even if more details have to be specified in each individual case. To be even more precise, many loan agreements also often refer to interest quotations from some specific major banks in that market as reference banks, in order to get the interest rate absolutely identified and fixed without referring to a general marketplace. The total interest rate for the customer also includes the margin as applied by the lending bank in each individual case, or as specified in the loan agreement. Trade finance transactions are generally based on bills or notes when it comes to supplier credits, but more frequently on separate loan agreements when it comes to buyer credits and structured trade finance transactions.

Short-term bills of exchange are often combined with a fixed interest for the entire period until due date, with the capital amount and interest rate compounded into a fixed amount to be paid at maturity. Promissory notes are often made in the same way, but for longer periods they have to be more detailed and are usually designed as short loan agreements, based on either floating or fixed interest rate. When it comes to buyer credits and other forms of structured finance, a separate and detailed loan agreement is always used for these longer periods.

If based on a floating interest rate they also contain a clear definition of how the interest should be calculated and fixed for each short interest period, with a successive number of roll-over periods of, for example, three or six months until final maturity. The borrower can often choose the length of these roll-over periods and at the end of each such period interest is due, together with amortization, if any. Many loan agreements also give the borrower the option to change currency at the end of each interest period, but combined with a maximum amount expressed in one base currency in order to cap the total outstanding loan in case of adverse currency exchange movements. This structure, with different optional currencies, floating or fixed interest rates and variable loan periods, can be adapted to suit the changing circumstances of the borrower during the lifetime of the loan and makes the international money market a very flexible source for short-, medium- or even long-term trade finance, based on a variety of financing techniques. One of the advantages with longer-term loans based on short-term roll-over periods is that they are simple to use and so flexible that, in principle, they can be adapted to any trade or financial transaction for almost any period.

The disadvantage for the borrower on longer periods can be the floating rate, which makes the credit costs difficult to evaluate in advance, but this problem is also easily resolved in most cases. The forward points system was described as the basis for establishing currency forward rates. The technique is similar for changing floating interest rates into fixed rates through interest swap agreements.

A five-year loan based on, for example, three-month LIBOR may be changed into a fixed interest rate loan at any time during the loan period. This is done through a separate interest rate swap agreement with a bank, whereby the borrower agrees to receive the floating rate needed to service the loan and deliver interest rates to the bank under the swap agreement. However, such a swap agreement also contains an additional risk for the bank should the borrower default during the period of the loan, thereby not being able to deliver the fixed interest.

It is, therefore, subject to a separate credit decision within the bank but the technique and the market liquidity make it possible to hedge the interest rate for very long periods. In the most traded currencies this can be done up to 5 or 10 years, thereby eliminating the potential disadvantage of using the money market's short-term interest rates.

7

Export Credit Insurance

A MUTUAL UNDERTAKING

In many cases, that may be difficult to achieve, because the buyer does not accept the proposed terms, the bank is unwilling to take the risks involved or the remaining risks may even be considered by the seller as being too high. The terms of payment must be negotiated in the same way as other parts of the contract, in which both commercial parties often have to make a compromise. In many countries there are established practices in the way payments are made and it may be difficult to agree with the buyer should the terms differ too greatly from these practices – particularly if they expect other suppliers to offer more competitive terms.

In other situations, the seller may have difficulty in finding financial institutions that are willing to accept the inherent risks in the discussed terms of payment, in particular related to the political and/or commercial risks in many countries in conjunction even with short-term financing, not to mention the medium- or long-term periods. In these cases it is crucial to try to structure the deal in a way that enables the seller to maximize the combined cover that can be obtained from banks, financial institutions and separate export credit insurance companies or institutions. The seller must then explore, in advance, what is achievable before commencing negotiations with the buyer.

Having the knowledge and capability to structure such transactions, together with banks and/or insurers, is of vital importance for the seller when dealing with political and commercial risks that might otherwise make the transaction difficult or even impossible to deal with. Insurance is generally based on a mutual relationship between the parties involved, where both the insurer and the insured enter into obligations towards one another. This is a major difference compared with a guarantee or bond, which is a one-sided obligation based on specified conditions.

Many forms of export credit insurance have been created to cover different parts of the transaction, for example coverage from shipment only or also including the production period. Each insurance cover is based on special terms and conditions, which the seller has to check with the preconditions applicable to the individual transaction. The most common of these conditions are related to the seller's own risk in the transaction, qualifying or waiting periods or conditions precedent, for example that an L/C has been issued, certain permissions in the buyer's country have been obtained or that certain guarantees have been received by the seller.

However, the seller also has obligations towards the insurer; for example, that the uninsured per centage should be retained during the whole insured period or, alternatively, that it might only be transferred under certain conditions. Other conditions could be that specified time limits must be adhered to or adverse changes regarding the buyer or the transaction should be reported, and/or that important changes to the transaction have to be approved by the insurer.

Incorrect, misleading, changed or unreported circumstances may, in the worst case, lead to the insurance being reduced or revoked. The seller must also take reasonable action during the insurance period to prevent or mitigate potential damage or losses under the insurance. It is, therefore, important for the seller to ensure that staff, who might not be aware of the conditions of the insurance, do not make changes or give concessions to the buyer that may jeopardize the insurance cover.

This applies in particular to the longer government-supported insurance. However, in the private sector insurance market, the normal situation is that all the commercial buyers are pre-evaluated and individual credit limits established for each buyer. The seller then only has to ensure that the individual credit limits are available and are part of the credit insurance contract. Even though many standard and special terms may apply, these terms are part of the same credit insurance contract and should therefore be well known to the seller's staff. If used correctly, export credit insurance can be a crucial part of the whole structure of the deal, whether it is to cover ordinary day-to-day short-term export transactions or the additional risk of an offered medium-term credit.

THE PRIVATE SECTOR INSURANCE MARKET

Goods and services exported to the most developed OECD countries on credit periods less than two years can only be covered by the private sector according to established OECD rules, while government-supported insurance is usually only allowed for longer periods or for covering other countries where the private insurance market generally is less competitive. For periods of 1–2 years, the commercial risk is the main risk element for exports to most OECD countries. But where both the commercial and political risks are increased, the terms of payment are generally shifted from open account terms to terms based on documentary payments, with stronger control over the goods until payment is received. For non-OECD countries, where the commercial/political risk is even greater, bank guaranteed terms of payment, usually in the form of an L/C, are often the norm.

The usual condition for obtaining insurance is that it covers the delivery of goods or services. However, the risks during the production period up to delivery can also be included, based on a signed contract between the parties. This basic payment structure is consistent with the structure of the market sector credit insurance, covering mainly commercial risk on shorter periods, or the combined commercial/political risk on government or semi-official institutions.

Political risk cover can sometimes be added to the policy for commercial buyers. The market sector insurance core business therefore comes from industrial countries, or countries in industrial development, in which relevant financial company information can be obtained and where the legal framework and financial systems are reasonably efficient. The advantages of an international network are also used in the marketing of other services provided by insurers in the market sector; for example, issuing various types of export-related guarantees or bonds in competition with the banks, or services related to the credit risk policies, such as credit risk assessment and collection of overdue payments.

The main advantages of private export credit insurance, taken from different leading insurance companies, are listed below:

- Capped and calculable costs;
- Economic security;
- Rapid and professional settlement of claims;
- Access to experience from various business sectors in many countries;
- Professional coverage of clients and outstanding claims;
- Access to an international network with local representation;
- Large databases of customer information;
- Release of administration and resources from clients;
- Increase in borrowing capacity from banks;
- Expanding sales to existing customers;
- Developing sales into new international markets;
- Professional credit management overview of receivables.

One of the advantages with market sector credit risk insurance, emphasized by the insurers themselves, is that in reality their combined services and not just the insur-ance tend to reduce the outstanding risk in the markets in which they operate, for example through local representation in the buyer's country and more professional supervision. The development of more sophisticated models for risk analysis, together with new techniques for database handling and the establishment of an international network, has led to a rapid restructuring of this segment of the insurance market, which now consists of only a few companies with a global presence. The cost structure for market export insurance is based on a number of factors such as risk assessment, customer relations, the volume of business generated and the competition. This means that the premium for individual transactions or for a package of transactions can vary considerably between insurers, even when considering the differences in risk cover and in other terms and conditions that may apply. Many credit insurance companies or brokers have standardized systems on their web sites, so-called credit insurance cost–benefit analysis, where the seller can do a simple analysis evaluating their total export portfolio.

By inputting the insurable yearly export sales, the average gross margin and an estimated average or worst-case loss ratio, this analysis shows not only the direct cost involved but also what incremental sales are necessary to pay for the corresponding average credit insurance premium. Not surprisingly, the seller will probably find that in most of these general and standardized calculations, the premium is a relatively small investment for covering the potential loss, and that the additional sales needed to cover this loss are of such magnitude that they justify almost any credit insurance programme. This is before taking other indirect advantages into account.

However, even if standardized calculations do not give the whole picture, the seller should study the cost–benefit of using a general credit insurance cover in their particular case, based on the seller's own preconditions and assumptions. A general cover often gives the best outcome in such an analysis owing to the business volumes involved and the automatic spread of risk for the insurer, and any new individual deal could be added to the cover at beneficial rates. When this analysis is done, it is easier for the seller to compare other alternatives and to make an informed decision as to whether to use such credit risk cover programmes. Another important evaluation for the seller is to look at the consequences of non-payment of larger invoices.

The insurance policies offered in the market sector are generally individually structured and can be combined with many other services, and the seller should try to find the optimal combination for them, either directly or through an insurance broker. By doing so, the seller can also check the various preconditions which might be needed for entering into a potential transaction or to cover a risk portfolio, for example regarding the terms of payment required.

This may also give a better picture of the costs involved in relation to different levels of risk coverage, together with a better analysis of how the risk is assessed by an individual insurer. This is why it is so important to establish early contact with banks and credit insurers when it comes to new transactions or unfamiliar markets or buyers.

MARKET SECTOR INSURANCE COVER

The dominant insurers tend to structure credit insurance policies in the international market in a similar way, but often with different product names and including additional, optional services. One general feature of this market's performance is the tendency to strive to cover not only individual deals or single buyers, but primarily all of the seller's export transactions.

This enables the insurer to obtain larger volumes of business with a more diversified risk structure, and to take advantage of the international network and additional services included in the offer. The description of the market sector insurance below is, therefore, of a general nature in order to highlight the basic structure of these insurance products. However, it also shows the different levels of services, the diversity of services and how these policies can be adapted to the needs of the individual seller based on business structure, risk aversion and affordability. It goes without saying that every request for insurance is evaluated according to the risk involved, which means that certain buyers and/or countries may not be insurable. Or, if they are, it could be at a low per centage indemnity and/or a prohibitive premium.

STANDARD EXPORT CREDIT INSURANCE

Most market sector insurers have designed a range of export credit policies suitable for small and medium-sized businesses, with cover against non-payment of debts owing to commercial and/or political risks. These policies are highly standardized in order to be cost-effective, often combining both domestic and export sales, with a risk assessment on the individual buyer and an indemnity level of up to 90 per cent.

They are generally structured and priced in order to induce the company to include most of its receivables, often combined with additional services for more effective credit control, and with collection and litigation support as additional and mostly optional services.

In order to facilitate the practical day-to-day handling of the credit limit process, the larger insurers may also offer their customers internet access to their internal underwriting systems, thereby enabling the seller to manage their credit limits online in the most efficient way, including:

- Applying for credit limits on new or existing customers;
- Monitoring current portfolios under existing limits;
- Making amendments to, or cancelling, existing buyer limits.

An additional advantage of standardized insurance – particularly important to small, growing businesses – is access to increased levels of export finance and the added security this cover will give the lender.

TAILOR-MADE CREDIT RISK INSURANCE

Many insurers offer more sophisticated integrated insurance packages, tailor-made for larger companies with greater volumes of receivables. They can also include global risk cover for the group's requirements and risk limitations on the turnover covered by the policy. Even insurance packages for smaller businesses are often more or less tailor-made, even though mostly not as complicated and of a more standardized character.

POLITICAL RISK INSURANCE

Apart from the political risk that is directly associated with the commercial risk in an individual transaction, many market credit risk insurers also cover pure political risks associated with trading or investments in countries where such cover may be needed.

Contract Repudiation Indemnity or Contract Frustration Policy

There are different names for this kind of cover. It is an insurance that can be combined with the commercial risk on a company in many developing countries, but covering risks of a political nature due to changed or revoked approvals, licences guarantees or other circumstances directly or indirectly caused by the government or any other public body. The cover can also include protection for similar events when interference from such institutions makes it impossible for the seller to fulfil their contractual obligations towards the buyer.

Bond/Guarantee Indemnity Insurance

This insurance provides cover against so-called 'unfair calling' of bonds or guarantees issued on behalf of the seller, related to the export sale. This includes both genuinely unfair callings, but also 'fair callings', caused by a public body or political interference, which makes it impossible for the seller to perform their obligations under the commercial contract and which might therefore trigger the calling under the guarantee.

Investment Insurance

This insurance covers events such as confiscation, expro-priation, nationalization or deprivation of the investor's fixed or mobile assets overseas. The cover can also be extended to include war, civil war, strikes, riots, terrorism, regulatory changes, currency inconvertibility, business interruption and the inability to recover leased equipment.

EXPORT CREDIT AGENCIES

Most industrialized and emerging market countries have established export credit agencies with roughly the same objective: to support exports from their own countries. There is, however, no such thing as a typical ECA. Some are private companies, which provide both domestic and export credit support; however, these companies tend to concentrate on credits of less than two years. In addition there are the official export credit institutions, which deliver guarantees and insurance on behalf of the national governments in a variety of ways. Some are government departments or agencies, while others are private insurance companies which, apart from doing insurance business on their own account, also act as an agency on behalf of the respective government, typically for credits over two years.

Most ECAs are part of the 'Berne Union', the leading international organization in the field of export credit and investment insurance, with members from both the public and the private sectors. Even if the obligations are guaranteed by the respective state, official ECAs should operate with reasonable confidence of breaking even in the long term, charging customers premiums at levels that are sufficient to cover the perceived market and buyer risks and administration costs. In addition to these costs, some also include a 'reserve margin' in the premium rate to accommodate potential individual large losses or general country/regional payment moratoriums. They also make every effort to recover amounts paid in claims – either directly from individual buyers or borrowers or through the Paris Club of Official Creditors.

The OECD has regulated the ways in which the official ECAs operate, in order to restrict the potential for governments to use their ECAs to win export contracts by offering to their own exporters terms and conditions that are too favourable. In order to stop this 'race to the bottom', the major exporting nations have negotiated the OECD Arrangement on Officially Supported Export Credits, also known as the 'Consensus' or the 'Arrangement'. The Consensus covers export credit support on periods of two years or more and includes the length of credit for different types of goods; repayment structures, minimum advance payments and maximum credit limits; minimum government-supported interest rate levels; and premium rates for sovereign/country risk. It is worth noting that the EU does not allow member states to issue state-supported insurance/guarantees for commercial risks to most OECD countries on periods of less than two years, an area that should normally be covered by the private insurance market.

However, for other countries there is no such restriction, and in these cases, many agencies issue insurance/guarantees for shorter periods. The agencies also work together in purely commercial matters, primarily in transactions involving suppliers from several different countries. In order to facilitate such transactions, one of them will normally take overall responsibility and cover the entire package with reinsurance from the other agencies covering their suppliers. These 'one-stop shop' programmes have several advantages for the project and for the lead supplier, who needs to have contact with only one agency.

COMPETITION AND MATCHING

The primary objective of an ECA is to supplement the private insurance market by assuming credit risks which this sector is unable or unwilling to accept at competitive terms. There are, however, two areas of business where OECD has tried to eliminate excessive competition between the countries in order to safeguard an equal playing field for government export support: commercial matching and tied aid matching. Commercial matching is related to decisions taken by individual agencies giving special advantages to their domestic exporters. Since the establishment of the Consensus between the major OECD countries in the 1970s, a system of transparency has been introduced together with strict notification and consultation rules.

Any deviation from agreed practices automatically leads to a matching procedure, where other agencies are free to give the same terms to their exporters competing for the same business. Tied aid is government-to-government concessional financing of public sector projects, primarily to the poorest developing countries. The financing is often provided as a jointly arranged financial package by the government aid agency, together with support from the official export credit agency, covering the risk on the commercial part of such a loan. The terms for this type of finance can be far better than any other terms available, often with maturity up to 20 years and with extremely low interest rates. In order to limit the use of tied aid for projects that should be commercially viable, and to separate them from real revenue-generating commercial projects, the major OECD countries also have agreed certain standards for this type of financing. One is that such financing should contain at least a 35–50 per cent pure aid element, depending on the economic status of the country. Government aid can also be formally 'untied' but combined with conditions which directly or indirectly favour exporters from a particular country.

SOME GENERAL PRINCIPLES

The agencies always apply some general rules or restrictions to their guarantees and insurances, but often with different terms and interpretations depending on the countries involved, covering:

- Foreign content or components;
- Used or refurbished equipment;
- Local costs;
- Environmental and human rights aspects;
- Illegal practices and anti-corruption guidelines.

A few agencies, such as the US Exim Bank, may also sometimes apply additional restrictions, for example shipping requirements with vessels from their own country for larger transactions, or economic or national impact assessments for strategic equipment, but such aspects will not be dealt with in this book. Individual agencies have somewhat different rules regarding cover for foreign content or components of the delivery. Some support relatively low levels of foreign content while others may support higher levels on a case-by-case basis, depending on size, structure, buyer country and other supplier countries involved. Used or refurbished equipment may also be eligible for support, but in most cases this depends on factors such as contract value, the origin of manufacture, foreign content, domestic costs for refurbishment and the remaining useful life of the equipment.

Local costs for goods and services that are related to the transaction, but are incurred in the buyer's country, may also be eligible for support up to a certain per cent-age of the contract value. Such costs are primarily associated with projects or larger transactions, including installation or construction, and should relate to the exporter's obligations as verified in the sales contract or in a separate exporter's certificate, but originating in the buyer's country. In most cases up to 15 per cent of the value of the exports can be covered for locally originated and/or manufactured goods and services.

However, restrictions may apply as to the size and nature of the transaction or the project. The OECD has also issued strict guidelines for a much broader perspective of government-supported international trade, for example its effects on the environment, sustainable development and human rights in the buying country. The larger the transaction and the more it is related to the infrastructure of these countries, the more important these considerations become. Illegal practices are also receiving more attention.

DIFFERENT FORMS OF INSURANCE/GUARANTEES

The insurance issued by the official ECAs have to comply with the rules laid down by the OECD and other directives. However, within that framework they are free to structure their programmes in order to meet the specific demand from their domestic business community. There are some basic programmes that are very much the same but differ with regard to name, terms and conditions, premiums and simplified procedures; or are specifically targeted towards smaller companies, which is a special target group for most agencies. The description below illustrates the diversity of cover available in different countries, but most agencies issue only some of these policies, even if under different names.

A. Export Credit Insurance/Guarantees	
Exporter Policies	
Single-buyer export insurance policy	Credit protection for general short-term credit sales, made by an exporter to a single foreign buyer
Multi-buyer export insurance policy	Same as above, this policy allows the exporter to insure all sales to eligible foreign buyers

Lender Policies

Working capital loan guarantee	This policy offers pre-export working capital loan guarantees to commercial banks, providing liquidity to the exporter to support new export transactions or related contract guarantees.
Buyer credit insurance policy	Protects lenders financing the export of goods and services directly to foreign buyers, both on short but more often on a medium-term basis.
Supplier credit insurance policy	Protects lenders that finance or purchase export-related receivables from the exporter on a non-recourse basis.
Bank letter of credit policy	This policy protects banks against losses on irrevocable L/Cs, when they are not prepared to confirm the L/C without such cover, owing to the uncertainty of the creditworthiness of the issuing bank.
B. Other Forms of Insurance/Guarantee	
Bond insurance policy	Protects the exporter against the risk of 'unfair calling' under a contract guarantee issued in favour of the buyer
Project and structured finance guarantee	A wide range of guarantee solutions may be offered for project suppliers and their international customers, covering limited recourse lending and structured financing
Leasing insurance policy	Cover may also be given to the leasing industry in the form of either an operating lease policy and/or a financing lease policy
Foreign currency insurance policy	Cover is also often available for transaction in foreign currency under most of the policies described in this chapter; however, this is usually restricted to a fixed per centage or a maximum exchange rate. Cover may also be available during the bid/ tender period
Overseas investment insurance	Covers the exporter or the financial institution against the political risks on long-term foreign investments

APPLICATION PROCEDURES

Every agency has established standard procedures for dealing with requests or proposals for cover, following the normal business cycle of its customers. The first stage is often in the form of a preliminary response, in oral or written form, when the seller is in the early internal process of preparing the offer. This response is without commitment, outlining only basic details for cover together with indicative terms and conditions. The second stage is usually a conditional offer, issued upon request by the seller when preparing an offer or a tender for contract. This offer, often fixed for a period of 90–180 days specifying the cover and the premium, but is subject to certain terms and conditions, and to the business details supplied by the seller.

The third and final stage comes when the contract is secured when an unconditional offer is issued, which specifies the final details and terms and conditions, with a validity for a period of 90–180 days to allow time for documentation and fulfilment of all outstanding conditions in the contract, upon which the policy will be issued. With this in mind, it is important for the seller to ensure that any signed contract is conditional upon the final issue of the insurance or guarantee, but also that any material changes thereafter in the commercial contract should have prior approval from the agency.

INVESTMENT INSURANCE

This form of insurance covers events such as confiscation, expropriation, nationaliza-tion or deprivation of the investor's fixed or mobile overseas assets. The cover can be extended to include war, civil war, strikes, riots, terrorism, regulatory changes, currency inconvertibility, business interruption, and the inability to recover leased equipment. This cover can be obtained from both the private insurance market sector and from many export credit agencies. The insurance programmes may differ in detail between the countries but are generally based on the same principle to cover the investor against the political risks in connection with their overseas investments. However, the cover can extend to breach of contract, where the host government or a local authority causes the underlying reasons, also often including the indirect consequences in case such events damage or prevent normal business operations related to the investment.

The schemes mainly provide cover for:

- Overseas direct investments as shareholder equity, loans or guarantees;
- Bank loans to an overseas company, when used for investment or purchase of goods from that country.

These insurance programmes have, over time, become very important for many investors which often are export companies creating production, storage or sales facilities abroad to strengthen their business opportunities in the region. The programmes generally cover long-term investments, some as low as USD 10–20,000, with cover for up to 10 or 15 years. During this period of time the investor can apply for annual renewals, sometimes at unchanged terms and conditions, including premiums, even if the situation in the country deteriorates. At the same time, the investor must normally take the long-term view on the investment in order to benefit from the cover, with an intended investment period of at least 3–5 years, or in the case of loans, with the same duration.

8

Globalization for Development: International Trade and Export Perspective

SYSTEMIC EVOLUTION OF THE INTERNATIONAL TRADING SYSTEM

The international trading system today incorporates a much broader range of economic issues, rules, disciplines, and commitments than did the pre-1994 regime of the General Agreement on Tariffs and Trade . Due to the expanded scope of World Trade Organization agreements, topics such as services and trade-related aspects of intellectual property rights – whose international dimensions were previously handled through sector- or subject-specific agreements and arrangements – have now been brought within the scope of multilateral trade policy.

As a result, not only goods but also the cross-border movements of services, and the protection of intellectual property are now included in the overall agenda of national, regional and international trade policy. Moreover, what were once considered non-trade issues are now being linked to market access conditions, particularly as part of the formation of a plethora of regional trade agreements and preferential trade agreements.

Governments, enterprises and civil society are thus called upon to be more comprehensively and cooperatively involved in trade policy formulation and implementation as part of holistic development strategies and policies. The development processes in developing countries are being comprehensively affected by the rules of the trading system, in addition to the trade policies of their major partners.

Developing countries need to strategically manage and balance many more variables in the trade and development policy matrix than ever before. Added to this is the challenge of calibrating and using national policy space *vis-à-vis* the growing panoply of international commitments and disciplines.

THE EVOLVING MULTILATERAL TRADING SYSTEM

Since 1995, the international trading system has undergone a number of major changes. In the pre-Uruguay Round environment, the multilateral trading system was focused mainly on border measures in trade in goods. It recognized the structural and economic challenges faced by developing countries, and provided them with some special and differential treatment. This took the form principally of non-reciprocity in trade concessions, such as preferential market access, the most important of which were the generalized system of preferences negotiated in UNCTAD and the Lomé Convention granted by the EU to African, Caribbean, and Pacific countries.It also comprised the dispensation from trade rules constraining domestic policy action.

In essence, these related to the flexibility to use import controls to protect infant industries and to deal with balance of payment problems, since contracting parties to the GATT were not obliged to become signatories to all or any of the issue-specific agreements or disciples on trade-related domestic policies. These included the plurilateral approach adopted in the Tokyo Round codes which allowed many developing countries to opt out from trade disciplines.

The pre-Uruguay Round GATT multilateral trade system was also accompanied by a series of international commodity agreements for coffee, sugar, rubber and tin, concluded under the aegis of the UN through UNCTAD, as well as for dairy and bovine meat, concluded within the GATT. Essentially, these agreements were multilateral undertakings on prices and supplies between the main exporting and importing countries. The post-Uruguay Round trading environment differs in several ways. The vast majority of developing countries, as well as countries with economies in transition, have now joined the World Trade Organization .

Established in 1995 as a result of the Uruguay Round of multilateral trade negotiations under the GATT, the WTO has brought about a profound transformation in the world trading system. As compared to the GATT 1947, the scope of the trading system was extended to agriculture, textiles and clothing, services, trade-related investment measures, and trade-related aspects of intellectual property rights. As tariffs were lowered and as trade disciplines were extended to development policies and measures previously falling exclusively within the domestic jurisdiction, the national policy space for developing countries contracted. On the other hand, the rule of law represented by the strengthened rules in the WTO worked to their advantage in several areas.

In particular, the strengthened, quasi judicial and automatic dispute settlement system that underpins the compliance of WTO members to negotiated disciplines and commitments, has provided effective trade justice avenues to them. Some developing countries are making effective use of the dispute settlement mechanism all though fuller utilization and benefit is constrained by factors like the lack of capacity of developing countries to ensure the enforcement of decisions.

THE MULTILATERAL TRADING SYSTEM AND THE WTO

Global trade relations and the bulk of world trade are now governed largely by the WTO agreements forming the multilateral trading system . Since the WTO agreements were based on the principle of a single undertaking, all members of the WTO are obliged to be party to all the agreements which cover a wider set of border as well as domestic policy issues than the GATT. These have reduced the extent of domestic policy space previously available to developing countries. Although developing countries still receive some form of special and differential treatment , these are mostly on the basis of temporary exemptions from some provisions of the new agreements and longer implementation periods.

As a result of a stricter application of the reciprocity principle, developing countries are now generally expected to have national trade regimes as open as those of developed countries. Thus, the new underlying logic in the trading system's approach to trade and development is equality in trade opportunities for developed and developing countries alike , rather than providing more meaningful responses to the specific structural problems of developing countries. LDCs have been granted a substantively greater degree of special and differential treatment under WTO agreements. However, unilateral trade liberalization and domestic market deregulation have left many of them with some of the most open national trade regimes.

There is no doubt that the freer trade enabled by the GATT/WTO system in the last six decades has contributed to expanding world trade, made for a buoyant global economy, as well as advanced trade-driven globalization. The extensive scope of WTO agreements in particular has had implications for the ability of developing countries to pursue proactive development strategies as well as to explore and experiment with various policy options. The broad coverage, scope, and depth of WTO agreements have increased the impact of the trading system disciplines to various governmental policies as well as measures taken for development purposes. WTO Agreements in areas such as agricultural and industrial subsidies, services, trade-related investment measures, and trade-related aspects of intellectual property rights have had a major impact on development efforts.

Some industrial policy tools – which were used extensively and successfully by developed countries in their industrialization and catch-up processes – were foreclosed indefinitely as viable policy options for developing countries. This has highlighted the need and importance of adequate and balanced policy space and flexibility in remaining trade policy measures. In this regard, SDT provisions and the less-than-full reciprocity principle constitute enabling tools for the progressive and sustained, integration of developing countries into the world economy.

CONTINUING CHALLENGES OF WTO ACCESSION

The universality of WTO membership is essential for the legitimacy of the trading system. The process of WTO accession continues to represent important challenges for 29 developing countries and countries with economies in transition in the accession process. Experience has shown that acceding developing countries continue to be subjected to requests for relatively deep liberalization and stringent reform commitments.

These include WTO-plus commitments which could go beyond the level of concessions and commitments undertaken by existing WTO Members of a similar level of development; or WTO-minus rights whereby concessions enjoyed by WTO members are not granted to the acceding country. For example, access to SDT provisions is not automatic – it is often subjected to negotiations on a case-by-case basis. It is crucial to ensure fair and equitable terms of accession to developing countries.

These terms should be commensurate with the trade, financial, and development needs of each acceding country. They should also be given increased support in all stages of the accession negotiations. Moreover, the specific needs of newly acceded countries should also be addressed in the Doha negotiations, given the extensive and deep commitment undertaken during the accession process.

If the terms and conditions are in keeping with each country's stage of development during accession to the WTO, economic policy and institutional reform will be stimulated and trading capacity enhanced. It has also being observed that WTO accession is a catalyst for developing countries to get their trade and economic reforms as well as institution building act together in a relatively short time.

TRADE PREFERENCES

Trade preferences constitute a key SDT pillar of the international trading system. Several initiatives by developed countries – and to a lesser extent by developing countries – have been developed to provide the latter improved market access for their exports and have brought important benefits. Such preferences for LDCs are a commitment of the international community, reiterated in MDG 8.

As a result many developing countries, especially LDCs are dependent on preferential access including duty free, quota free access into major developed country markets. Such access enables them to secure more FDI for productive capacity-building and makes their exports more competitive than otherwise. Preference have served as a stimulus to trade and development in many beneficiary countries and for sectors affected. They continue to provide important competitive advantages to many small and vulnerable economies and represent for a number of them a most significant trade policy instrument for development. However with continuous unilateral, regional and multilateral liberalisation and lowering of tariffs, preference margins are being continuously eroded rendering trade preferences an international trade and development solidarity measure with diminishing returns.

The challenge for preference dependent developing countries and the international community is to cushion the adjustment shocks of preference erosion and to fashion SDT and solidarity measures going beyond tariff preferences. Thus it would be useful to look at easing market entry of these countries through help in the standards and conformity related infrastructure for example, including through aid for trade. Also, existing preference need to be improved especially as regards their product coverage and predictability as well as realistic rules of origin requirements and simplified administration procedures.

The EU's 'Everything but Arms' initiative for LDCs, and the United States' African Growth and Opportunities Act provides increased trading opportunities for some of the poorest developing countries. Other developing countries benefit from non-reciprocal trade preferences. However, such trading regimes are time-bound and will expire.

The Cotonou Partnership Agreement's trade component expired in December 2007. New WTO-compatible trading arrangements have been negotiated in the form of interim economic partnership agreements that are being implemented for some ACP States from 1 January 2008. Other developed countries – such as Japan, Australia, Canada, Norway and the United States – have instituted a generalized system of preferences for developing countries and LDCs which have been enhanced. The two major importers – the EU and the United States – recently revised their GSP programmes. The EU's GSP scheme was revised in January 2006, and is valid until December 2008. While the revised scheme is simpler and has wider product coverage than the previous one, it also includes some stringent rules for the 'GSP Plus' benefits which some vulnerable countries are entitled to.

At present, 15 countries are beneficiaries of the 'GSP Plus' benefits. Also, the graduation criteria are tighter in the current scheme as compared to the previous one. Except in the case of textiles and clothing, which are reviewed annually, graduation will be assessed at the end of 2008. Under the revised scheme, 80 per cent of Chinese exports will be graduated. In December 2006, the United States' GSP programme was extended for a further two years, until 31 December 2008. The criteria set for GSP graduation was tightened in the current GSP programme by adding a new statute. Previously, GSP products became subject to graduation if their exports exceed the competitive need limit , but such products could have a CNL waiver under certain conditions. In the current GSP scheme, the President can revoke any existing CNL waiver that has been in effect for at least five years if it meets certain conditions. Under the new criteria, some products from Brazil, Cote d'Ivoire, India, Philippines, Thailand and Venezuela have been graduated. The coverage rates and the utilization rates of trade preferences.Between 1995 and 2005, developing countries' utilization rates of the GSP scheme have improved. Thus imports from developing countries into developed countries under GSP schemes increased. However, the coverage rates deteriorated. Thus the universe of goods from developing countries that can benefit from preferences has declined. For LDCs conversely, the coverage rates made notable improvement, while the utilization rates showed mixed results. The coverage rates for developingcountry beneficiaries decreased from 73 to 44 per cent for the EU, 43 to 26 per cent for Japan, and 39 to 16 per cent for the United States.

The declines are due to the increase in dutiable imports along with the rise in total imports from developing countries, while imports covered by the GSP schemes declined. For Canada, the coverage rate in 2005 increased by 7 per cent as imports covered by its GSP increased along with the rise in the dutiable imports from developing countries. In contrast, the coverage rates for LDC products have made substantial improvement. The rates increased from 15 to 79 per cent for Canada, from 95 to 97 per cent for the EU, and from 6 to 68 per cent for the United States. For Japan, the rates decreased from 27 to 6 per cent. The preference utilization rates for developing-country beneficiaries increased from 41 to 59 per cent for Japan and from 62 to 77 per cent for the United States, while they decreased from 63 to 56 per cent for Canada.

For the EU, although the figures indicate substantial increase, it should be noted that the 2005 figure includes the imports which received preferences under the ACP scheme and the Euro-Mediterranean Free Trade Area. Disaggregated data is not available, and it is not possible to assess the utilization of the EU GSP scheme for 2005. For LDCs, the utilization rates increased from 64 to 96 per cent for Canada, while they declined from 95 to 93 per cent for Japan, and 56 to 51 per cent for the United States. For the EU, the rates increased from 26 to 68 per cent, but the 2005 figure includes the imports received under the ACP preference, and the LDC utilization rate cannot be assessed. The experiences with trade preferences granted to exports indicates that these are meaningful only when they are utilized by the beneficiary countries.

The utilization rate is affected adversely by restrictive rules of origin and other non-tariff barriers, which prevent these preferences from being fully exploited. Hence, the deficiencies in preferential regimes and market entry barriers need to be addressed and removed in order to ensure genuine market access opportunities. In addition, supply capacity constraints severely limit the capacity of many developing countries to exploit duty-free and other preferential opportunities. Thus, the development of competitive production capacities is a key aspect in enabling developing countries to take fuller advantage of market access opportunities.

GROWING IMPORTANCE OF NON-TARIFF BARRIERS AND STANDARDS

A notable trend in the international trading system is that, with the decline in tariffs as a result of eight rounds of multilateral trade negotiations, the relative importance of non-tariff barriers has risen, both as instruments of protection and for regulating trade.

For instance, during 1994-2004, besides traditionally applied NTBs such as anti-dumping and countervailing measures, governmentmandated technical measures increased seven times worldwide. The nature of the most applied NTBs has also changed. In many developed countries, regulatory policy now focuses on the protection of the environment, public health and safety, and often includes higher standards for the domestic market than existing international standards. While these regulations do not contravene WTO rules, they entail greater compliance costs than would otherwise be the case, especially for those developing countries that are mainly standard-takers and not standard-makers.

The challenge to them can be gauged by the fact that, even for developed countries, standards have become a major concern in each others' markets. This is all too evident in the market access barrier reports brought out by the USA, EU and Japan, and in the context of transatlantic regulatory harmonization being considered between the USA and EU. The increased use of requirements concerning the technical specification of products places additional costs and burdens on companies in developing countries in accessing markets. The products of export interest to developing countries most often affected by NTBs include food and beverages, fisheries products, electrical equipment and electronics, pharmaceuticals and chemicals, as well as textiles among others. In general, costs arise from the translation of foreign regulations, the hiring of technical experts to explain foreign regulations, and the adjustment of production facilities to comply with the new stringent, frequently changing requirements and shifting goal posts.

Overall it is estimated that presently due to measures relating to Sanitary and Phytosanitary Measures, and Technical Barriers to Trade , potential export earnings of developing countries are being decreased by at least 10 per cent. Additional costs are also incurred when legal and regulatory frameworks need to be improved to support both the participation of national firms in international markets and enhance their competitive-ness. Accordingly, classifying, quantifying and assessing the development impact of NTBs will be very important in assuring that market access granted to developing countries is not obviated by these newer non-tariff protectionist measures. Meeting international standards for quality, safety, health, environment and consumer interests is increasingly becoming a precondition for competing in international markets. The modernization of standards systems in developing countries, including institutions and infrastructure for certification, is essential for operating in the current global trade environment. Lack of such trade related infrastructure has also become a major factor constraining many exporters, particularly in the LDCs, from benefiting fully from preferential access initiatives.

Thus assistance involving the provision of hardware like testing equipment, financial support for institution building, and technical assistance for raising capacity to comply with regulations and standards should be strengthened. Moreover, the participation of developing countries in international standard setting activities should be facilitated. The promotion of mutual recognition agreements between developed and developing countries, as well as among developing countries, will also help in reconciling frictions and disputes caused by different regulations between trading partners, and lead to large cost savings for exporting firms worldwide. Greater reliance on internationally evolved standards in which developing countries have participated rather than on unilaterally determined measures and standards is called for. This would ensure greater systemic transparency and equity as well as discipline the abuse of standards that are prepared, adopted or applied with a view to or with the effect of creating unnecessary obstacles to international trade.

MAINSTREAMING DEVELOPMENT INTO THE MULTILATERAL TRADING SYSTEM

Against this background, the Doha Round of multilateral trade negotiations offers a unique opportunity to mainstream development into the MTS. The completion of the Round is also imperative in realizing Goal 8 of the Millennium Development Goals of 'an open, equitable, rule-based, predictable and non-discriminatory' multilateral trading system. The system stands at a crossroads.

Following the Sixth WTO Ministerial Conference held in Hong Kong, China in December 2005, the Doha Round has entered its most crucial phase. There is urgent need to find solutions on key issues: agricultural market access, domestic support in agriculture, and industrial tariffs as well as services. Agriculture remains central to the negotiations. A genuine structural adjustment in agricultural policy is important to enable an ambitious, balanced and development-focused outcome. It remains imperative that a substantial development content that reflects the needs and interests of developing countries – including real commercial opportunities for them – be firmly included on a contractual basis in the final outcome of the Doha Round. The timeline for concluding the Doha Round has been overtaken several times. There is risk that the Round will continue indefinitely. In the event that the

Round is successfully concluded, any negotiated outcome will be implemented over the period leading to 2015 and will define trading conditions for the coming decades. Thus, it is the shared responsibility of all members to support and contribute to upholding the credibility of the MTS at this juncture, and to ensure that the Round leads to development-friendly results.

PROLIFERATION OF REGIONAL TRADE AGREEMENTS

At the same time, RTAs have proliferated worldwide to become a defining feature of today's international trade landscape. The WTO web site on RTAsnotes that "some 380 RTAs have been notified to the GATT/WTO up to July 2007. Of these, 300 RTAs were notified under Article XXIV of the GATT 1947 or GATT 1994; 22 under the Enabling Clause; and 58 under Article V of the GATS. At that same date, 205 agreements were in force. If we take into account RTAs which are in force but have not been notified, those signed but not yet in force, those currently being negotiated, and those in the proposal stage, we arrive at a figure of close to 400 RTAs which are scheduled to be implemented by 2010. Of these RTAs, free trade agreements and partial scope agreements account for over 90 per cent, while customs unions account for less than 10 per cent."

Currently, the trade between RTA partners accounts for almost 50 per cent of global merchandise trade. This trend towards RTAs will continue on a North-North, North-South and South-South basis, thereby affecting the trading patterns and prospects of developing countries. The vast majority of RTAs are South-South agreements. These constitute important instruments for trade creation, investment, and regional development. South-South RTAs and cooperation face the daunting challenges of deepening and expanding integration measures as well as the rationalization of their membership so that they could serve as effective development instruments.

Challenges arise for developing countries to design policies and approaches that would maximize gains from both multilateral and regional integration processes. It is important that both processes are mutually supportive and complementary in terms of their scope, pace and sequencing of policies and measures committed to. North-North and North-South RTAs represent a particularly significant systemic challenge to the MTS. They could divert attention and commitment away from multilateral trade negotiations, and have a stronger negative impact on the MFN principle enshrined in the MTS.

They also pose important adjustment challenges for developing countries as these agreements tend to impose deep trade liberalization between major trading nations and weaker trading nations. Doha negotiations on WTO rules on RTAs aim to clarify and improve existing rules to effectively discipline the proliferation RTAs, as well as take a better account of the developmental aspects of RTAs. A Transparency Mechanism on RTAs was adopted by WTO members on 14 December 2006 as an interim measures will help to enhance transparency as well as compatibility of RTAs with the WTO as well as assess their systemic effects.

TRADE ADJUSTMENT ISSUES

Multilateral and regional trade negotiations and the resultant trade agreements engender changes in policies, legislations and strategies to comply with, adapt to and take advantage of the new trading dispensation. Such trade liberalization is expected to generate trade and welfare gains in the long run, at least in the absence of externalities. However, there are often short- to medium-term adjustment implications of trade reforms. This is because, as economies open up, imports use existing channels while new exports often come from different sectors that have to gear up production and find new markets. As this transition takes place, the structural unemployment that occurs is, perhaps, the major social cost of adjusting to trade reforms.

Countries as advanced as the United States recognize that, unlike job losses that are the consequence of technological change or competition, any form of trade liberalization that affects domestic industries and employment is a policy choice. Thus, the State has an obligation to ensure that the costs are not borne by the most vulnerable workers alone. This can be witnessed for example from the proposed United States' Trade and Globalization Adjustment Assistance Act of 2007 to assist workers, communities, firms, and farmers affected by trade liberalization with any country. Developing countries need adjustment assistance that goes beyond implementation support to see them through the liberalization process at least as much as – and most certainly more than – developed countries. A key role can be played here by both the donor community and international financial institutions to provide adjustment support, including through the aid for trade initiative. This is particularly so where the affected countries are already heavily in debt.

TRADE AND GENDER

Empirical evidence on trade, trade liberalization and gender is scant. The available limited research establishes that trade has gender-related effects. This is not surprising given that women, like men, participate in various levels of production and trade whether locally or internationally. More interestingly, available empirical evidence suggests a direct link between exports and female employment, especially in the manufacturing sector with dynamic growth potential and a large concentration of women. For example, increased exports were associated with increased female employment in such countries as Mauritius, Tunisia, Sri Lanka, Bangladesh, Malaysia, and the East Asian 'Tigers. In labour-rich developing countries, the expansion of exports are related to a substantial increase in female employment and an increase in women's share in employment.

Moreover, researchers found that industrialization in the newly industrialized economies of Taiwan Province of China, Hong Kong China, South Korea, and Singapore is as much female-led as it is export-led. Conversely, in countries with low level of trade integration and dominance of commodities, the impact of trade on women in the labour market appears less positive. This is witnessed for example in several countries in sub-Saharan Africa.The level of women participation and remuneration with trade liberalization and growth however cannot be easily verified with empirical evidence. This association between trade and women empowerment can be positive but it cannot be assumed to be either automatic or generalized. Establishing the details of this association requires in-depth analysis and research on the impact of trade and globalization on gender in generally and in specific countries.

Studying the linkages between trade performance and gender empowerment is important. It will help to enhance awareness of the extent of association between trade and women. This can also help identify policies and actions that can be designed and implemented to strengthen women participation in trade and in turn acts as a further stimulus to trade growth. This can provide useful ideas about best practices at the national level and development cooperation at the international level to strengthen the participation of women in trade and promote pro-poor growth and development. Women empowerment in trade can be a powerful engine of dynamic trade expansion for the whole economy.

FOSTERING AN ENABLING ENVIRONMENT: A FAIRER AND MORE OPEN TRADING SYSTEM

The underlying logic in the trading system's approach to trade liberalization and development is the equality of trade opportunities for developed and developing countries alike. However, because of the existing and often widening inequality in capacities, this makes for an unequal approach to development.

There is need for coherence in policy to ensure stability, predictability, security, and fairness in the rules governing trade with a view to achieving a more open, equitable and development oriented trading system. Attendant support mechanisms should be provided for effective flexibilities which respond to the specific structural problems of developing countries and accompanying market access opportunities.

The Doha Round provides an opportunity to correct some of the imbalances in the multilateral trading system. It is also an opportunity to install a development dimension into the MTS system of rights and obligations to ensure that trade liberalization is pursued not as an end in itself but as a means to development and poverty reduction as well as the attainment of internationally agreed development goals.

All countries and all stakeholders have a shared interest in the success of the Doha Round and the realization of its core development agenda. This was in fact mandated by the Doha Declaration, when it stressed the imperative for the Round to ensure that the needs and interests of developing countries are placed at the heart of the Round and its final outcome. This has been further emphasized by the UN Millennium Summit and the 2005 World Summit.

Six key elements of a development package must be delivered to ensure greater coherence in, and the credibility of the MTS. First, the Doha Round must result in significantly enhanced and additional real market access and entry for the exports of manufactures, commodities, and services of developing countries in the major markets of developed countries to enable the growth and prosperity of the former. This implies tariff elimination, the removal of tariff escalation and peaks, providing access in the services sectors offered by developing countries , and addressing NTBs. The provision of duty-free and quota-free treatment to all LDCs for their products on a lasting basis is a prerequisite. In this respect of strengthening gains from trade flowing to LDCs, UNCTAD had proposed a Trade Marshall Plan for LDCs.

Its critical aspects, which are interrelated and constitute a comprehensive package of measures, relate to: secure, predictable and stable market access for LDCs through binding duty-free, quota-free treatment in the WTO on all their products; accompanying actions to discipline non-tariff barriers and market entry barriers facing LDCs, especially in the area of SPS/TBT measures, and help them build effective standards-related capacity and infrastructure to comply with such requirements; a targeted package in services to operationalize LDC priority areas in supply-side capacity building and technology transfer, as well as commercially meaningful expansion of market access in the temporary movement of persons supply services at all skill levels and in sectors of key interest to LDCs; and an aid for trade fund to building LDCs' export supply capacity.

Paying priority attention to LDCs in services liberalization, including in terms of services sectors and modes of interests to them and greater flexibility in liberalization commitment is important. Further, WTO Members should ensure the implementation of the modalities for the special treatment for in services that was adopted in September 2003. Meaningful liberalization is expected to generate substantial welfare gains. One estimates points out that global welfare would increase by over US$260 billion annually as a result of eliminating all trade barriers. About US$50 billion of this would come from agricultural liberalization, and a further US$80 billion from liberalization of manufactures. The rest of about US$130 billion would arise from liberalizing services trade.

Developing countries would capture some of these gains. Second, the Doha Round should improve the rules that address and remove existing asymmetries as well as enhance the fairness and equity of the MTS. Reducing and removing trade distorting agricultural subsidies substantially is indispensable for levelling the playing field for fair competition in agricultural trade. An appropriate pacing and sequencing of market opening as well as institutional and regulatory reform are also important, particularly in the services sector. These should be accompanied by flanking policies as well as support for building domestic supply capacity. Also important is infusing a development-orientation into both existing and new WTO disciplines in order to provide the flexibility and predictability that developing countries need in order to promote trade and development. For instance, the flexibilities recognized under the TRIPS Agreement for access to essential medicines can be operationalized and implemented.

Given the importance of access to technology for develop-ment and poverty reduction, the objectives and principles of the TRIPS Agreement regarding the transfer and dissemination of technology can also be operationalized in a manner conducive to social and economic welfare. Likewise, in negotiations regarding rules on fisheries subsidies, there is need to integrate the concerns of small and vulnerable coastal States for appropriate SDT in any disciplines, particularly in respect of access fees and development assistance, fiscal incentives to domestication, fisheries development, and artisan fisheries. Third, the development dimension signifies an adequate and sufficient degree of policy autonomy for economic governance that would allow countries to effectively manage and regulate their domestic economic policy in the light of national development and public policy objectives, within the multilateral framework of rights and obligations under the WTO.

This translates into such measures as SDT and less than full reciprocity; the preservation of tariff revenue; the promotion of domestic nascent industries as well as pre-empting de industrialization; the preservation of long standing trade preferences; safeguarding food security, livelihood security, and rural development; providing for the use of policies and measures to foster commodity production, diversification and competitiveness; universal access to essential and infrastructure services; as well as access to essential drugs. Implementation-related issues, and the concerns of small and vulnerable economies and LDCs, also need to be addressed.

Policy flexibility should be available to developing countries that need it in specific areas so as to reduce the cost of implementation and adjustment, to ensure the sustainability of the adjustment process on the economic, social, environmental, and political fronts, and to deploy proactive measures with a view to building competitive supply capacity and productivity for exports. Some degree of flexibility has already been introduced in existing agreements and in the ongoing Doha negotiations. However, what is more important in the long run is mainstreaming the development dimension into the architecture of the WTO and making it fully operational. Fourth, development solidarity is required from the international community to developing countries for under-taking adjustments and meeting implementation costs, as well as building traderelated infrastructure and supply capacity in order to take full advantage of increased market access and new trading opportunities. With trade liberalization and reform, developing countries face important implementation and adjustment costs, along with the need to create and strengthen supporting institutional and infrastructural capacities.

Such solidarity would be in keeping with MDG Goal 8 on global partnership for development. In this context, the Aid for Trade initiative is an essential complement to trade liberalization in the trading system. It can play an important role – along with improved market access, balanced rules of trade liberalization, and sound domestic policies – in helping developing countries realize the potential gains from trade and mitigate its potential costs. Fifth, it is important to ensure coherence and a positive interface between RTAs and the MTS.

Given the rise of regionalism, a robust progress in and a development-oriented conclusion of the Doha Round is the best guarantee against the erosion of the MTS. Specifically, the WTO rules on RTAs – under negotiation in the Doha negotiations – need clarification and improvement so as to improve compliance and better take into account the developmental aspects of RTAs. Sixth, it is necessary to regularly monitor and assess protectionist threats to the goal of an open, equitable, rule-based, predictable and non-discriminatory multilateral trading system. Such assessment could help to highlight such tendencies and lead to measures and actions which can curtail protectionist threats against freer and fairer trading relations.

THE IMPACT OF INCREASED INTERNATIONAL TRADE DYNAMISM

THE GROWTH AND CURRENT DYNAMISM OF INTERNATIONAL TRADE

The last decade, as well as the prognosis for the future, is marked by the increased dynamism and impact of trade on development and the world economy. The sheer size, scale and growth of trade and its impact on development are the main features of globalization. World exports of goods and services doubled between 1995 and 2006 to reach over US$14 trillion in 2006. Since 1995, world merchandise trade has been growing at an annual average rate of 7.5 per cent. Since 2000, it has accelerated further to an average of 13 per cent.

In the period 2000-2006, developing countries average export growth was about 15.9 per cent, while that of developed countries and countries with economies in transition was 11 per cent and 21.3 per cent respectively. The evolution of trade in goods exports over the 1995-2006 period. World merchandise trade value has increased by 130 per cent while that of developing countries by 190 per cent. As a consequence, an upward trend in the participation of developing countries in total trade is observed. The share in world trade of developing countries which was 28.1 per cent in 1995 reached 35.5 per cent in 2006 The share of trade among developing countries has also increased significantly. In 2006, this share is almost equal to 16 per cent of world trade. It was about 11 per cent ten years ago.

A major contributing factor has been the spectacular growth in the share of international merchandise and services trade of several dynamic developing countries. This growth has resulted in new and enhanced opportunities for trade and development. Another related feature has been the dynamic rise in trade between the countries of the South. Their share in merchandise global exports jumped from around 20 per cent in 1970 to an all-time record of around 36 per cent in 2006.

DEVELOPING COUNTRIES IN INTERNATIONAL TRADE

The overall trade performance of developing countries is very telling. During 1995 to 2005, the share of developing countries in world trade saw a three-fold increase, reaching an impressive US$3.7 trillion. It accounted for 36 per cent of total merchandize exports – an all-time record. The trade to GDP ratio increased for almost all groups of countries, indicating a greater openness on the one hand, and trade dependence on the other . The importance of export earnings as a source for development finance also increased

Table. Trade to GDP Ratios.

Economy	1995	2000	2005
World	43.3	50.3	56.4
Developing economies	38.3	44.5	49.4
Developing economies	61.7	69.9	78.0
Least developed countries	46.7	53.1	63.8

Developing countries have also significantly increased their presence in developed economies since the mid 1980s. Led largely by the developing Asia, particularly China, exports from the South in 2005 accounted for 32 per cent of total imports by developed economies, as compared to 25 per cent in 1985. As regards exports from developed countries to the South, it remained at around 23 per cent during the same period, suggesting that the South is capturing a greater market both in the North and in the South. Among developed countries, Japan reveals the strongest trade linkage with the South.

More than 60 per cent of Japan's imports are from the South, and more than a half of its exports are destined to the South. The United States' imports from the South accounted for 52 per cent in 2005, having steadily increased from 35 per cent in 1985. As for the EEC- 15, the share of the South in its import slightly fell between 1985 and 1995, reflecting a reduction in imports from Africa. It then increased to 20 per cent in the period between 1995 and 2005, which is about the same level as that of 1985, owing primarily to a substantial increase in imports from China. The aggregate trade performance of developing countries has been impressive. However, it has been neither a continuous process nor uniformly spread across developing regions. The newly industrialized economies and China together account for almost the entire rise in the share of world exports of developing countries taken as a group. China's trade growth continued to outstrip other major traders. China's merchandise exports grew by 27 per cent. In the second half of 2006, its merchandise exports started to exceed those of the United States, but for the whole year US exports still exceeded those of China. The four regions with the highest share of fuels and other mining products in their merchandise exports recorded the strongest annual export growth in 2006. Except for a few industrializing economies in Asia and some dynamic developing countries, the exports of other developing countries still concentrate on a limited range of natural resource-based products and/or manufactured products with low value-addition.

These have made for small returns. These developing countries have also suffered from worsening terms-of -trade, highly volatile world prices, as well as actually experienced a decline in their share in world trade. For example, the export share of the 50 LDCs – the majority of which are in sub-Saharan African and are commodity dependent – fell from 2.5 per cent in 1960 to about 0.5 per cent in 1995, and have since hovered around this level, rising slightly to 0.8 per cent in 2006.

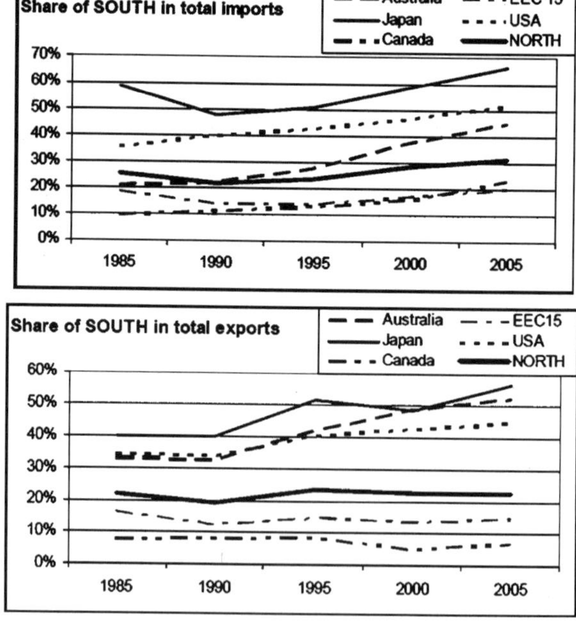

Fig. Chart of Developing Countries Trade with Developed Countries.

On the import side, the developed countries remain the major market. Nevertheless, the share of developing countries in world merchandise imports has also been increasing, rising to 32.1 per cent in 2006, up from 28.6 per cent in 1995. The strong growth in developing country import demand in the last decade has been dominated by rapidly growing/developing Asia. This is particularly true of China which, in 2006, absorbed about 6.5 per cent of world imports, up from 2.5 per cent in 1995. Thus, while the exports of developing countries have increased, so too have their imports from all sources. This proves that their increased exports have led to increased income growth which has led to increased demand and import growth, thus spreading the benefits of trade-driven globalization.

NEW AND DYNAMIC SECTORS OF WORLD TRADE

It is also clear that increased participation in dynamic and new sectors of world trade is critical to successful export performance and to development in general. The dynamic sectors of world trade are those that have grown five times in value since 1995, and now constitute at least US$10 billion in value. New sectors are also growing rapidly , and include niche and specialty goods and services for which the returns are very high. Dynamic and new sectors are driven by a sustained rise in demand, shifts in consumer preferences, and technological and skill-related developments. These sectors include beverages; marine products; energy-based products ; minerals and metals in commodities; manufactures such as electronics and electrical products; automotive parts; textiles and clothing items; renewable energy equipment; and services.

As a group, these dynamic sectors grew on an average of 12 per cent annually over the last decade. Many of them are based on new technologies with high value addition.The increasing participation of developing countries in world trade in these sectors is a positive trend. Over the last ten years, the share of developing countries in the top 25 new and dynamic products rose to 35 per cent in 2005. Even in niche products such as organic and environmental goods and services, their contribution is rising. Such participation in new and dynamic sectors enables developing countries to increase export earnings, augment value-addition and diversification, as well as improve both the terms of trade and build technological capacity. Sectoral reviews of new and dynamic sectors have been carried out by UNCTAD for the purpose of strengthening developing countries participation through identifying policy pre-requisites for successful productive capacity-building, competitiveness and better market access.

Such reviews have covered South-South trade in new and dynamic sectors, energy, electronics, fish and fishery products, steel and related specialty products, IT-enabled outsourcing of services, renewable energy products, including bio-fuels, and textiles and clothing. Particular attention is given in these sectoral reviews to the needs of LDCs and African countries. These specific sectoral reviews indicate that the ability of developing countries to participate and benefit from new and dynamic sectors depends on productive capacity, competitiveness, and market access and entry conditions. Also, participation in global production, value and distribution chains through trade and investment links is important to enable developing countries to take advantage of opportunities in this regard. Of special note among the dynamically growing sectors of world trade are creative industries and the creative economy.

Since 2000, creative industries globally have grown at an annual dynamic rate of over 7 per cent, to reach an estimated global market value of US$1.3 trillion in 2005. These industries – with strong cultural and creative components – include a number of sub-sectors from traditional art and crafts, the visual and performing arts and music, to the more technological and services-oriented fields such as publishing, audiovisuals, design, and the news media.Recent growth in trade in creative industries has been particularly high in OECD countries as well as in a number of leading developing countries. Between 1996 and 2005, world trade in the creative industries nearly doubled to stand at US$208 billion in 2005.

A notable feature of these trends has been the sharp rise in the share of developing countries in world exports in this category, increasing from 24 per cent in 1996 to 40 per cent in 2005. The increase was accounted for mainly by exports from Asian developing countries, which arose from 22 per cent of world trade in 1996 to 37 per cent in 2005. There is much potential also for LDCs to benefit from production and trade in creative industries as also for Latin American, Caribbean and African countries. LDCs could benefit from production and trade in their traditional and distinctive arts and crafts as well as music.

ANALYZING TRADE AND DEVELOPMENT PERFORMANCE: THE TDI

Regarding overall trade performance, interesting findings emerge from the systematic examination of the interaction between structural/institutional context, trade policies/processes and the trade and development performance provided by UNCTAD's Trade and Development Index 2007.The TDI provides both a quantitative indication and an analytical framework to identify how well trade and development are integrated in an individual country, based not only on its trade and development performance, but also on key factors affecting this joint performance.

In addition, the TDI also offers a useful new tool for comparative studies among countries/regions regarding their trade and development performance. TDI national scores are a composite quantitative indication describing the interaction between development and trade performance. TDI scores have improved in all the regions, with the exception of a marginal decline for North America. All the seven emerging economies have shown a 'climbing up' in

TDI scores. The major exporters of energy as well as commodity dependent countries have also shown positive improvements in TDI since 2005. Nominally, TDI scores have risen the most in sub-Saharan Africa, the Middle East and North Africa. However, this improvement still leaves huge gaps in development levels between developing countries, transition economies and developed countries. It is also interesting to note that several developing countries with a formerly centrally managed economy or a strong governmental planning role have witnessed the most exceptional economic and trade performance in recent years. This is so despite the fact of their not having bilateral trade or investment agreements, or any significant 'guidance' by the Bretton Woods institutions. Their experience with trade-led globalization could provide important development lessons for other countries. The TDI-2007 incorporates a number of refinements following suggestions from governments and the academic community.

Thus three new components have been added to the structural and institutional context dimension, namely: domestic finance resources, international finance resources, and macro-economic stability in addition to six components contained in the TDI-2005. Further more, two new components, trade performance and economic and social well-being have been added to the newly defined 'trade and development performance' dimension.

In addition, a number of new indicators have been added, including: gross domestic savings, total external debt service and short-term debt, regulatory quality and control of corruption, the inflation and current account balance, female to male income share and female labour force participation in total labour force, and the adult literacy ratio as an education indicator. The third TDI dimension – 'trade policies and processes' remained the same as in the TDI-2005. As a result, the new TDI incorporates 3 dimensions, 13 components and 34 specific indicators. UNCTAD's TDI is an example of policymaking tools available to UNCTAD member States for identifying existing strengths and weaknesses of their institutional and policy environment, and development strategies including in achieving the MDGs by 2015.

FOSTERING AN ENABLING ENVIRONMENT: EASING MARKET ACCESS, MARKET ENTRY AND RELEASING THE COMPETITIVE PRODUCTIVE CAPACITIES OF DEVELOPING COUNTRIES

One size or one set of rules does not fit all. This fact must be taken into account in global rulemaking while trying to ensure optimum trade and development outcomes. Trade rules affect a much greater array of domestic policies and regulations than ever before, thus placing an additional strain on policymaking and institution building, especially in developing countries. Successful development outcomes from trade are mediated by policies and institutions that direct the surplus earned through trade towards activities that promote economic growth, thereby initiating a cumulative trade/

growth/development spiral. The transition to greater reliance on formal institutions is not easy. The design, targeting, sequencing and pace of the transition require care for the transition to be successfully accomplished. Developed countries and institutions could make their contribution through aid for diversification, institutional and technical support, and through the provision of better market access and entry for the exports from developing countries. For their part, successful trade policymaking in developing countries will depends upon cooperative and collegial approach among all national level stakeholders with an interest in trade-related matters.

Governments need to place more emphasis on mainstreaming trade into development and, for this purpose, extensively and continuously consult with all stakeholders in the public, private, and civil society, including academia. In turn, these stakeholders have an interest in participating and contributing actively to trade policy formulation and decision making so that they can use trade as an engine of development. UNCTAD's TDI can serve as an innovative diagnostic and policymaking tool for assessing the overall interactions and interdependence among various factors in the trade and development process. Identifying the ways and means of strengthening the trade integration of developing countries that are marginalized from the dynamism in international trade and development gains has to be an important plank of coherent national and international efforts.

Central to this approach must be a focus on improving market access, market entry and competitiveness of developing countries.Promoting trade agreements and negotiations at the multilateral, regional, and bilateral levels to build up market access and entry as well as enabling conditions for the continued expansion of the trade of developing countries will be important in this regard. Addressing non-tariff barriers in major markets has to be central in providing genuine market access and entry for the export of goods and services from developing countries.

Augmenting the competitive productive capacities of developing countries and enhancing their participation in value-chains with higher returns deserves a more focused, in-depth and sustained attention that is both coherent and also coordinates international support measures with national development priorities. It is necessary to adopt specific strategies for selecting sectors with existing and potential comparative advantage in a developing country. Then actions can be undertaken to build supply capacity and competitiveness through appropriate enabling and supportive policies as well as private sectors initiatives. Public-private partnerships in trade and investment can promote international trade with a focus on promoting development as well as meeting global and national development priorities. In order to strengthen the participation of developing countries in new and dynamic sectors, publicprivate partnerships will be needed. A trend-setting example in this regard is the UNCTAD-Philips initiative on the electronic/electrical sector in southern Africa .

As the Philips initiative shows, moves to set up trade-related industries and FDI in sub-Saharan Africa could set an example of the corporate world undertaking responsibility for development and of creating stakes for developing countries in trade-driven liberalization and globalization. Public-private partnerships serve a variety of purposes relating to FDI and the transfer of technology, and productive capacity-building. Global enterprises can take up these challenges *vis-à-vis* weak and vulnerable enterprises that have been prevented from participating in the new, dynamic and high-return segments of international trade.

This is particularly true of commodity-dependent countries, small and vulnerable economies and LDCs. Systematic monitoring and the research and analysis of international trade flows, trends and patterns will be essential for providing updated information and data for trade policy formulation, trade negotiations and business operations. All these will also be necessary for the exploitation of new trading opportunities in promoting trade, economic growth and development.

THE DYNAMIC SOUTH AND SOUTH-SOUTH TRADE AND ECONOMIC COOPERATION

DYNAMIC SOUTH AND SOUTH-SOUTH TRADE DYNAMISM

North-South trade remains important, with the North providing the main markets for developing countries as whole. In parallel, South-South trade has emerged from the peripheries of world trade to becoming more and more central, both in terms of quantity and quality. As more and more developing countries especially large, populous and dynamic ones grow economically, accelerate the pace of their development and diversify their productive base, they provide bigger and higher value markets for the South's commodities, manufactures and services. In turn, they draw upon South's rich natural resource base and cost/quality competitive goods and services to power their economic growth, meet their food and energy security and build infrastructure. This emergence of South-South economic interdependence is already setting new modes of trading and investing.

If such trade and cooperation is conducted in mutually beneficially manner, it has the potential to be highly development "transmitting". Integral to this major change has been the rise of a group of dynamically growing, trading and investing developing countries that are spawning global enterprises involved in production, trade, and investment in both developed and developing countries. These active developing countries are climbing up the value chain in international trade to produce and sell higher value-added products. Moreover, countries like Brazil, China, India and South Africa are combining the two key ingredients of global competitiveness in trade – low-cost labour and a growing high-tech knowledge base – and are thus spurring the competitiveness of the South. This has lent a major impetus to South-South trade and the promise of new trade and economic complementarities. Moreover, the dynamic South helps raise the buying and selling power of the South as a whole, providing an engine of global growth. As new drivers of trade integration, the dynamic South is contributing to the maximization of advantages from trade, investment, and technology, as well as technical and financial flows into other countries of the South and the North.

There has been a marked shift in the composition of the exports of developing countries taken as a group, with manufactures now accounting for about 70 per cent of their exports. The manufacturing sectors also represent a large part of South-South trade, rising from 35 per cent in 1995 to 42 per cent in 2005. The most traded goods in 2005 included high-end manufacturing goods, such as electrical machinery and equipment, computers, other machinery and mechanical appliances. These also formed the most dynamically growing sectors in world trade.

Fuel is the second-most traded sector , followed by base metals and products , and textiles and articles . The share of fuels' share in total South-South trade increased from 13 to 21 per cent between 1995 and 2005, reflecting the rise in oil prices. South-South merchandise trade has expanded dynamically, increasing from US$577 billion in 1995 to US$1.7 trillion in 2005 – a threefold increase in 10 years. This has resulted in the concomitant increase in the South-South share of world merchandise exports, rising up to 15 per cent in 2005, up from 11 per cent in 1995. South-South trade performance in recent years has indeed been impressive. In 2005, 46 per cent of the total merchandise export of developing countries went to each other, as compared to 40 per cent in 1995.

Developing countries are increasingly trading with each other. With such current growth rates it is likely that, by the end of the decade, over one half of the trade of developing countries will be with each other. A few developing countries dominate South-South trade, however. Those with the highest value of exports to the South in 2005 include China, Hong Kong China, the Republic of Korea, Singapore and Saudi Arabia. The share of South-South exports in the total exports of these countries was generally higher than the South's average . The majority of developing countries have yet to be more fully integrated into South-South trade and to benefit from its recent dynamism.

TRADE BETWEEN DEVELOPING COUNTRIES AND COUNTRIES WITH ECONOMIES IN TRANSITION

The recent period of 2000-2006 witnessed a surge of merchandise trade between developing countries and countries with economies in transition. Exports from developing countries to the latter increased by more than 382 per cent in 2000-2006, from US$ 14.1 billion to US$ 68 billion.20 The growth of their imports from countries with economies in transition was also impressive. During the same period, such import increased by 123 per cent, from US$ 31.1 billion to US$ 69.4 billion.

In terms of export product structure, the most dynamic exports from developing countries were: animal and animal products , various vehicles , base metals and products , aircraft, ships and boats and other manufactured articles. On the other hand, the most dynamic products of developing countries' imports from countries with economies in transition were: fuels , vegetable products , ores and minerals and miscellaneous manufactured articles. Analysis of these trade flows, which, to a large extent, are only now emerging, suggests that a strong pattern of complementarity is gradually evolving in trade between these two groups of countries.

FOSTERING AN ENABLING ENVIRONMENT: DEVELOPMENT-TRANSMITTING SOUTH AND SOUTH-SOUTH TRADE

There is a new window of opportunity for developing countries and the international community to support the emergence of the dynamic South in the wider effort to assist developing countries in maximizing development benefits from trade and investment driven globalization. The tendency to resort to neo-protectionism measures – especially in industrialized countries – against rising merchandise/services exports or investments from South should be arrested, even ruled out. This should be done through awareness and confidence building measures, and policy deliberations with all the concerned stakeholders. UNCTAD, as in the past, can play a constructive mediating role in such dialogue.

The emerging South is also rapidly building trade and economic relations with other developing countries, including LDCs. What is important to emphasize is that unlike in the 1960- 1970s, the dynamic South-South cooperation is driven today by economic factors and, in fact by the globalization itself. These positive and encouraging trends should be strengthened, widened and deepened so that developing countries still at the periphery of South-South cooperation can be mainstreamed and become beneficiaries of the new trade geography, in addition to their efforts to integrate into the international trading system. A simulation exercise shows that the removal of South-South barriers has the potential to generate gains 40 per cent larger than those obtained with the opening up of all Northern markets to all developing countries.

The results imply that giving greater emphasis to removing barriers between as well as within continents could prove a successful Southern survival strategy. Moreover, with South– South trade liberalization, interregional exports within developing regions increase dramatically. Compared with North–South liberalization, South–South liberalization is accompanied by a larger overall impact in manufacturing sectors relative to agricultural products sectors. This is mostly the consequence of the removal of initially relatively higher tariff rates imposed on South-South trade in manufactures. Ultimately, South-South liberalization should add to multilateral liberalization and stimulate global trade generally. There is also a need to support the new dynamism in South-South trade to ensure that it sustains its role as a major motor of world economic growth, especially against the latest developments and predictions regarding economic slowdown and even potential recession in the leading developed economies from 2008 to 2010.

Such support will also require effective and coherent policies for regional development, coordinated at sub-regional, regional, and interregional levels.The dynamic South and South-South trade dynamism equally demands institutional and regulatory changes, adaptation and innovation, both in respect of South-South and North-South cooperation. In particular, South-South trade liberalization needs to be consolidated and pursued further, including through more rapid and complete implementation and rationalization of South-South RTAs. Investments in R&D and technological cooperation at the regional level will be required as well to build the scientific and technological basis for future South-South trade and economic relations, including raising levels of technological complementarity among developing countries. The impact of a dynamic and rising South is already prominent in the international trading system in the form of the proactive participation and the decisive role of developing countries and their groupings in WTO trade negotiations in all areas. The Doha negotiations marked a departure point not only because they formally placed development at the heart of the work programme, but also because developing countries have been effectively pursuing a positive agenda whilst also trying to secure their policy flexibility related to larger development concerns.

This positive agenda of developing countries addresses issues in both market access and systemic multilateral rules with a view to ensure that in the outcome of the Doha Round, development dividends will be meaningful and operational. Developing country issue based coalitions such as G-20, G-33, NAMA-XI, G-90, G- 110,have been playing a key role. It is also significant that the Quad which used to be composed of developed countries alone has been complemented by the G-4 involving USA and EU and developing countries like India and Brazil.

This is a sign of the times and an indication that the MTS and the global trade governance it represents is and should be increasingly adapting to the new realities in the geography of international trade. More needs to be done, however, to reflect the expansion of WTO members to 152, the majority of which are developing countries, and to respond effectively to their varying trade and development conditions and specific needs. In North-South RTAs and free trade agreements too, there is a shift by leading trading nations like

EU and US to enter into such agreements with countries not only geographical contiguous to them but also with regional and subregional groupings of developing countries further a field. Examples include the EU-Mercosur or EU-ASEAN free trade agreement negotiations. Moreover, countries like China, Japan, India and the Republic of Korea which previously shun RTAs and relied on multilateral trade liberalization are engaging other regional and extra-regional partners.

There is now a new generation of North-South RTAs emerging, many of which are replacing unilateral preferences in favour of developing countries with reciprocal concessions among countries at substantially different levels of development. This is a new phenomenon which requires careful analyses to ensure that these agreements provide real, effective and additional market access for developing country exports, and promote broader development partnerships. At the same time calibrating developing countries' participation in these RTAs to sequence and pace liberalization in a manner consistent with their trade, development and financial capacities will determining the pro-development outcome of such arrangements. An enabling environment for development of the South and South-South trade can include, among other things: opportunities for greater FDI flows to and from the South; facilitating R&D and technological cooperation and transfer to the South in key areas of transformational production and development including in pro-poor technologies; increasing universal access to essential services; and promoting energy efficient, eco-friendly technologies and renewable energy sources.

Trade agreements should spur industrialization, help improve agricultural productivity and food security as well as help build competitive services sectors and new export capacity. Aid to trade and development should be made available to cushion partly the adjustment costs for developing countries arising from trade liberalization and reforms on account of RTAs and WTO agreements. Deeper productive capacity and infrastructure building should be a key objective and outcome of RTAs to enable developing countries to take advantage of trade liberalization opportunities. Trade, investment and development cooperation policies of the developed countries are critical for continued dynamism of 'development multiplying' South's engines of regional and global trade as well as for 'development transmitting' stimulus of South-South trade, investment and technology transfer.

To some extent, adaptations in this direction are already happening in that the developed countries are entering into RTAs with South-South groupings. Arrangements such as the EU-ACP economic partnership agreements should be so tailored as to enhance both a market access package and a substantial capacity developing package which will have an impact sub-regionally and regionally. At the same time, as stipulated in the Cotonou Agreement, ACP countries should be provided concrete special and differential treatment. Preferential trade schemes, both unilateral and "free trade" concessions provided by the North to the South as part of RTAs, could include South-South cumulation provisions in the rules of origin. This would stimulate South-South investment and trade and ensure that the dynamic South's globalisation drive is harnessed to boost the rest of the South's trade. In addition, participation of some developing countries in Northern enterprises led global production and distribution chains is also generating South-South trade.

This form of intra-firm triangular cooperation , however, needs to be further encouraged especially in terms of increased value chain participation by developing countries. Some duty free, quota free schemes have been notified or announced by developing countries for LDCs as a measure of development solidarity.

These countries include China, India, Morocco, Pakistan, Sri Lanka and Turkey.As regards other trade related institutions and policies of global economic governance, it is evident from the G-8's and OECD's outreach programmes directed at dialogue with some big emerging economies, that developing country voice and perspective is essential if global economic governance is to be credible, inclusive and effective.

With regard to the international monetary and financial systems too, need for institutional adaptation to reflect the growing trade and development role and impact of developing countries is being recognized. There is a move albeit not as much and as fast as it should be, to increase the voice and participation of developing countries in multilateral financial institutions – the World Bank and the IMF and their decision making process. Global macroeconomic policy management, including addressing global trade and current account imbalances in a coherent way along with multilateral surveillance and disciplining of monetary and financial markets is imperative and must involve developing countries.

It is important that the dynamic trade performance by some developing countries should not be mistaken for their having overcome their inherent and persistent trade and development constraints and challenges. It must be realized that most still deserve development support and special and differential treatment in terms of both trade and aid policies. Recent studies by the World Bank highlights how big development challenge even dynamic low-income trade and economic performers like China and India face in catching up with developed countries even when their per capita income is measured in PPP terms.

Similarly, UNCTAD's Trade and Development Index shows that the emerging developing countries are still quite low in the rankings on account of widespread poverty, infrastructure deficits, weak financial intermediation facilities, and structural and institutional shortcomings. They, like in the North, but probably even more face the daunting task of ensuring more equitable and widely distributed trade and development gains for all their regions and populations including the urban and rural poor and women. The inequality gap within developing countries, often accentuated by trade driven globalization needs to be bridged. Reliance on a trickle down of economic growth will not be adequate to address such inequalities - proactive policies need to be followed by developing countries to spread the benefits of trade growth more inclusively.

The emergence of changes in South-South trade call for new and well adapted South-South institutions, strategies, policies and measures at all levels. Development strategies of the South should and are increasingly factoring in economic cooperation with other countries of the South especially as regards trade, investment, technology transfer and social development programmes. Awareness raising about successful development models, projects and best practices and their replication would be an important area of South-South cooperation.

Institutions for sharing such experiences and models at regional and interregional levels would be required and would involve government, private sector and civil society participation. A new look needs to be given to initiatives such as the South Bank both as regional and interregional concepts. Initiatives such as the Global Network of Export Import Banks and Development Financial Institutions promoted under UNCTAD auspices could play a significant role in supporting South-South trade and development finance. Regional and inter-regional monetary unions and arrangements are also ideas whose time may have come for operationalization.

The Bank of the South launched in December 2007 by several Latin American countries is a concrete step towards promoting financial and monetary cooperation among these countries in support of their mutual trade, investment and development. Developing and implementing regional standards on TBT and SPS can be effective in South-South trade promotion. The South Fund for Development and Humanitarian Assistance, launched at the Second South Summit could useful support and sustain the South-South dynamism. This is a seminal period for the evolution of South-South trade and investment models in sectors ranging from minerals, metals and fuels, manufacturing and services. There is some expectation that as developing country enterprises operate and deal with other developing countries, there will be greater mutual understanding of development imperatives and conditions.

Similarly, there is indication that South-South trade and investment cooperation, export credits and project implementation especially in infrastructure, need to be moulded so as to be 'development transmitting' models. This would involve public-private partnerships that help build permanent capacity, physical and social infrastructure, transfer technology, create jobs, contribute to value addition, and build competitive productive structures and institutions. The flying-geese model that worked in the Asian regional context needs to be adapted to inter-regional Asian, African and Latin American contexts, while respecting their traditions and individual development paths. A "one-size-fits-all" approach will not work here as it has not worked on a global scale. Considerable expansion in inter-regional South-South trade especially since 2000, with a number of developing countries among top five global trading partners, represents an exciting new phenomenon of international trade. The major change in South-South economic and trade interaction is in terms of the reality that the new dynamism is market driven with enterprises of the South and the North linking up Southern economies and markets through intra- and inter-firm and intra- and interindustry networks and transactions.

Increasing complementarities and capacities of developing country enterprises have played an important part. However, policy driven South-South trade liberalization still remains rather limited, inconclusive and needs to be advanced, while trade promotion and facilitation combined with deeper economic integration and institutional cooperation should play a more critical role in expanding South-South trade and investment both regionally and inter-regionally.

Although South-South RTAs have been active in driving regional economic integration for over several decades, their implementation in terms of coverage and commercial benefits requires a lot better performance. Many of them have hub and spoke formations with some key developing countries propelling such integration in accordance with their perceived interests. These have given rise to increasing regional division of labour in general, greater complementarities and new value chain creation. However, new institutional mechanisms for tapping and encouraging the entrepreneurial, capital, technological and labour related resources of the South for the benefit of the whole South need to be evolved.

Regional trade liberalization needs to be deepened and complemented by a provision of finance and capital for building the required physical, air, rail, road and maritime transport infrastructure and trade related institutions such as those for standards, testing and conformity assessment, and mutual recognition of qualifications, technical regulations and standards. Special and differential provisions for less developed participants of South-South RTAs are also required as expression of economic wisdom and development solidarity.

Such new generation arrangements should enable developing countries to leverage their existent and dynamically progressing comparative advantage *vis-à-vis* each other and in their relationships with the North, including in possible triangular cooperation arrangements, which should be clearly defined and not confined only to ODA-type projects, but also based on economically viable commercial and investment endeavours. In this regard, the private sectors both from South and North should play a leading role supported by government facilitating policies. In this regard, comprehensive and progressive inter-regional South-South trade liberalization is being attempted through the third round of negotiations under the Global System of Trade Preferences among Developing Countries that were launched at UNCTAD XI. As a first step, modalities for tariff liberalization on applied rates with special consideration for LDCs and requisite rules are being finalized towards adoption at UNCTAD XII.

It will be expected that this will lead to further negotiations to cover NTBs and services in subsequent rounds. The GSTP has the potential to become a true catalyst for a deeper and more inclusive South-South trade liberalization, particularly by giving impetus to inter-regional South-South trade and investment and to economic cooperation among developing countries generally. Trade between developing countries and countries with economies in transition is emerging strongly. New initiatives in terms of trade agreements, institutions, and trade promotion activities can be developed and implement to build up such trade further to the mutual benefit of developing countries and countries with economies in transition. Finally, the emerging big Southern performers are themselves benefiting increasingly from trade and economic expansion.

The challenge is also to ensure that these economic gains are more equitably distributed inside their societies, while their policies aim at providing universal access to the benefits of impressive economic growth, especially in case of poor segments of their populations. The emerging South's ever increasing population and enterprises with progressively augmented purchasing power and rising demand for resources has already become a major impetus to regional and interregional trade and economic development, as well as a substantial driver of global trade and economic growth in recent years. Other countries of the South also benefit from larger and fast growing markets which they can access and get better terms of trade and returns for their exports.

It enables them to diversify away from their dependence on Northern markets for their exports and imports as well as for FDI and technologies. For North too, this is a win-win scenario as rapid and increased economic growth and trade capacity in dynamic developing countries and markets enables the North to increase their exports, particularly of high value-added goods and services, while putting off pressure, to some extent, on their imports from emerging economies.

Furthermore, both developing country and developed country consumers benefit from cost quality competitive imports from the dynamic developing countries. In this regard therefore it would be counter-productive to view the rise of new dynamic engines of the South in international trade and investment as anything but a positive-sum phenomenon for all. The fact that more and more developing countries are increasing their stakes in freer and more open international trade should be welcomed and encouraged.

RE-LAUNCHING THE COMMODITY AGENDA

OPPORTUNITIES OFFERED BY THE RECENT COMMODITY BOOM

Since 2002, there has been a 'commodity boom.' International commodity prices showed a strong upward trend after their sharp fall in 1995-1997 to 2002. UNCTAD's commodity price index in current US dollar terms has risen 96 per cent since 2002. The rise in prices has been driven by the boom in the prices of metals and minerals which have increased by 191 per cent, and those of crude oil which have risen by 140 per cent. Price increases for agricultural raw materials and tropical beverages taken as groups averaged between 58 per cent and 45 per cent, respectively. The relative importance of factors behind the price increases differs from commodity to commodity. However there are some common factors. These include the strong growth in import demand of developing countries, owing to the rapid pace of industrialization, especially in China , India and other emerging developing countries; the increased production of biofuels which mainly affects the markets for food products by pushing up the price of land and adding to effective demand for some products that are used both for food and for biofuel ; as well as emerging supply constraints in some commodity markets.

A sustained increase in the demand for commodities by emerging countries – which appears likely – will continue to provide additional opportunities for increased commodity exports by developing countries. Although the Asian import demand has centred on industrial raw materials, the rising consumer purchasing power in the developing Asia region has also boosted the demand for some agro-food commodities which had been facing stagnant or falling demand in the traditional OECD markets. This additional source of demand has contributed to a general recovery of commodity prices and improved prospects for commodity producing countries. Sustained growth in the United States and economic recovery in Japan and Europe have also been contributing factors. As regards minerals and metals, world supply has not been able to catch up with strong demand growth since investments in new production capacity have been low over a long period due to a prolonged period of low prices.

The long lead times in mining investment have made it harder for mining companies to meet the growth in demand. Inventories of metals have been drawn down, and have remained at extremely low levels for the past few years. Also, while supply-and-demand fundamentals determine the direction of the price trend, speculators seeking higher returns than those offered by financial assets have enhanced the tightness of the metals markets. From 2002, copper, nickel and zinc prices increased by 136, 118 and 74 per cent, respectively. This trend continued in the first half of 2006, with zinc and copper prices rising by 70 per cent on their 2005 level, and nickel by 45 per cent. Oil prices continued to rise in 2006 and reached US$78 per barrel in July of that year and US$100 in 2007.

As in the case of metals, Chinese demand growth, as well as speculation were significant factors. Worries about potential disruptions to supply also played a role, and reinforced speculative sentiments. The rise in oil prices has also an impact on other commodity markets. In some cases – for instance, natural fibres, rubber, and sugar – the price increases resulted partly from the substitution effects engendered by the jump in international oil prices. Rising hydrocarbon prices made some synthetic materials less competitive. This strengthened the position of natural materials such as cotton and rubber, resulting in an increase both in demand and prices. In the case of sugar, higher oil prices have led to an increased demand for ethanol and, consequently, to higher international sugar prices.

LOOMING CHALLENGES FOR COMMODITIES

The recent increases in commodity prices notwithstanding, these have not been enough to offset the consequences of severe price declines suffered in the past. For instance, in the case of coffee, the rise in international prices has not been sufficient to make up for the fall in prices following the 1997 crisis. Expressed in current US dollar terms, non-fuel commodity prices are still lower than what they were in the early 1980s. In real terms, by the end of 2005, commodity prices were about 30 per cent lower than the average for the period 1975-1985. The prospects for individual commodity markets vary.

For instance, the prices of rubber and cotton are influenced by developments in the oil market owing to substitution effects between natural and synthetic products. However, the main reason for the increase in the price of natural rubber lies in the rapidly growing demand for rubber products – particularly tires, and mainly highly quality tires of natural rubber used in high growth areas such as heavy trucks and aircraft. Meteorological conditions and trade policies have influenced supply conditions for other cash crops. Global economic conditions also affect different markets in different ways from the demand side. For instance, the rapid pace of industrialization and income growth in China has had a much stronger impact on the prices of industrial raw materials as compared to food prices. This difference is likely to persist in the short-to-medium term. However, food imports by China are likely to increase in the longer term, raising the likelihood of future price increases for agricultural commodities.

The international market for a wide range of commodities tend to be characterized by alternating short periods of higher prices – like the current period since 2002 – and longer periods of lower prices, with high volatility within these cycles. Commodities fall into three categories: petroleum and other energy resources, minerals and metals, and agricultural commodities.

Aside from petroleum – in itself a special case – a distinction should be made between minerals and metals on the one hand, and agricultural commodities on the other. With increasing globalization, countries dependent on the export of these different categories of commodities experience the impact of the commodity problematic in different degrees, thus requiring responses tailored to their specific circumstances in order to maximize development gains from them.

COMMODITY, POVERTY REDUCTION AND DEVELOPMENT

A majority of developing countries are dependent on the commodity sector as their largest source of revenue and employment, and a major source of external finance for development. Some 83 developing and least-developed countries derive more than 30 per cent of their export earnings from the export of primary commodities. A single commodity accounts for more than 40 per cent of export earnings for 42 of these countries: 15 rely on agricultural, fishery, and forestry products; 9 on mineral and metals; and 18 on petroleum. While price trends and behaviour are of major importance to all categories of commodity producing countries, the situation of low-income countries dependent on the export of traditional agricultural commodities provides a unique challenge for reducing poverty and assuring development gains from international trade.

Since the early 1980s, the prices of those commodities on which many LDCs and other more vulnerable developing countries are the most dependent have shown a long-term declining trend, both in nominal and real terms. Besides the problem of prices, the marketing and processing of these commodities is largely skewed against the developing countries that produce them. Also, despite the current respite in the downward trajectory of most commodity prices, low-income commodity-dependent developing countries continue to face difficulties in retaining international market shares. Thus, it is vital that issues relating to commodities be urgently and adequately addressed at the international level. Both sets of problems are related to the workings of the international trading system.

Persistent supply/demand imbalances on world commodity markets have been mainly due to trade-distorting domestic support and export subsidies in certain industrialized countries. These not only displace the exporters of developing countries on world markets but also reduce world prices . They also pressure low-income commodity-producing countries to increase export volumes even in the face of declining world prices so as to expand the level of foreign exchange earnings, and thereby sustain debt servicing and import capacity. Typically, low-income commodity-dependent developing countries rely on one – or a few – export commodities. With their populations dependent on these commodities for their livelihood, these countries are highly vulnerable to trade shocks, and face an unpredictable existence at both the micro and macro levels. For example, declining and volatile commodity prices adversely affect the incomes of farmers, agricultural wages, rural employment, the prospects for rural development, and poverty reduction immediately. Price volatility creates uncertainty on investment returns, and reduces both the willingness and capacity of farmers and entrepreneurs to invest.

As a consequence, commodity producers in these developing countries are at a disadvantage when attempting to adapt to increasingly harsh international competition and changes in the international market place. At the same time, in the mining sector , the predicament of small miners – of which there are over 30 million in developing countries – needs to be addressed. At the macro level, declining and volatile commodity prices often have a direct and negative impact on macroeconomic stability, fiscal balance, and balance of payment.

A collapse in commodity prices usually has an immediate adverse economic multiplier effect. As farmers and workers have less to spend, local businesses contract or shut down. The Government also faces a reduction in revenues and taxes. These induce or aggravate fiscal deficits which require correction by a reduction in spending. A fall in Government spending leads to more job losses. It also results in the reduced ability of the Government to provide basic services such as health and education and to invest in infrastructure such as roads, ports, water supply and electricity. Reduced foreign exchange earnings put further pressure on foreign exchange reserves, limiting import capacity, reducing external creditworthiness, and making debt servicing less sustainable. Hence, the importance of reducing and managing the volatility of commodity prices to arrest this negative spiral and turn it into a positive one.

FOSTERING AN ENABLING ENVIRONMENT: COMMODITY-BASED DEVELOPMENT STRATEGY

Over the medium to long term, the prospects for continued growth in world demand for most commodities appear good. Commodity prices can be expected to remain relatively high. The main underlying reasons are the expected rapid economic growth and import demand of developing countries, particularly in Asia, juxtaposed against weak commodity supply capacities, and the increased diversion of the supply of some commodities to the production of biofuels. However, it is unlikely that the growing imports of primary commodities into Asia alone will lead to a reversal of the long-term decline in real commodity prices. Nonetheless, the prospect of better prices for a considerable period of time – maybe as much as ten years – may mean that commodity-dependent developing countries will potentially generate sufficient finances to invest in their development and poverty reduction. However, any success in planning their development based on commodity production and trade will depend both upon the existence of an enabling international environment and the ability to build capacity, as well as undertake necessary institutional changes. Governments of developing countries experiencing windfall revenues from commodity price booms need to deal first with the problem of translating higher prices into higher revenues, investment into local infrastructure, jobs and poverty reduction through appropriate revenue sharing, and taxationrelated policy and agreement *vis-à-vis* domestic and foreign investors. They also have to pursue their core policies of targeting local infrastructure and productive capacity, diversification and value addition, job creating industries and poverty reduction schemes.

Harnessing the present boom in commodity prices from changing market conditions for the purposes of development is an urgent matter for both developing countries as well as the international community. The challenges include: the adaptation – in real terms – of international trade rules within which most international commodity trade takes place between countries that have historically been at the periphery of world trade, and have not been part of the rule-making process; the mobilization of financial resources to support this trade, including from financial institutions which are traditionally focused on financing trade within the North; and the suitability of legal regimes governing investment *vis-à-vis* the new flows of investment capital between developing countries.

All these challenges call for enhancing coherence at all levels in order to ensure that institutional change facilitates and supports the shift in commodity trade patterns, and eventually makes for sustainable economic development and poverty reduction. The degree of success with which the world can meet these challenges depends crucially on the progress made in enhancing the enabling environment at all levels so as to strengthen productive capacity, trade and investment. Only then will commodity-dependent developing countries be able to exploit the window of opportunity provided by the new market environment. To support a viable commodity-based development strategy, there is a need to address several issues at the international level. Firstly, there is the need to address some of the causes and mitigate the adverse consequences of long periods of commodity price declines and sharp price fluctuations – the key causes of oversupply and market failure.

Secondly, there is the need to facilitate and ensure an equitable distribution of the gains from trade in commodities, encourage value addition and competitiveness within commodity value chains, and improve market access for commodity-based products. Thirdly, there is need to improve: the access of commodity-dependent countries to international finance for the purposes of development and to commodity exchanges; investment in the upgrading of traditional commodity sectors; and investment in the diversification of traditional commodities into non-traditional ones . And fourthly, there is a need to address the proliferation of new generations of product presentations, technical processes, and sanitary and phytosanitary standards for market access , especially in OECD markets.All these elements – which are part of a holistic strategy for development from a commodity base – require substantial investment in infrastructure and supply-side capacity-building.

In this context, the Aid for Trade initiative – along with UNCTAD's involvement – could play a critical role in supporting improvements in the competitiveness of traditional commodity sectors, the vertical and horizontal diversification in commodity-dependent countries, and the mitigation of the short-term impact of commodity 'shocks' at the national level. The latter could include the financing of safety net programmes for small and resource-poor producers seriously affected by commodity 'shocks'. A holistic approach would require reinventing and putting into place institutions that can more effectively carry out some of the useful functions that previous marketing boards had performed. The problems of institutional vacuums, missing markets and access to financing are all too evident in most commodity-dependent countries, particularly in Africa and other LDCs.

Commodity financing should be a priority for small producers marginalized by globalization, and for the mechanization and up scaling of agricultural production and trade. Small producers need assistance in order to reinforce and upgrade their productive capacity, competitiveness and be integrated into international supply chains. They also need other inputs such as better infrastructure, timely information, as well as financial and other support necessary to gain access to national, regional, and international markets. They need help to organize themselves and to bargain better with global supply and distribution networks.A roadmap for a comprehensive approach to commodities was provided by the outcome of the first UNCTAD XII pre-event: the Brasilia Conference on the Global Initiative on Commodities, which was jointly organized by the ACP secretariat, Common Fund for Commodities, UNDP and UNCTAD, and hosted by the Government of Brazil.

SERVICES – THE NEW TRADE AND DEVELOPMENT FRONTIER

THE INCREASING IMPORTANCE OF THE SERVICES ECONOMY

Services contribute to economic growth and development through the creation of a competitive economy, by providing new jobs, by enhancing access to essential services, and by stimulating trade. Service sectors such as business and finance, telecommunications, construction, environment, distribution, health care, education, and cultural services provide the backbone of an integrated and effective economy, nationally, regionally and globally. An improved services economy contributes to improved performance in merchandise trade since the increased sophistication and availability of producer services enhances international competitiveness in the export of primary and manufactured goods.

The informal services sector is also an important aspect of the services economy in developing countries. With globalization, the potential for developing countries to expand and diversify their economies through the increased development and trade in services is immense. Moreover, increased services trade can generate significant development gains – *i.e.* far more than can be realized through the narrow focus on increasing the exports of primary commodities and manufactures alone. Thus, services hold a huge potential as en engine for realizing development gains in developing countries. Globally, the services economy continues to expand, with its contribution to GDP, employment and trade increasing significantly, including in many developing countries. Between 1980 and 2006, the share of services in GDP has grown from 60 to 73 per cent in developed countries, and from 41 to 51 per cent in developing countries.

Services today account for over 70 per cent of employment in developed countries, and around 35 per cent in developing countries. World trade in services has nearly tripled to reach US$2.4 trillion, while the FDI inward stock has quadrupled to nearly $10 trillion in the wake of the globalized production of goods and services. Particularly significant sectors and modes for services exports include the temporary movement of natural persons supplying services and outsourcing , but also in Mode 3, and sectors such as health, tourism, construction and business services. Regarding tourism, the "Trade and development implications of tourism services for developing countries" was discussed at an UNCTAD XII pre-event from 19–20 November 2007 in Geneva. The event identified best practices that developing countries are increasingly pursuing in promoting tourism with the aim of ensuring that benefits from the sector translate into long-term economic, social and environmental gains.

The overall performance of the trade in services in developing countries has been exceptional. Since 1990, the export of services from developing countries has grown at an average annual rate of 8 per cent, compared to 6 per cent from developed countries. Thus, the share of developing countries in world export of services has climbed from 19 to 24 per cent. Travel and transport continue to represent the major proportion of the services exports of developing countries while business services now account for about one-third of all services.At present, services trade of developing countries is dominated by a small number amongst them. Developing countries in Asia account for 75 per cent of the services trade of all developing countries. While Africa/Latin America and the Caribbean accounted for 10 and 15 per cent, respectively.

Over half of developing country services exports originate in only 6 countries, and the top 15 developing country services exporters account for 80 per cent of all developing country services exports. An increasing number of countries are successful in exporting services such as tourism, transport, construction, audiovisual, computer and information services, business and professional services, particularly through Modes 1 and Mode 4. South-South trade is also expanding, within which regional trade agreements play an important role.

FDI INFLOWS AND OFF-SHORING SERVICES

FDI inflows to developing countries are increasingly targeting the services sector. The services sector attracted only 32 per cent of FDI inflows to developing countries in 1990 compared to 50 per cent in 2005. Accumulated FDI inward stocks in their services sector have also climbed during this period by some 800 per cent from US$150 billion to US$1.3 trillion. FDI inward stock in the services sector of developing countries is now nearly twice the value of FDI inward stock in their manufacturing sector and accounts for 22 per cent of total world FDI inward stock in the services sector. Developing countries themselves have become a major source of these investments. Total FDI outflows from developing countries to the world's services sector rose from only US$2 billion in 1990 to nearly US$38 billion in 2005 and most of these outflows were destined for other developing countries.

Off-shored services are a small component of the world outsourcing market for a wide range of services, including IT and IT-enabled business services, as well as pharmaceutical and R&D services. Current estimates indicate that the magnitude of the global off-shoring market exceeds US$50 billion. With developing countries capturing a sizable and growing share of the market, the potential of their benefiting from the trend of off-shoring services appears to be large. The recent growth in the global market for off-shoring services increasingly offers new export opportunities to developing countries, as well as significant cost-savings benefits to countries importing these services. Key benefits for exporting countries include increased export earnings, job creation, higher wages, and the upgrading of skills. FDI in off-shoring can create further positive spillovers in terms of raising the competitiveness of human resources and improving the ICT infrastructure.

Development gains from increased services trade include enhanced inward FDI flows and the transfer of technologies to the services sectors of developing countries, including producer services. Improving the availability, capacity and competitiveness of domestic producer services is a critical requirement for enhancing their export performance in primary and manufactured goods. At the same time, improved market opening commitments by trading partners in the trade in cross-border services , as well as in the movement of natural persons supplying services would unlock new opportunities for developing country services exports in areas where many have an established competitive advantage, including in IT-enabled services, business, construction and health-care services. However, the potential of the development of the services sector and trade in services is yet to be fully realized by many developing countries especially in sub-Saharan Africa and in small and vulnerable economies including small island developing States and LDCs.

LDCs, for instance, continue to be marginalized from the international flows of services, with their share in world service exports being only about 0.5 per cent. Also, most services in the informal sector are not tradable, thus reducing their propensity to benefit from trade-led globalization. Positively integrating these countries into the services economy and trade, and assuring that they derive development gains, remains a major challenge for development.

FOSTERING AN ENABLING ENVIRONMENT: MEANINGFUL AND PRO-DEVELOPMENT COMMITMENTS IN SERVICES LIBERALIZATION AND BUILDING COMPETITIVE SERVICES PRODUCTIVE CAPACITIES

The WTO Doha Round of negotiations regarding services are a major forum for creating an enabling and progressive liberalization of trade in services as well as delivering global governance objectives through the formulation of possible disciplines, including in the area of domestic regulation. The negotiation on services offers an important avenue to liberalizing trade in services in a development-friendly manner and from the perspective of developing countries.

Such liberalization can create new opportunities for the development and trade in the services sector to be seized by developing countries. Quality integration in the services economy necessitates securing favourable terms and conditions for the participation of developing countries in world trade in general, and in the multilateral trading system in particular. Despite the continuing growth of the services sector, and the fact that services negotiations were already mandated as the built-in agenda of negotiations in the GATS, current negotiating dynamics do not offer services the same prominence as NAMA and agriculture.

In general, developing countries have been asked to make binding commitments on services at the actual level of openness or beyond. This raises important questions about the flexibility available to developing countries in ensuring the appropriate pacing and sequencing of liberalization, and about the development flexibilities and the positive-list approach of the GATS. For developing countries, any movement in services depends upon pro-development aspects in – and in balance with – other areas of negotiations, notably agriculture and NAMA. A pro-development solution in services negotiations would require 'meaningful' commitments in the sectors and modes of export interest to developing countries. However, clear progress on market access issues is still outstanding. Currently, there are 70 offers and 30 revised offers.

However, most of them are not effectively meeting the Mode 4-related market access expectations of developing and least developed countries. Also, the effective operationalization of the modalities for the special treatment for LDCs remains outstanding. Combining GATS commitments with flexibility to review – and roll back – commitments in the light of development impacts may offer a safety-valve, making it easier for Members to offer commitments in the first place. The use of an emergency safeguard mechanism could also be of value. In the domestic regulation area of GATS negotiations, the main development challenge lies in striking a balance between preserving the right to regulate and achieving clear and specific international disciplines to underpin any market access commitments, including for Mode 4.

Despite much efforts, many important issues remain outstanding, with Members disagreeing on the overall direction and level of ambition any future disciplines should achieve. A pro-development approach would include a strengthened section on development, combined with an effective development angle for each and every discipline, rule and obligation. Members may also wish to borrow from the approach used in the Trade Facilitation negotiations, where the extent and the timing of entering into commitments shall be related to the implementation capacities of developing and least developed country Members, and where least developed country Members will only be required to undertake commitments consistent with their individual development, financial and trade needs and their administrative and institutional capabilities.

In other areas of rule-making, progress remains notably absent. Regarding the development of disciplines regarding the trade distorting effects of subsidies, the respective mandate in the GATS requires that negotiations shall recognize the role of subsidies in relation to the development programmes of developing countries. Hence any disciplines would require equilibrium between granting developing countries the respective flexibility, and the means to address the potentially restrictive effects of the trade distorting subsidies of developed countries on their exports. Finally, an emergency safeguard mechanism for services remains an important development issue. The impact of Modes 4 and 1 on development should not be underestimated. Even a relatively modest but meaningful liberalization in Mode 4 could bring welfare benefits that would strengthen the development component of the Doha round.In fact, the gains from Mode 4 alone are estimated to outweigh the combined expected gains from the liberalization of agriculture and NAMA.

For example, it has been estimated that an increase in developed countries' quotas on the inward movements of both skilled and unskilled temporary workers equivalent to 3 per cent of their workforces would generate an estimated increase in world welfare of over $US150 billion annually,as compared to projected gains in agriculture of about $50 billion and in manufactures of about $80 billion.In Mode 1, developing countries can gain not only from business process outsourcing but also by capturing export opportunities in IT-enabled services, and by moving up the value chain to knowledge process outsourcing . The KPO market is projected to reach US$17 billion by 2010.However, the realization of gains by developing countries in both Modes 1 and 4 are currently hampered by growing protectionist sentiments in the markets of destination.

Thus, there is need for coherence in the policy and commitments made at the international level vis-à-vis practice at the national level. There is also the need for coherence between national/federal/regional legislation and policies in destination markets for developing country exports. This will ensure that the commitments made are adhered to, that restrictions are rolled back, and access liberalized even further. Many developing countries are apprehensive of government procurement in the services sector .

However, it has been indicated as an area that could provide development and export opportunities for some developing countries if undertaken on a unilateral/bilateral basis, and with a development outcome in mind. International solidarity – particularly through the provision of finance but also in terms of technological support and investment – is important not just in order to build competitiveness in the services sector but also to move towards the development of pro-poor services, including through the provision of universal access to essential services.International solidarity initiatives to create an enabling environment in the services sector can be of two kinds.

The first is in the context of infrastructure building, both physical and social. This is an essential complement to services liberalization. Governments have a key role to play in this context. While private sector participation and financing in infrastructure building is important, it is clear that the private sector alone cannot provide for necessary infrastructural needs that tend to be capital intensive. Thus, there is a need to also explore the use of private-public partnership as and the essential role that multilateral financial institutions and donor finance can play in terms of international public funding. The second initiative is the use of the 'Aid for Trade' initiative, particularly for LDCs, as a tool to build competitiveness in the services sector, thereby facilitating productivity in the whole economy. The AfT initiative could be used for building national services strategies, including strategies for development, sectoral assessment, and regulatory frameworks.

The use of AfT would help beneficiaries identify and build on the services sectors of export potential move up the services value chain, and diversify both within the services sector and across other sectors, including manufacturing and agriculture. The enormous potential contribution of the services economy for – and its actual contribution to – trade and development means that any inadequacy in the services supply capacities and competitiveness of developing countries will result in their marginalization from the modern economy and global trade. The latter is a problematic facing most developing countries, especially LDCs. Particularly noteworthy is the challenge of exploiting the potential of the expanding service economy and trade in services *i.e.*, moving from the informal to the formal, and from low to high value-added sectors; overcoming over-reliance on one particular sector ; and diversifying into other sectors that are less vulnerable to external shocks.

However, these all still remain as challenges since development gains are not automatic. Reaping such gains requires sound and coherent national developmental policies and strategies, regulations and institutions, the fostering of enabling conditions, and minimizing detrimental effects. Appropriate content, the pacing and sequencing of reform and liberalization, as well as coherence with other economic sectors is important. While a few developing countries have set inspiring examples of development and trade in the services sector, other countries are being increasingly marginalized. In this regard, the 'development benchmarking' of polices governing the services sector is important. Such benchmarking should assess whether or not these policies can deliver increased capacity, up-scaling, modernization, technology transfer, job creation and social benefits.

The first challenge facing developing countries is to design and implement comprehensive policy frameworks for the services sector. These frameworks can include carefully negotiated market access commitments that can ensure dynamic gains from a greater opening of their services markets, and the effective use of the private sector including public-private partnerships. These contribute to the creation of a competitive services sector, including in infrastructural services and in the building up of SMEs in the services sector. The second challenge is to build effective national and regional regulatory frameworks and institutions for their services economy. In the context of both policy and regulatory frameworks, the development of a National Services Strategy is essential.

Comprehensive national assessments and policy reviews of services and trade in services have a central role to play in assisting developing countries and the international community in meeting the challenge of integrating developing countries into the services economy. Such assessments enable countries to appropriately pace and sequence policy reforms affecting the services sectors. Such policy reviews can facilitate intergovernmental deliberations and consensus-building on best practices, lessons learnt, as well as policy options for services development.

Follow-up capacity-building support in countries and regional groupings are also important in developing and implementing services agreements, putting in place regulatory regimes, and developing competitive services supply capacities. At the same time, the human and social development implications of the service economy and regulations have to be addressed in terms of universal access to essential services such as education, energy, health, water, and telecommunications services. The international community can greatly help in this regard.

THE REALITY OF LABOUR MOBILITY AND DEVELOPMENT GAINS

In 2005 about 200 million people were living outside the country of their birth as compared to 175 million in 2000.Regional demographic projections in major developed and emerging markets indicate a reduction of the total labour force by 29 million by 2025, and by 244 million by 2050.This trend is in contrast to the projections for the South, where the labour force is seen to increase by about 784 million by 2025, and by 1.55 billion by 2050. The flow of temporary migrants to developed countries has increased recently. This is partly in response to policy changes in some of these countries, which have eased the requirements for admission for certain occupations. For instance, the United Kingdom has increased its work permit approvals from 85,600 in 2000 to 115,700 in 2001, including in education, health care and computer technology.

In Japan, the figures increased by 10 per cent for the period 2000-2001. Germany's 'green card' programme, instituted in August 2000, has tripled the employment of foreigners in the health care sector and has granted more than 13,000 green cards to foreign computer engineers. The European Union employs almost 500,000 seasonal agricultural workers from countries outside the EU. With demographic and economic imbalances between the North and the South persisting, migration and labour mobility is expected to rise continuously, aided also by a variety of economic , political/security, and social/cultural push-and-pull factors. Labour mobility is becoming a hallmark of the latest wave of globalization. The migration of labour covers the whole gamut of movements of people, regardless of purpose and duration of stay – temporary or permanent.

There are also increasing opportunities for labour integration and mobility in the context of trade and investment-led globalization as never before due to several factors. These push-and-pull factors, combined with global production, distribution chains, and technological developments have created a global pool of labour which is accessible to businesses and consumers on a cost-quality competitive basis, with beneficial trade and development results for all. The benefits and costs of migration apply to both sending and receiving countries. The challenge is to ensure that there is more 'gain' than 'drain' in the process of migration. There is scope for win-win gains for both developed and developing countries from liberalizing the movement of people.

Labour movements could be realized through unilateral, bilateral and multilateral schemes, most notably under Mode 4 of the GATS in the WTO. However, in overall terms, current liberalization in market access remains relatively limited. This is due to political and security pressures as well as perceived negative wage and employment effects. That there has been a growth in the demand for labour from developing countries at all skill levels is generally acknowledged. However, current international trade and economic governance structures and agreements do not provide favourable conditions for meeting this demand, and this situation is not resolved due to the lack of progress made in Mode 4 liberalization in the WTO. Developed countries have tended to resort to targeted recruitment and bilateral arrangements rather than multilateral accords to regulate liberalized sectors.

Most countries regulate foreign markets through unilateral regimes and schemes that are unpredictable, and in which the developing countries have no say. Even within the limited labour mobility visible today, there are neo-protectionist concerns revolving around the 'export of jobs'. Many factors underlie these concerns: the importation of goods and services from low-wage countries at various skill levels; investment by OECD transnational corporations in manufacturing and services in developing countries; new ways and areas of outsourcing and off-shoring to developing countries; and wage depression and social security erosion in the home countries, giving rise to concerns over 'social dumping'.

There are several ironies and issues of coherence that hamper labour market integration and the cross-border movement of labour from contributing fully to trade and development. These include the fact that cost-quality competitive labour is one of the strongest endowments of most developing countries. And yet, this comparative advantage is largely being left out of the ambit of trade liberalization, both at the multilateral and regional levels.

Market realities and actual labour flows on the ground far outstrip formal international agreements and frameworks for liberalization. Political populism against labour integration in policy discourse nationally and internationally often minimizes the recognition of considerable socio-economic, welfare, and efficiency gains – regardless of whether they are direct or indirect, short-, medium- or long-term – for all the economies concerned. Moreover, there is often a gap between corporate interests and labour interests when, in real terms, economy-wide interests and benefits point to the coherence of these interests, including in net job creation and savings, in the generation of new consumers and markets, and in the ensuing additional purchasing power in both the sending and receiving countries. While labour integration is an important component of goods, finance, entrepreneurship and information-related trade, the freer movement of labour is continually being resisted.

Thus, the impact of an inadequate understanding of the costs and benefits of labour integration and globalization for all countries – both developed and developing – may well mean that the most win-win and inclusive phase of globalization for development through labour market integration has been forestalled for some time to come. Significant global welfare gains are estimated from the liberalization of the temporary movement of natural persons to provide services abroad. One estimate finds a global welfare gain of US$150-200 billion from the relaxation of entry conditions for the temporary movement of workers or service providers at all skill levels, with greater gains expected from the liberalization of the movement of less-skilled workers.The estimated gains are greater than the total gains expected from all other areas of negotiations under the WTO Doha Round. An earlier study found that the elimination of global restrictions on labour mobility would bring worldwide efficiency gains ranging from 15 to 67 per cent of world GDP.

However, when only skilled labour is allowed to migrate, welfare gains are smaller since skilled labour is only a small proportion of the labour force in developing regions.Despite the existence of a real demand for foreign workers in developed and some developing countries, barriers to entry and stay continue to exist.

Barriers to service suppliers include quotas, economic needs, and labour market tests, lack of recognition for diplomas and competencies acquired outside of the destination country, language and residency or citizenship requirements, as well as complex and expensive visa and permit acquisition procedures. Also, once allowed in, foreign workers are prone to a host of challenges like abuse in employment contracts and conditions, including lower wages, under employment, absence of social security protection, and vulnerability to exploitation.

MAXIMIZING THE GAINS FROM LABOUR MOBILITY

Labour exporting countries can benefit from several socio-economic benefits including: the inflow of remittances and foreign exchange; the return of skilled workers increasing local human capital stock, and transferring skills and links to foreign networks ; and technology transfer, investments and venture capital contributed by citizens in the diaspora. However, a brain drain occurs when highly skilled workers are recruited, thus reducing the quality of essential services, especially in occupations such as health and education that are also much in demand at home. Remittances from migrants form a substantial proportion of foreign exchange earnings for sending countries, and are a stable source of finance for development.

In 2001, the remittances sent home to developing countries from workers living abroad were equal to 42 per cent of the total FDI inflows to those countries, and double that of ODA flows. Recorded remittance flows have doubled over the past five years, and stood at US$249 billion in 2005 - $180 billion of which is accounted for by developing countries. These figures could be twice as much if unrecorded flows are captured. Of the top thirty recipients of worker remittances, Remittances play a key role in the economies of some countries. For instance, for about 20 developing countries and countries with economies in transition, the share of remittances in the GDP range from 11 per cent to as high as 31 per cent. This share is estimated to be about 13 per cent for the Philippines with its 80 million inhabitants, Remittances provide direct income benefits to the recipients in source countries, thereby helping them ease household consumption expenditures, and encouraging more household investments in education, health, and entrepreneurship. World Bank household surveys indicate that remittances have led to declines in the poverty headcount ratio in some countries, such as declines of 11 per centage points in Uganda, 6 in Bangladesh and 5 in Ghana. With regard to their impact on poverty reduction, a World Bank analysis based on household surveys indicates that remittances have been associated with declines in poverty headcount ratio in some countries as follows: 11 per centage points in Uganda, 6 in Bangladesh, and 5 in Ghana.

Gender-specific data provide some examples suggesting a significant increase in the temporary cross-border employment of women. For example, in Sri Lanka, 2002 figures reveal that 70 per cent of the 970,000 Sri Lankan overseas contract workers were women, resulting in a positive impact on the economic and social empowerment of women. As remittances have grown in recent years efforts are being made to mobilize and channel these funds to maximize their impact on the development of the sending countries in general, and for the well-being of the migrants and their families in particular. For example, several countries have introduced remittance-backed bonds to raise funds at lower interest rates on the international bond market.

In India, the government floated specialized bonds for development purposes, raising close to US$10 billion.Efforts could also be made to tap the skills of diaspora populations and the networks they have established abroad. It has been documented that Chinese and Indian IT specialists have either invested back in the countries of their origin, or have gone home to set up their own business ventures, with some even setting up a commercial presence in other countries. Other government initiatives targeted at assisting the reintegration of returning migrant workers so as to stimulate investment include the provision of facilities for importing capital goods and raw materials, business counselling and training, access to loans, and encouraging entrepreneurship for development.

On the cost side of migration, there are several actions that sending governments could consider for mitigating the negative effects of the brain drain. These include: compulsory public service for critical occupations such in health care and education; paying back for their training and the costs of their education; devising some form of rotation schemes to ensure the availability of an ample supply of qualified nurses domestically; encouraging return migration by acknowledging their training abroad and giving them some visiting scholar positions ; encouraging them to serve as trainers; requiring those who leave to post a bond to ensure their return to the country; adopting a human resource programme which would encourage the retention of staff through salary increases and other incentives, and an expansion of domestic training capacity. Governments could pursue bilateral country-to-country or institution-to-institution initiatives in order to forge and maintain bilateral cooperation arrangements.

Some of these could include: facilitating the movement of workers; requiring some compensation from host countries for every foreign worker taken in; exploring the possibility of regularly inviting some of their own experts, practitioners and specialists to conduct training on advances in the relevant field on a short-term basis as compensation for the loss of skilled workers; and arranging special visa schemes which will ensure that the employment and stay of foreign workers remains temporary in the host country, thus ensuring their return migration.

FOSTERING AN ENABLING ENVIRONMENT: LEVERAGING HUMAN RESOURCES IN TRADE

A key challenge in the formulation of policies is to ensure that there is 'gain' rather than 'drain' from migration. Measures can be taken that encourage temporary migration, with better means to ensure the return of migrants and curb illegal migration; promote policies and management that achieve 'brain gain and brain circulation'; ensure the consideration of 'ethical approaches' in the codes of practice in recruitment; craft domestic measures that ensure the return of workers; and other measures that maximize the utilization of remittance receipts. In the long run, developing countries should not become over-reliant on labour export to the neglect of other productive and export sectors. All countries must generate adequate economic growth and employment opportunities to meet the needs of their peoples.

Those developing countries that have a critical mass of human resource pools should incorporate the labour export component into their trade and development strategies at the national level. Ensuring the sufficient availability of skills for the domestic economy while, at the same time, leveraging human resources in international trade requires a major and sustained investment in the development of skills through education, training, and institution building. To be truly competitive in global labour markets, the quality and quantity of labour needs to be skilled within certain parameters. Also, developing countries need to include an enhanced and predictable access to export markets for their skilled labour as a priority in their trade negotiations agenda. They also need to enter into the development-oriented return of their workers as well as a 'brain gain' agenda for their skilled personnel.

This should be done in cooperation with the destination country governments and diasporas. At the international level, the best approach towards the promotion of a more open and predictable yet rule-based market access to all developing countries wanting to export labour is for meaningful commitments to be made in GATS. Such commitments should cover service providers at all skill levels, from all developing countries, and be complemented with facilitation initiatives in terms of procedure as well as administrative and qualification requirements. Bilateral and regional trade agreements have also served as very useful instruments in this regard.

Even in terms of unilateral liberalization schemes, developed country governments could liberalize *de jure* to the extent of the de facto situation prevailing in these countries, thereby making it easier to reduce the gap between what they are willing to commit to multilaterally and the effective market access which they are granting. A number of countries have set examples of a 'market access plus' approach to support the temporary movement of developing country workers. These then return to their home country in the 'brain gain' mode. The GATS negotiations can be an important avenue to facilitate the temporary movement of natural persons supplying services at the multilateral level. However, no substantive progress in this area of the Doha negotiations has been achieved. This has been so due to difficulties in finding an agreed upon methodology at the multilateral level for managing the movement of services providers to ensure that such movement is temporary and not permanent.

Transparency of rules and regulations to facilitate access to export markets, as well as facilitating the accession of developing countries to existing mutual recognition arrangements have also been sought. Some countries have resorted to bilateral and regional arrangements in facilitating the movement of workers. However, these must remain supplementary to the multilateral means. For example, the US-Singapore free trade agreement provides Singapore with a quota for service providers under the H1B visa programme.There is a need to raise awareness – in both developed and developing countries – of the actual cost and benefits of labour integration, together with a sustained dialogue between labour and global enterprises.

This would include economy-wide analysis of labour requirements sectorally – both domestic and foreign as well as in the short to medium-term – to determine the best policy mixes on migration. International cooperation for a better-managed migration policy would certainly be useful. This would include devising rules and regulations on employment and labour, visas, human resource development, structural adjustment policies and social safety nets. Policies could be geared towards better managing these movements through the regulated entry of temporary workers rather than through outright prohibition which often leads to illegal migration and other attendant problems.

ENERGY, TRADE AND DEVELOPMENT

THE PROBLEMATIC OF RECENT HIGH ENERGY PRICES

The past few years have witnessed wide fluctuations in oil prices, which reached record levels in the summer of 2006 and continue to rise. Generated by the unexpected increase in world consumption and geopolitical upheavals, this price volatility has led to a global consensus on the need for a strategic and development-conducive energy portfolio. Higher oil prices affect the economies of developing countries at both the macro- and microlevels. An important part of the effects are transmitted through changes in the terms of trade. According to UNCTAD estimates, the terms of trade of countries in whose exports fuel products play a substantial role increased by 30 per cent during 2002-2004. All fuel-importing developing countries with manufacturing-dominated exports experienced deterioration in their terms of trade during this period.

The terms-of-trade losses for East and South Asian economies with predominantly manufacturing exports ranged from 8 per cent for the Taiwan Province of China to over 14 per cent for India in 2003 and 2004. The effects were less pronounced in economies such as Colombia, Costa Rica, Viet Nam and South Africa whose exports include significant shares of both manufactures and primary products. In the case of Malaysia and Mexico – for which fuels account for one tenth of exports – the positive contribution of higher fuel prices largely offset the negative impact of deterioration of terms of trade in manufactures on their overall terms of trade during the same period.

While the intensity of oil use has declined in developed countries since the first oil shock in 1973, developing countries have significantly increased the use of oil as a commercial fuel, especially with increasing industrialization. According to the IEA, Africa's oil use intensity in 2002 was 2.34 times higher than that of the OECD. Thus, the impact of high oil prices is felt strongly when oil prices rise. This is particularly so in net oil-importing countries with very low per capita income. On average, the impact is estimated to be a 1.5 per cent drop in GDP for a US$10 per barrel price increase, and a drop of up to 3 per cent for very poor countries. During the first two oil shocks of the 1970s and 1980s, inflation and unemployment increased dramatically in Africa and in LDCs.

During the present upturn in oil prices, the experience has – to some extent – been reversed by the application of prudent monetary and fiscal policies. However, there are signs that inflationary pressures are beginning to take hold. Companies are struggling with lower demand and higher energy costs as well as with the demand for higher wages. A number of countries, including Burundi, Seychelles, and the Democratic Republic of the Congo have already seen inflation climbing rapidly. The African Development Bank predicts that current high oil prices, if sustained, will translate into an average increase in inflation of 2.6 per centage points for oilimporting African countries in 2006. One other obvious effect of the oil price increase is higher oil import bills.

A survey of African importers by the African Development Bank shows that oil accounts for more than 15 per cent of total imports in 12 countries and for 10 to 15 per cent in 16 countries. Oil-exporting countries are experiencing different problems. Oil revenue has risen to unprecedented levels, generating massive windfall gains. In 2004 and 2005, the windfall gains that accrued to the Governments of nine oil-exporting countries in Africa exceeded US$15 billion. Research by the Overseas Development Institute estimates the surpluses generated by the eight largest oil exporters in Africa to be as high as US$22 billion in 2006, growing to US $35 billion in 2015 at current prices.In the oil-exporting countries of Africa and LDCs, the revenue flow resulting from high oil prices has caused real exchange rates to appreciate.

This may weaken the competitiveness of a country's other exports and cause its traditional export sector to shrink. The effect, described as the 'Dutch Disease', requires remedies to reduce excess liquidity such as by investing overseas revenues that are surplus to the absorptive capacity of the economy. The issue of how to invest the surplus is also receiving growing attention. While prudence would dictate that the excess funds should be invested conservatively so as to provide income for future generations, it could be argued that it is possible to invest in development without straining the absorptive capacity of the surplus country – for instance, by placing the surplus in a fund for regional development. Discussions about possible arrangements are under way in African institutions such as the African Development Bank.

Outside the oil sector itself, a rise in oil prices has similar implications at the micro-level in both oil-importing and oil-exporting countries. Rising prices reduce the real disposable income of households outside the oil sector, particularly of urban households. They also raise production costs in most sectors, including both industry and agriculture, and may damage competitiveness. Moreover, oil accounts for virtually all the fuel used in the transportation sector in the developing countries of Africa and other LDCs. Thus, understandably, the impact of rising prices on these economics is great. Without the shield of price controls, increased transportation costs resulting from high oil prices have a direct impact on the movement of goods. For instance, Ethiopia has made progress in increasing the rate of economic growth.

However, current high oil prices have pushed up transportation costs, thus raising production costs. This affects the competitiveness of the country's major export, coffee. Furthermore, a shortage of truck fuel is hampering drought relief in the south of the country. As is evident in the case of coffee, the impact on export-oriented agriculture can be particularly severe. Agriculture employs the majority of the population in most African countries, and remains of great importance both for food security as well as foreign exchange earnings.

However, farmers are now faced with increasing costs of fuel needed to operate farm equipment and irrigation systems. Also, higher costs of energy-intensive supplies lead to the diminishing use of these supplies and, thus results in lower productivity. Moreover, rising oil prices also affect Government finances. Often, poverty reduction programmes in oil-importing countries get affected because funds are reallocated to cover the rising costs of fuel. Many countries have attempted to alleviate the effect of energy prices on poverty with the help of subsidies. While subsidies may help to mitigate the immediate impact of oil price increases, they may not be the most appropriate instruments to deal with high oil prices in the longer term. The burden of subsidies on government budgets may be unsustainable for most countries.

Moreover, subsidies may also delay the necessary adjustments in consumer behaviour and demand structure. Indeed, in some countries, there appears to be considerable scope for the reduction of energy costs through market liberalization . However, the removal of subsidies has often caused public unrest in several developing countries. In 2005, a decision to increase fuel prices by 30 per cent in Indonesia was met with widespread protests. In 2005, several cities in Nigeria were paralysed by strikes protesting against fuel price increases under a policy of deregulating the downstream sector.

DEALING WITH OIL PRICE RISE

One consequence of the increase in oil prices is that the Governments of oil-importing countries have an incentive to make their domestic oil markets more efficient. Since the 1980s, many developing countries have opened their energy markets to competition. However, competition in importation is difficult to achieve owing to the limited size of the markets and deficiencies in infrastructure, such as poor port facilities. Thus, the refining and distribution of oil products tend to be natural monopolies that have to be regulated. However, with regard to oil procurement, there appears to be room for increased cooperation between developing countries, including on tendering procedures. Financing oil imports is another area where gains could be made, particularly by using structured financing techniques more intensively. All strategies which might be adopted by oil-importing countries to deal with oil price increases would entail some sacrifices.

The strategies differ mainly in the timing of the sacrifices. Cutbacks in expenditure are one way of absorbing the consequences immediately. If the consequences can be postponed and spread over a longer period, their impact on development may be less pronounced. Governments can avoid the impact of oil price increases by hedging oil imports through the purchase of derivatives such as options, futures, and swaps. No doubt this would have to be done much in advance of the price increase. Governments may also use the compensatory financial mechanisms provided by international financial institutions, even though they would usually be subject to conditionalities. Existing multilateral schemes for compensatory financing do not fully meet the needs of developing countries – they are often not large enough in proportion to the shocks, and are often provided too late. Indeed, there is much scope for strengthening South-South and regional cooperation in this area. Measures to enhance efficient use of energy are also essential. With regard to oil-exporting countries, strategies focus on ways of avoiding the expansion of export revenues, which leads to excess liquidity and causes the 'Dutch Disease'. Such strategies usually have two elements. The first is a decision or rule that attempts to put a brake on government spending. This is usually done by estimating a rate of growth of potential output, and avoiding expenditure increases that are not compatible with this estimate. The second uses the method of both sterilizing revenues that are surplus to current requirements as well as ensuring that such revenues are put to good use. The use may vary.

However, the focus is either on preserving inter-generational equity by reserving funds for a future date , or on smoothing out cyclical economic fluctuations by releasing funds when oil prices fall as also when other indicators point to the economy needing an infusion of funds. The issue of where funds should be parked in the interim has attracted increasing attention recently.All this has resulted in the balance of power shifting in favour of national oil and gas companies . Many of them – especially those from resource-rich states that have profited from soaring prices for oil and gas – may be taking a more prominent role on the global markets, perhaps competing more strongly with the major international oil companies.

Moreover, high oil prices and the increasing clout of state-owned/ controlled companies have transformed the mergers and acquisitions market. Indeed, the energy industry has undergone the biggest merger boom since the wave of consolidation among major oil companies at the end of the 1990s. In 2006, the total value of deals involving energy companies was US$566 billion, up from US$372 billion in 2005. In 2007 the value of deals is set to be higher still: announcements for 2007 already nearly match the 2005 total at US$356 billion. NOCs spent $57 billion on acquisitions last year, accounting for a third of the value of all transactions in oil and gas exploration and production worldwide. Much of the recent activity has been domestic, such as the acquisitions of Rosneft and Gazprom, as well as the asset deal between China's Sinopec and China Petrochemical, both stateowned.

However, a rising number of the deals are international, such as China's CNOOC which paid US$2.7 billion to South Atlantic Petroleum for a 45 per cent stake in the Akpo field in Nigeria, and India's ONGC which purchased the Colombian assets of Omimex for US$850 million. While China and India are making deals overseas to secure resources, companies from other resource-rich states are taking advantage of ample liquidity to expand overseas. Perhaps the most momentous development is that NOCs from resource-rich countries are taking their interest in the 'security of demand' to its logical conclusion by trying to buy consumer-focused companies in destination countries.

Because natural gas is overtaking coal to become the second most important global energy source after oil, international trade in natural gas is predicted to evolve progressively towards worldwide integration. The fact that the traditional business model in the gas industry is changing is evident in the flexibility of LNG ships increasingly allowing sellers to bring gas to markets with the highest value.

The rapidly growing LNG market-share already transfers price signals among markets as distant as Japan, Spain and the United States. With the Atlantic LNG market set to equal the Pacific market by 2010, a definite trend towards the establishment of a global gas market is becoming evident. The tremendous growth in LNG trade as well as the increasing importance of gas in the current and future world energy mix are attracting more and more attention to the evolution of the LNG markets and their implications for all market players.

ENERGY SECURITY IN THE GLOBAL MARKET CONTEXT

The concept of 'energy security', which first emerged in the 1970s, has broadened and assumed the utmost importance. Consuming countries focus on the 'security of supply' – *i.e.* the reliability and availability of energy at reasonable prices. Exporting countries, on the other hand, are more concerned about the 'security of demand' – *i.e.* a sufficient access to markets and consumers that will justify future investment. The Russian Federation placed the theme of 'energy security' as the central issue during its G8 presidency. A further examination of the issue reveals that the differences are even sharper. For the Russian Federation today, energy security is about the state retaking control of the 'commanding heights' of the energy industry and extending that control downstream *i.e.* over the critical export pipelines that provide a substantial part of government revenues. In contrast, Europe's concerns centre not so much on oil but on natural gas, as well as on the debate about its critical dependence on gas imports.

For other countries, the question is quite different: how can they compensate for the deficit in domestic energy resources? Countries like China and India need to make sure that the energy problem does not hold back the economic growth they need for development, which could result in social turbulence. In the United States, energy security has a double focus: one is to offset any possible disruptions in supply; and the other is to achieve the goal of 'energy independence,' first articulated as early as in the 1970s – although, in the years since, the United States has moved from importing a third of its oil to as much as 60 per cent today. In recent statements, OPEC ministers have indicated that, without the guarantee of a market in the future, they may slow down investment in production capacity. OPEC members have expressed concern that increased efficiency, alternative fuels, higher taxes on oil, and subsidies for alternatives to oil will diminish and, perhaps, even reverse the growth in petroleum demand. Meanwhile, cooperation between countries that produce and export energy resources, particularly natural gas, is on the increase. There are discussions about bilateral ventures in natural gas, of how to coordinate efforts in third countries, and how to work together on some deposits in the countries of both parties. Talks of plurilateral cooperation have resurfaced in the Gas Exporting Countries Forum and in the Shanghai Cooperation Organization. Indeed, while gas producing countries consider how they should coordinate their actions, especially with regard to the pricing of gas and the establishment of the main gas routes, fears have been expressed by some that such cooperation constitutes the first steps towards the establishment of a 'GASPEC'.

Any 'solution' of the issue of international energy security that includes only a part of the energy chain will remain a partial solution. This applies to both upstream and downstream links in the chain. It may be noted in this connection that, when the G8 leaders vowed 'to reduce barriers to energy investment and trade,' they also added that: 'It is especially important that companies from energy producing and consuming countries can invest in and acquire upstream and downstream assets internationally in a mutually beneficial way and respecting competition rules.'

Increasing oil price volatility and the growing seriousness of global warming have driven countries and institutions to diversify by exploring alternative energy sources, especially renewable and climate-friendly ones. In connection with climate change concerns, it is clear that carbon emissions will continue to rise and the sustainability of the current energy system will increasingly be questioned. If current government policies do not change, CO2 emissions will increase by 55 per cent between 2004 and 2030.This provides an incentive for the consideration of alternative energy sources that promote both climate change mitigation as well as energy security and enhanced energy efficiency. Policy intervention will be needed to address the issues of energy security as well as climate change concerns in such a way as to achieve both reduced energy security risks and deeper cuts in greenhouse gas emissions.

FOSTERING AN ENABLING ENVIRONMENT: REALIZING TRADE GAINS FROM THE ENERGY SECTOR

The new energy paradigm has brought into focus the 'international rules of the game' that apply to the energy sector, how they are implemented and how they can be strengthened. Oil and gas industries have traditionally been dominated by state-owned, vertically integrated utilities engaged in the production, transport and distribution of energy products. This has left little margin for trade and competition in energy services. Energy goods have been largely exempted from trade rules, and are based on GATT general exceptions for national security and the conservation of exhaustible natural resources. These exceptions have promoted the perception that, in general, international trade in oil is governed by its own distinctive rules. This perception was strengthened by the fact that the main oil and gas producers and exporters were outside of the WTO. Indeed, some still are, most notably Algeria, Islamic Republic of Iran and the Russian Federation. At the same time, energy trade and investment have been subject to the rules of the Energy Charter Treaty, which has emerged as the international legal framework for the energy sector.

The Energy Charter provisions on trade are drawn from those of the WTO, in the most part by direct reference to the WTO rules. The Charter Treaty addresses specific challenges for the energy sector that are not covered by the WTO, in particular the issue of investment protection and the specific characteristics of energy transit through electricity grids and pipelines. Some provisions in the Energy Charter have been subject to much criticism. It has been suggested that: they make the control of the transport network – considered a security issue – more difficult; the dispute settlement mechanism foreseen for transit disputes gives too much power to the conciliator; and the investment provisions should not apply exclusively to the post-investment phase.

The provisions envisaged on access to technologies as well as on the sovereign rights of a State over its national resources are also considered by some to be insufficient. With the accession to the WTO of Mexico , Venezuela , Oman , Qatar , Saudi Arabia , as well as the ongoing accession process of the Russian Federation, attempts have been made to put energy on its agenda. A range of energy-related issues were raised in the accession negotiations, as well as during the Uruguay Round. These included the issue of dual pricing and, more specifically, the problems that arise in finding acceptable mechanisms to keep domestic prices lower than world prices. In 2002, Saudi Arabia requested that energy taxation, subsidies and incentives be included in the negotiations. Their concern was that the energy and environmental policies of developed countries – which include energy and environmental taxes and subsidies – may have negative economic implications for developing countries. Moreover, countries pursuing environmental objectives may contravene their WTO obligations in a number of areas, while others may seek to protect their domestic interests under the guise of environmental protection.

Qatar has recently been promoting natural gas as the economic and environmental fuel of choice in the WTO Committee on Trade and Environment. It has also argued for the liberalization of trade on goods, equipment and technologies used in conjunction with natural gas. In 2006, the EU Trade Commissioner mooted the idea of a new WTO round of negotiations that would address the energy sector, and seek to treat oil and gas in the same way as other traded goods.This could potentially require oil and gas producers to liberalize distribution networks, thus opening up access to gas pipelines, currently under monopoly control. Energy-importing developed countries would like to eliminate barriers to trade in energy as increasing global demand for oil and gas drives up prices. If producers do not support liberalization, it is suggested that they be offered in exchange additional investment, as well as more security for their energy exports.

In a related development in the WTO services negotiations in February 2006, a group of energy-importing nations and a few major energy exporters – including Canada, Saudi Arabia, the US, Australia and the EU – tabled a 'collective request' to a group of developing countries – including Brazil, China, Colombia, Ecuador, Egypt, India, Kuwait, Nigeria, Qatar, and the United Arab Emirates—asking them to open up their markets to freer trade in energy services. The proposal covered sectors that encompass the core activities of oil and gas production, processing and distribution. However, these are limited in scope when compared to what the EU has proposed. Subsidies for oil, coal, gas and nuclear power are often cited as a very significant barrier to renewable energy.

As a general matter, it is open to question whether WTO dispute settlement proceedings would be a realistic option to challenge such subsidies: Governments might be reluctant to deploy legal arguments that could result in challenges to their own support programmes.On the other hand, to break out of the pattern of just a handful of countries participating substantially in renewable energy deployment, it may be necessary to shift away from subsidies and preferential public procurement in the renewable energy sector itself. It is accordingly important to examine whether and to what extent trade regimes could be used to challenge or discipline policies that disadvantage renewable energy and, conversely, whether and to what extent Government policies to promote renewable energy might be challenged as non-tariff measures.

TRADE, ENVIRONMENT AND SUSTAINABLE DEVELOPMENT

Globalization has led to increased public awareness of the environmental effects of trade growth and the important developmental implications of issues in the interface between trade and environment. There is a general recognition that increased trade flows that result from globalization have to be accompanied by environmental sustainability and poverty reduction to truly achieve sustainable development. Environmental impact is perceived as an increasingly important factor of production that directly bears on production costs, competitiveness and opportunities in international trade.

If properly implemented, trade liberalization can lead developing countries to access new environmentally sound technologies, goods, services, and production methods. These can facilitate transition to environmentally sustainable production and consumption patterns and augment their international competitiveness. For the first time in the history of the GATT/

WTO, trade and environment issues have become a negotiating subject of global liberalization. Hence the environmental effects of enhanced trade are being much emphasized, and are becoming more and more the centre of public discussion. Issues at the intersection of trade liberalization, environmental protection and economic development have become more closely integrated with globalization. These are climate change and biodiversity; new environmental, health, and food-safety requirements; and access to environmental goods, services and technologies, and related sustainable production methods.

They will pose formidable challenges for the international community in the years to come as any attempt to reduce poverty will have to take the natural environment into consideration.It is the poor who are the most dependent upon the natural environment to meet their daily food, health, livelihood, and shelter needs. Thus the effects of environmental degradation are felt most immediately and keenly by the poor.

TRADE, CLIMATE CHANGE AND SUSTAINABLE DEVELOPMENT

The international community has now reached a consensus regarding the fact that the increasing emissions of greenhouse gases such as carbon dioxide and methane – most of which are linked to the human use of fossil fuels – are causing changes in global climate systems. Climate change currently poses one of the greatest risks to environmental, social and economic development globally.

Private and public responses to the climate crisis are bringing significant changes in several economic sectors, especially related to energy. This section highlights the broad range of relationships among climate change, trade and development: how trade policy might impact on climate change through economic transformation; how significant competitiveness and market access concerns may be affected; how climate change may physically impact economic structures, in particular in agriculture and services, as well as infrastructure; and how trade rules interact with measures for climate change mitigation.

The UN Development Programme's Human Development Report 2007/2008 focuses on potentially dramatic impacts of climate change upon agricultural production and food security, water stress and insecurity, rising sea levels and flooding, ecosystems and biodiversity, and human health.The Inter-governmental Panel on Climate Change outlines mitigation options for the following sectors: energy supply, transport, buildings, industry, and agriculture, forestry, and waste - reflecting the extent to which climate measures are affecting nearly every aspect of the economy.The new sense of urgency behind efforts to curb global warming may provide the stimulus for a more proactive approach to integrating trade policy within sustainable development strategies. Global concerns on the impact of climate change have emerged as a key development theme with globalization.

Impacts of Trade and Investment Upon Climate Change

International trade may impact climate change in a multi-faceted way through its scale effects, resulting in increased economic activity; composition effect leading to changes in the structure or patterns of economic activity; boost and changes in technology; and direct GHG emission effects, *inter alia*, from increased maritime, truck and air transport. The scale effect of trade will generally have a negative climate change impact, because higher production of most goods and services will generate more GHG emissions.

The composition effect of trade liberalization tends to shift production to goods and services in which countries have a comparative or absolute competitive advantage. Depending on national policies, this might lead to a more or less carbon-efficient economy. The overall outcome, however, could be a global reduction of GHG emissions, provided there is internalization of the environmental costs of GHG emissions. The technological effect of enhanced trade and investment flows can make a significant contribution to material and energy efficiency, and thus to climate change mitigation.

Conversely, more trade and investment generally lead to directly higher GHG emissions from increased maritime, truck and air transport, in addition to higher electricity consumption by global computer and telecommunications networks.The right mix of specific trade and investment policy measures can optimize multi-faceted impact of trade and investment liberalization on climate change. In this regard, tariff liberalization for renewable and clean conventional energy and related equipment, as well as energy-efficient goods or inputs for energy- and carbon-efficient production processes is one promising cluster of trade policy tools. Another is the reduction or removal of subsidies for conventional energy sources and energyintensive sectors.

A third cluster is the use of technical requirements and standards to encourage carbon-efficient modes of production and consumption. Fourthly, government procurement can be used to encourage consumption and investment in low-carbon goods and technologies. Last but not least, investment policies can be geared to gradually redirect investment into carbon-efficient sectors and simultaneously enhance carbon efficiency in energy-intensive industries. This implies greater opportunities for energy-efficient and carbon-neutral industries and stimulating technological innovation. Also, changes in the energy mix will often support local energy and development needs more effectively than fossil fuel imports. The Clean Development Mechanism of the Kyoto Protocol offers significant opportunities for attracting and directing investment into carbon-efficient or carbonneutral areas, including changes in the energy mix.

In order to restructure markets towards carbon neutrality, consumers, corporations, and governments need to consider certain increased costs as medium to long-term investments. Businesses directly involved in GHG-intensive activity need to be supported to make the necessary transition to minimize dislocation in the interest of broader societal benefits. Developing countries that invest private capital and direct their public policies towards climate-friendly products will stimulate domestic innovation, reap the advantages of technological "leapfrogging", and are likely to increase their export potential.

Developing private and public sector strategies with climate change in mind also often offers local environmental protection and other benefits as well. Countries that fail to do so risk consolidation in dirty industries on the lower end of the value chain, and damage the environment.

Possible Tensions between Trade Law and Attempts to Address Climate Change

Although the UN Framework Convention on Climate Change and the Kyoto Protocol have no specific trade obligations, they have significant trade implications as they aim to modify the carbon impacts of the ways in which goods and services are produced and consumed. The interface between trade rules and climate change concerns the WTO disciplines on tariffs, technical barriers to trade, government procurement, subsidies, investment policies, and border tax adjustment. The growing importance of national measures to address climate change, the UNFCCC as an element of international economic governance, and climate change as a factor in international commerce will heighten the importance of the interface between trade and environment policy but does not pose an inherent conflict. Rather, it does necessitate enhanced coordination among policymakers.

The principle of differentiated level of obligations among the parties according to their different stages of development – adopted in Agenda 21 in 1992 – is the basis of the UNFCC and the Kyoto Protocol. There are prospects for evolving post-Kyoto commitments frameworks with a potential for further engagement by some developing countries. The United Nations Conference on Climate Change in Bali resulted in the adoption of the Bali roadmap. The Bali roadmap charts the course for a new negotiating process to be concluded by 2009. This will ultimately lead to a post-2012 international agreement on climate change. There is also increasing interest in ensuring access to low-carbon technologies and to additional financial resources for implementing climate change policy.

Competitiveness and Market Access Concerns

The competitiveness concern arises regarding two issues. On the one hand, the likelihood that a country that takes stronger climate change mitigation measures might put its companies or industries at a disadvantage relative to foreign competitors in countries that do not adopt similarly strong measures. This may lead to a "carbon leakage" problem, where strong mitigation measures may encourage companies to relocate to other countries.

On the other hand, there is concern that even among countries taking similarly strong climate change mitigation measures, there is unfair competition due to differentiated employment of such measures. The World Bank finds that "there is some evidence – although it is not very pronounced – of leakage of carbon/energy-intensive industries to developing economies that could be attributed to more stringent climate change policies and energy efficiency standards."Sectoral characteristics also matter, *i.e.,* how energy intensive is the economy and to what extent companies and the sector are in a position to pass on cost increases to customers.

Developing countries face a significant challenge due to their industrial structure and its carbon intensity. Investment in energy-intensive industries in developing countries may expand, resulting from domestic needs for industrialization, energy security, physical-infrastructural development, but also redeployment of carbon-intensive industries from developed to developing countries.

For example, "environmentally-sensitive industries" represent a growing share of exports for several Latin American countries.Within these sectors, developing countries often concentrate on the bulk market segment where higher carbon/energy prices are difficult to pass onto consumers. A potentially significant problem for developing countries is the competitiveness and market access impact of technical measures to trade, caused by requirements on energy efficiency product and process standards or related eco-labelling programmes. In its recent study, based on a simple two- country trade model, the World Bank singles out energy-efficiency standards as likely to have the most significant trade impact of all trade policy tools for climate-change mitigation.

Impact of Climate Change on Trade and Investment

Climate change will have significant implications on trade flows arising from its impact on agriculture, forestry, trade-related physical infrastructure, and services such as tourism. Weather extremes and related natural disasters can disrupt specific sectors, notably agriculture, and negatively impact infrastructure, in particular along coast lines. Tourism is likely to be impacted by weather conditions and fundamental ecological changes.

Rising temperatures are also likely to modify the competitive advantage in agriculture based on ecological factors. The Intergovernmental Panel on Climate Change forecasts imply gradual but colossal shifts in production patterns, cultivated crops and yields, the spread of pests and diseases, as well as accelerated desertification and droughts. The introduction of climate response measures through the emerging carbon market and the Kyoto Protocol will have trade and development implications as they are introduced in several sectors of the economy, such as transportation, energy use, electricity generation, agriculture and forestry. Many developing countries, in particular the small and vulnerable ones, will be particularly hard hit by these climate change impacts. For example, sea-level rise is causing enhanced soil erosion, loss of productive land, increased risk of storm surges, reduced resilience of coastal ecosystems, and raising attendant costs of responding to and adapting to these shocks.

Countries in temperate zones are likely to be far less affected or may even benefits from a longer vegetation period, more cultivable crops and higher yields. As a result, international trade patters in agriculture will change over time because of different supply and demand patterns, as well as yields.

BIODIVERSITY, TRADITIONAL KNOWLEDGE AND TRADE

The international approach to the protection of biodiversity continues to focus on innovative ways to promote sustainable use, bringing economic, social and environmental benefits to nations and their people. Biodiversity-rich countries are taking advantage of new trade and investment opportunities for biodiversity products and services in the emerging market, with increasing participation of the local private sector.

UNCTAD's BioTrade Initiative has estimated that the world market for natural ingredients used in the cosmetic and pharmaceutical sectors amounts to over US$1 billion annually. Greater scientific certainty, public awareness, growing trade and investment activity levels, as well as the availability of statistical data on environmental and economic losses associated with certain patterns of development, have all led to more discussions and the promotion of more pragmatic policy options aimed at sustainable development. Harnessing the knowledge-for-development focus will require assisting developing countries to benefit from their own resources: their rich traditional knowledge, innovations and practices.

TK is the main asset of the poor who use it to derive goods and services from their natural environment. Yet TK is being lost at alarming rates worldwide, as globalization and environmental degradation are accelerating the break-up of traditional communities and endangering livelihoods. There are also concerns that TK is being inappropriately exploited and patented by third parties without the consent of the original holders of that TK, and without the fair sharing of resulting benefits.

There is need for concerted action at the national, regional, and international levels to redress this. A key example is organic agriculture, whose production systems are built on a synthesis of local TK and the results of modern research. In this way, producers who use local varieties adapted to local conditions can achieve higher incomes and greater security than would be the case with conventional agriculture. Further, the protection of TK as intellectual property is an important means of harnessing the potential benefits of TK for trade and development gains by the owners themselves.

NEW ENVIRONMENTAL, HEALTH AND FOOD SAFETY REQUIREMENTS AND MARKET ACCESS

- An important trend at the trade-environment-development interface is the growing impact of new environmental, health and food-safety requirements on the access of developing country products to key export markets. The proliferation of private voluntary standards on EHFSRs and sustainablility standards in international trade, and their impact on market access and national development of developing countries is a major concern. In contrast to the proliferating standards, there is a dearth of empirical knowledge both about their impact as well as about successful adjustment strategies to these standards taking into account national developmental priorities. Four developments are particularly challenging:New EHFSRs are becoming more stringent, frequent, complex and multidimensional. This constitutes both serious challenges as well as opportunities for export competitiveness, sustainable production, and consumption methods at the national level.
- There is a growing trend towards the 'privatization' of many EHFSRs, with voluntary requirements imposed by the private sector co-existing and inter-acting with mandatory governmental requirements. Governments set product characteristics, product-related processes, and production methods ; the private sector and NGOs follow by imposing specific non-product-related PPMs to meet the product characteristics. As it is open to question whether or not private standards fall under the WTO disciplines, they pose serious challenges in terms of justifiability, transparency, discrimination and equivalence.
- Besides their function of providing technical quality-assurance, private standards often play a governance role in global supply chains, leading to significant dependencies and the shifting of costs and risks away from buyers, often to the disadvantage of producers/ exporters in developing countries.

The new bread of private voluntary standards, but also some sustainability standards of NGOs, poses particular challenges for small farmers in developing countries. It is not so much the lack of quality or productivity of small growers, but the enhanced management and coordination costs in implementing and complying with PVS that are causing very high recurrent adjustment costs, on average about 20 per cent of turnover or up to 50 per cent of total income of small farmers, often causing massive drop-outs of small producers from PVS compliance schemes. According to a recent study on horticultural exports from Ghana, Kenya, United Republic of Tanzania,

Uganda and Zambia to the United Kingdom, over 50 per cent of small producers participating in PVS compliance schemes have dropped out of these schemes between March 2005 and September 2006. The mushrooming of new EHFSRs has to be dealt with in a proactive and coordinated way. This requires the development of national adjustment strategies that minimize the costs and maximize the benefits of the new requirements. It also requires actions to seize production and export opportunities including through 'front-of-pipe' solutions on production processes, materials for environmentally friendly goods and services.

These would include organic agriculture products, other biodegradable products, natural colorants and flavours. Of particular importance is conceptual clarity on the design of national programmes on Good Agricultural Practices that in a modular way allowing producers to meet national and regional requirements with buyer recognition in lucrative overseas export markets. In these national GAP programmes, governments need to pay special attention to support the participation of small producers through supportive/ flanking measures, which lower adjustment costs, provide bridging funding, support the creation or continuation of stable and wellmanaged groups of small producers, and provide improved extension and training services.

DEVELOPING ENVIRONMENTALLY PREFERABLE PRODUCTS, SERVICES AND PRODUCTION METHOD

International public attention on the problems caused by climate change, material and pollution intensity of economic growth and unsustainable life styles as well as the pressure from new EHFSRs have heightened the interest in environmentally preferable products, services and production methods. These are the strategic markets of the future. Developing countries need to identify market niches and the opportunities open to them as well as the policy initiatives needing to be launched in time to turn these opportunities into reality. The growing consumer demand for environmentally preferable products presents new opportunities for those producers and countries that can produce them in more energy-efficient and environmentally friendly ways, especially if they can effectively communicate this to consumers.

A prime example of this is the rapid expansion of organic agriculture markets: global growth rates have been over 12 per cent over the past decades, and compare favourably with the overall agriculture market growth of only 2-4 per cent. In addition to the economic advantages accruing from premium prices and expanding sales, organic agriculture offers developing country producers an array of environmental, health, social, cultural, and food security benefits . Other examples of EPPs include energy-efficient electronic goods and certified wood products. Yet even here, differing standards can become obstacles to trade. Thus, further harmonization and equivalency are needed to fully reap the gains in trade and sustainable development.

INTERNATIONAL TRADE AGREEMENTS FOR MANAGING THE TRADE AND ENVIRONMENT INTERFACE

In the Doha Round, and for the first time in the WTO history, trade and environment has become a negotiating subject. The main challenge to the negotiations provided for in paragraph 31 of the Doha Ministerial Declaration on environmental goods and services is to make three main objectives – environmental sustainability, development and trade liberalization – converge in a mutually supportive way. The current positions span a wide range of approaches. On the supply side, there is the very pragmatic approach of putting forward self-defined lists of environmental goods. On the demand side, there is the environmental project approach, which seeks to strengthen the hands of the individual countries reflecting their divergent environmental situations and developmental priorities. Still other approaches seek to bridge both sides in the negotiations.

Irrespective of which negotiating approach prevails, it will have far reaching implications in the longer term. The risk lies in the absence of criteria, which may lead to a precedent, an inadequate introduction of this subject matter in trade liberalization rounds, with consequences for the following rounds and tendency to deal with the issue on the basis of negotiating power. Climate change policy highlights the growing interface between energy and environmental goods and services. Goods, equipment and technologies used in conjunction with renewable energy sources - renewables - are one case in point. The strength of the international commitment on climate change may play a catalytic role and influence the modalities for cooperation, including in the WTO, be it as a separate "WTO climate initiative" or in the context of the negotiations conducted under the mandate provided for in paragraph 31 of the Doha Ministerial Declaration regarding the reduction or, as appropriate, elimination of tariff and non-tariff barriers to environmental goods and services..

As climate change does not form part of the negotiating history in the Doha Round, there is a need to carefully manage the interplay between the on-going work and any new initiatives. There is a growing consensus, however, that the negotiations on environmental goods and services should include renewables, and possibly technologies for cleaner utilization of conventional energy sources such as natural gas-driven turbines, low-emission coal combustion, and carbon capture and storage. They could also include climate positive goods such as biofuels and energy-efficient construction materials and appliances or even goods derived from more GHG-efficient processes and production methods. The expansion of product coverage in the negotiations to include these goods is not without problems. While the existing HS can capture most renewables, the ubiquitous nature of some goods and their component parts means that the dual use problem will remain over and above what could be sorted out by a greater specificity in the tariff codes.

As for GHG-efficient goods or goods produced in a GHG-efficient way, there are simply no HS codes to match, not to mention that climate or energy efficiency is a moving target. The inclusion of goods derived from GHG-efficient processes and production methods is especially problematic as it may dramatically increase the scope for protectionist measures.

The relative importance of tariffs and non-tariff barriers is another sticky point. Lowering the tariff reductions may well be a simpler task, but NTBs are considerably more important for the liberalization to be commercially meaningful. Another important issue is that climate positive technologies and the export of related goods tend to be concentrated in developed countries. It is important to balance market opportunities brought about by climate positive technologies and access to these technologies by developing countries.

"Technology will play an essential role in our collective response to climate change".The ultimate goal is to capture the "public goods" nature of innovation and international trade. More than 50 countries with 80 per cent of the world's population now have measures in place, both mandatory and voluntary, for energy efficiency. And yet there is a significant gap between expectations and actual impacts. At the same time, energy efficiency standards affect trade flows and market access. As the marketplace for energy and environmental goods and services becomes increasingly global, so too is the need to ensure cooperation in the development of these standards. Financial flows and official development assistance targeting climate positive technologies may play a catalytic role in the development of renewables in developing countries through increased trade, investment and technology transfer.

Some developed countries are involved in a number of projects in developing countries. The international consensus on climate change provides an important incentive framework for various types of cooperation arrangements. Countries increasingly use bilateral and regional trade agreements to manage the trade and environment interface. A variety of instruments has been deployed, ranging from environmental chapters and side agreements to consultation, cooperation, and exception clauses. Among the OECD members, Canada, EU, New Zealand and the USA have included the most comprehensive environmental provisions in recent RTAs. The 'Global Europe' communication of November 2006 announced a set of new bilateral negotiations by the EU.

Environmental concerns have a very important role in these negotiations, which will be seeking substantial commitments from both sides, with possible market access and development assistance incentives. Among non-OECD countries, Chile's efforts to include environmental provisions in its trade agreements are particularly noteworthy. Few trade agreements among developing countries include environmental provisions like ASEAN and MERCOSUR.

FOSTERING AN ENABLING ENVIRONMENT: PROMOTING TRADE AND ENVIRONMENTAL SUSTAINABILITY

The interface of trade-environment-development with globalizations necessitates a transition to environmentally sustainable production and consumption patterns as well as international competitiveness. Trade policies and trade liberalization should facilitate access to new environmentally sound technologies, goods, services, and production methods. In meeting this challenge, dealing with climate change has major trade and development implications that the world as whole has to address. Three sets of policies are accordingly being developed at the international level to ensure a coherent approach that will minimize the detrimental effects and maximize possible opportunities. One set of policies concern 'Cap-and-Trade' policies on carbon pricing, taxation, emissions trading, and regulation.

These policies will ensure that people face the full socio-economic costs of their actions. A second set of policies promotes home-grown technological solutions and incentives that will drive the development and deployment of a wide range of low-carbon and high-efficiency products and services. A third set of policy measures will aim to remove barriers to energy efficiency, and to inform, educate and persuade individuals on what they can do to respond to climate change in each sector of the economy. Effective action to counter climate change impact requires a global policy response. These typically involves: mitigation, or the reduction of greenhouse gas emissions; and adaptation, or by 'climate proofing' economies.

If the future global climate regime is going to contain emission reduction commitments involving some developing countries, developed countries should assist them in capacity-building, technology transfer, and adaptation. In parallel, the impact of efforts made towards reducing emissions in those developing countries which are highly dependent on the production/export of fossil fuels should also be examined. Special support should be provided to them. The long-term nature of the climate change problem makes technological change a central issue in policy considerations. Specific financing mechanisms should be made available to them to help in the process of developing and adopting new energy technologies. Renewable energy sources comprise an important means to reducing climate change.

Developing countries have two advantages contributing to the competitiveness of their renewable energy sources. They tend to have strong renewable energy resources and a lower costs profile for the production of equipment, components, and biofuels . These two factors point to the scope for trade and cooperation in renewable energy. However there are major considerations that still have to be addressed. These include tariff barriers affecting trade in renewable energy, market deployment policies for renewable energy and other carbon-reducing energy technologies. Financial flows and official development assistance targeting climate positive technologies may play a catalytic role in the development of renewable energy sources in developing countries through increased trade, investment and technology transfer. Some developed countries are involved in a number of projects in developing countries.

The Kyoto Protocol provides an important incentive framework for various types of cooperation arrangements. Addressing new EHFSRs is another emergent issue on the international agenda in the area of trade and environment. The concern is how to design appropriate proactive adjustment strategies to address new EHFSRs. This requires conceptual clarity, a good understanding of the role of supportive or flanking policies, effective public-private partnerships as well as policy coherence at the national level. At the initiative of several developing country members, the WTO SPS and CTE Committees have recently begun discussing the salient issues of private sector standards and WTO disciplines.

The development of regional standards by developing countries – as part of proactive adjustment approaches – is a worthwhile initiative because, apart from facilitating access to overseas markets, such standards can also ease regional trade. Liberalization efforts in the WTO on environmental goods and services should be considered in conjunction with the possibilities for supporting and financing these efforts, and to make them commercially, financially and technically viable. So far, no institutional linkages have been established between the negotiations and the different fora dealing with development finance and assistance. There is a need to promote coherence in the negotiations between the WTO and other environmental infrastructure projects financed by multilateral financial institutions, especially in terms of meeting financial needs and building capacity.

The key driver in introducing environmental provisions in RTAs is ensuring a level playingfield among the parties. This can be done by giving a legal expression to a commitment to maintain high levels of environmental protection. Another motivation is to enhance cooperation in environmental matters. The fact that an increasing number of RTAs serve as a framework for cooperation in environmental matters does not necessarily make such cooperation traderelated. In fact, most cooperation agreements are not trade-related. They have typically taken place among countries with shared ecosystems. Indeed, a lot of regional arrangements for environmental cooperation pre-date the respective RTAs.

Finally, there seems to be a missing link between international trade negotiations and the need to be responsive to broader development goals, such as the MDGs. There is a need to look at the technical issues arising in the negotiations on trade and environment from a broader development perspective. The MDGs are one case in point. There are many potential target areas to be derived from MDGs such as the supply of drinking water, drainage systems, sanitation, the disposal of sewage, waste disposal, and the development of renewable energy sources. The choices the WTO Members make could also be linked to multilateral environmental agreements. Bringing a development dimension to negotiations on environmental goods and services is important to promote sustainable development.

ENSURING FAIR COMPETITION

TRADE, COMPETITION AND GLOBAL ENTERPRISES

Trade liberalization alone is often not enough to maintain an optimal level of competition in all economic sectors. Private actors – fearful of the consequences of trade liberalization and stronger competition – may be inclined to protect their interests and market shares by introducing cross-border anti-competitive practices. These include international cartels, abuses of dominance, and the abuse of intellectual property rights.

In some circumstances, such practices can limit international trade even more severely than high tariffs and just as severely as non-tariff barriers. Market entry may be restricted, for instance, where suppliers enter into exclusive arrangements with their distributors, or large retailing chains refuse to distribute traded goods on reasonable terms and conditions. International cartels established to fix prices and allocate markets would prevent competition from alternative sources of goods or services from undercutting the high prices imposed by cartel members.

If an effective competition law is in place, such anti-competitive practices can be challenged. However, in countries where there is no competition law, the benefits of trade liberalization could be lost through such anti-competitive conduct. It is increasingly clear that anti-competitive practices, both domestic and cross-border, impair the process of development in developing countries more significantly than has previously been thought. This is true for at least four reasons. Firstly, given their narrow domestic industrial base, developing countries have to rely on imports of intermediate goods. To the extent that such intermediate goods are subject to anti-competitive practices – either within national borders or by the foreign suppliers of these imports– the developing country in question will be penalized by higher prices for both the intermediate goods and the goods for which they are used as production inputs.

In a number of papers, UNCTAD has documented the extent to which international cartels still operate in markets where developing countries have to import a lot, including in markets for intermediate goods. There is also increasing concern that the agricultural exports and imports of LDCs are dominated by small numbers of traders, facilitating cartelization or collective abuses of dominance which would lead to higher import prices or reduce the benefits from exports. Secondly, to achieve their developmental goals, developing countries need to rely on exportoriented strategies. However, the gains expected to arise from liberalized market-access conditions at a multilateral level or through preferential schemes will be severely limited if private anti-competitive practices are still in place. Thirdly, foreign firms feel freer to engage in across-the-border anti-competitive behaviour when the countries to which they export do not have a domestic competition law, and can neither individually nor through cooperation with foreign competition authorities challenge the market behaviour of the firm. Thus, countries that do not have a domestic competition law will be the prime victims of international anti-competitive practices.

Even where such laws have been adopted, taking enforcement action against foreign firms is a daunting task for developing countries which, in many cases, still need capacity-building assistance to sufficiently establish their competition authorities, as well as international enforcement cooperation. Fourthly, effects on trade arise from the conditions under which foreign direct investment is established and operates. The impact of FDI is not always pro-competitive. Where, as often happens, FDI takes place through the acquisition by a foreign corporation of a domestic enterprise, or the establishment of a joint venture between a foreign and a local firm, the foreign investor may gain a dominant position in the relevant market, enabling it to charge prices above competitive levels but often temporarily. Another scenario often encountered in developing and transition economies, is where the affiliates of two transnational corporations compete with each another in a particular market and the parent company overseas undertakes the merger. With the affiliates no longer independent of one another, competition in a host country may be adversely affected, even if the merger does not significantly affect competition in the markets of the TNCs' home countries. In both scenarios, the effects would be felt in the domestic markets of the host country as well as on its international trade since higher prices in the domestic market would encourage imports. With globalization and technological change, there is a trend towards the establishment of global production and distribution chains, as well as network-based industries such as in computer software. There is a danger that such trends – together with recent trends relating to mergers and acquisition – may be leading to a concentration of market power in a few global enterprises and reduced competition in the markets involved, thereby facilitating anti-competitive practices. Such anticompetitive practices may reduce domestic and global efficiency gains as well as the welfare benefits that should arise from liberalization. They will also adversely affect the trade and development prospects of developing countries, their enterprises, especially SMEs, and their consumers.

EFFECTS AND IMPLICATIONS OF THE WAVE OF MERGERS AND ACQUISITIONS

In recent years, there has been a strong increase in the numbers and transaction value of mergers and acquisitions across the world, especially within some sectors, such as in the oil and gas, food, metals and minerals sectors, automobiles and, in particular, in some services sectors such as financial services . Thus, since widespread deregulation has permitted the integration of banking, asset management and insurance, the global annual average number of mergers and acquisitions involving a financial company increased from 954 in the period 1990-1995 to 1556 in 1996-2000, with a slight drop to 1436 in 2001-2003.The transaction values of deals in 2005 stood at US$93.8 billion.

In the mining sector, there was a dramatic rise in the number and value of mergers and acquisitions in 2005 and 2006– amounting to a transaction value of around US$60 billion by the third quarter of 2006. Such mergers would reduce the number of competing rivals and may thus facilitate anticompetitive practices, which may adversely affect developing countries. Risks of cartelization may also be heightened by the enhanced avenues of communication among firms arising from new technologies and globalization, as well as from the fact that there is often relatively more frequent contact among multinational firms because they operate in several geographical markets. For example, developing economies are estimated to have been overcharged between US$12.5 and US$25 billion for several products which were the subject of international cartels during the period 1990-1995.

Moreover, evidence confirms that cartels with multi-continental effects raise prices higher than other types of international cartels and that, despite evident increases in cartel detection rates and the size of monetary fines and penalties in the past decade, a good case can be made that current global anti-cartel regimes are not sufficiently robust and are not serving as a deterrent.

FOSTERING AN ENABLING ENVIRONMENT: PROMOTING COMPETITION AND CONTROLLING ANTICOMPETITIVE PRACTICES

Exploiting the opportunities arising from liberalization requires both national competition policies and international cooperation to deal with both domestic and cross-border anti-competitive practices, particularly those that hamper trade and investment. Yet there are serious deficits at the national, regional, and multilateral levels in respect of applicable legal rules and enforcement capacity for controlling such anti-competitive practices, particularly when these practices are of a cross-border nature. One element typically found in competition law is the prohibition of any merger, acquisition, or takeover which is likely to substantially lessen competition or which leads to the acquisition of a dominant position in the relevant market. Thus, any adverse consequences of mergers and acquisitions involving TNCs, for instance, can be avoided if an effective competition law is in place in the host country.

As UNCTAD points out, competition law enforcement signals to firms that any inward investment that is motivated by the pursuit and eventual abuse of a dominant position will be dealt with severely by competition law. It is also argued that an economy that has implemented an effective competition law is in a better position to attract foreign direct investment than one that has not. This is because most TNCs are accustomed to the operation of such a law in their home countries, and know how to deal with any concerns that the competition authority may raise provided that the competition authorities act with impartiality in cases involving domestic and foreign firms, as well as between foreign firms. While it may not be feasible to ban more than a few mergers outright, competition authorities often impose conditions in return for allowing such mergers.

In recent years, some developing countries have occasionally examined the domestic effects of international mergers upon their markets and imposed requirements upon the local subsidiaries of the companies concerned as a condition for approving such mergers. For instance, as a condition for approving a merger between two large international shipping companies, the South African Competition Commission required one of them to divest its assets, rights and obligations in respect of its liner shipping activities on the South Africa/Europe and South Africa/North America routes.

Moreover, after its investigations, it also shared information with the European Commission, which also investigated and imposed conditions relating to this merger in respect of EU markets. However, there is ample evidence that developing countries face special enforcement difficulties when addressing anti-competitive practices with international elements. It is indeed open to question whether a developing country's competition authority ordering the prohibition of a merger between two global companies in order to prevent anti-competitive effects upon its markets will actually be able to enforce it. Thus, enhanced international cooperation on competition law and policy is also required to address anti-competitive practices which lead to losses by developing countries.

The general consensus regarding the benefits of competition policy for development led to the unanimous adoption of the Set of Multilaterally Agreed Equitable Principles and Rules for the Control of Restrictive Business Practices by the General Assembly in 1980Since the Set's adoption, there has been a universal trend towards the adoption, reform and the enhanced application of national competition laws and policies. There has also been a substantial increase in international cooperation in this area, resulting in relevant bilateral and regional agreements. Of the approximately 300 RTAs which are in force or under negotiation, over a 100 contain competition-policy related provisions. Yet much remains to be done to help ensure that anticompetitive practices do not impede or negate the realization of the development benefits arising from liberalization in globalized markets.

The objective of such action should be to facilitate stronger international cooperation. This should include: the identification of how competition rules in bilateral and regional agreements might be developed further, and better cater for developing country specificities, and how they can be more fully implemented. It should also work towards strengthening the consistency and coordination between national action and international cooperation in the area of competition law and policy.

Global coherence in dealing with anti-competitive practices, particularly those affecting more than one country, would also require addressing the following:

- International mergers and market concentration, abuses of dominance and export and international cartels affecting developing country markets and their effective market entry opportunities;
- Enhancement of legislation and institutions for implementing competition law and policy;
- Coherence between competition policy and other policies, including possibilities for cooperation between competition and trade authorities;
- Exchange of experiences and best practices, networking, provision of capacity-building to competition agencies in developing countries and voluntary convergence on standards and rules;
- Strengthening of consultations, exchange of information and cooperation in the competition area at the regional and multilateral levels; and
- Preferential or differential treatment for developing countries.

AID FOR TRADE AND DEVELOPMENT–BUILDING CAPACITY

MEETING ADJUSTMENT COSTS AND BUILDING PRODUCTIVE CAPACITIES

The Aid for Trade initiative is an essential complement to trade liberalization in the international trading system. It is necessary both in realizing potential gains and in mitigating the costs of trade liberalization, whether multilateral, bilateral or unilateral. There is general agreement also that the AfT initiative should not become a substitute for a development outcome to the Doha Round, but should rather complement to it. The need to help developing countries and LDCs build competitive supply capacities, make better use of market access opportunities, and diversify their exports has long been recognized as being part of a long-term development strategy in which trade operates as an effective engine of growth, development and poverty reduction.

However, there is also an important immediate need to help developing countries cope with the trade shocks associated with liberalization as well as the difficult transition into a more liberalized global trading environment. Thus, adjustment assistance is indispensable, particularly when countries lack their own social safety nets. The AfT initiative is thus novel in the sense of responding specifically to trade liberalization under the WTO, as well as a long-awaited response to the need to generally provide trade-related assistance and support to developing countries to build up their trade capacities to participate effectively and benefit from international trade. Trade-related adjustment costs cover a wide range of issues but primarily include those relating to preference erosion which particularly affects countries dependent on textiles and clothing and agricultural commodity exports.

Other adjustments needing assistance include the loss of revenues from trade taxes; increases in food prices for net food-importing countries; shortfalls in export earnings; and other social costs such as the loss of jobs/livelihood activities due to the contraction of import-competing sectors and/or export sectors faced with the loss of trade preferences. Another category of costs that require AfT assistance are those associated with compliance to the commitments, rules and standards of the international trading system.

Such costs include those incurred in the process of setting up domestic regulatory mechanisms and institutional frameworks to support the liberalization of services; the implementation of a new agreement on trade facilitation; the creation of standard-setting institutions, certification agencies and testing laboratories; and compliance with the TRIPS Agreement.

Because of inadequate trade-related infrastructure and supply-side capabilities, many lowincome countries need to make substantial investments in these areas before they will be able to take full advantage of market access opportunities. Trade-related infrastructures include both physical infrastructure, as well as institutional infrastructure, such as an efficient banking and financing system, business services and other trade support institutions. This involves focusing attention on developing competitive services sectors.

The strengthening of supply-side capacities also calls for strategically targeting support at the enterprise and producer levels. This involves support to enhance entrepreneurship and enterprise development, the upgrading of skills as well as technology absorption and innovation. All these are aimed at strengthening export production capabilities and competiti-veness, building trade facilitation capacities, and facilitating entry into new markets and a more beneficial participation in global supply chains.

FOSTERING AN ENABLING ENVIRONMENT: IMPLEMENTING THE AID FOR TRADE INITIATIVE

Although the concept of the AfT initiative has been accepted as a necessary systemic response to trade marginalization, it still needs to be operationalized. It will assist the implementation of new Doha Round agreements; help ease adjustment costs to economic reforms; and facilitate the utilization of new market access. It is urgent that the mechanism be supported with substantial resources that should be additional to development aid, without being unpredictable and/or debt creating.The recommendations of the WTO Task Force on AfT provide a framework for transforming the commitments of the Aid-for-Trade initiative into action. The Task Force affirmed that the effectiveness of its recommendations for operationalizing AfT requires substantial additional targeted resources for trade-related programmes and projects, as pledged at the WTO's Hong Kong Ministerial Conference.

During the conference Japan announced that its development assistance spending on trade, production, and distribution infrastructure would be increased to US$10 billion over three years; the United States announced AfT grants of US$2.7 billion a year by 2010; and the EU and its member States announced trade-related development assistance spending of €2 billion per year by 2010. At St. Petersburg G, the G8 leaders expressed their expectation that AfT funding would rise to US$4 billion by 2010. Moreover, the broader international commitment at the International Conference on Financing and Development in Monterrey, as well as the G8 summits in Gleneagles and St. Petersburg , promised to significantly scale up development assistance by 2010.

The OECD estimates that these commitments entail an increase in ODA, which will include assistance for trade, by about US$50 billion per year by 2010. The delivery channels for AfT are also important. The multilateral versus exclusively bilateral channelling of AfT funding is an important issue, involving predictability and effectiveness in dealing with some of the challenges and gaps in current AfT identified by the Task Force. Accordingly, the Task Force has recommended that donors should 'consider channelling Aid-for-Trade funds multilaterally, when appropriate'. The provision of AfT through global programmes – such as those currently provided by international organizations such as UNCTAD – should be an avenue for delivering trade-related assistance for the benefit of all countries.

In this context, the assistance expected under the AfT initiative should not replace existing operational mechanisms which are already delivering trade-related assistance through the UN agencies at the global level. In this context, it is worth considering the experience of the Integrated Framework for LDCs . In existence since 1997, it is an important instrument for delivering the Aid for Trade initiative to LDCs. The IF experience has shown that assessing needs and setting priorities at the country level can be time-consuming ; that country ownership is weak when there is uncertainty or lack of funding at the end of the process; and that in a system with diffused responsibility for management and implementation , implementation will be weak and programme objectives will not be met.Because of this experience, IF stakeholders have agreed to implement an enhanced facility. The Enhanced IF will have a full-fledged multilateral institutional, managerial and governance structure, and increased predictable financial resources to support the implementation of priority projects and actions. This is, perhaps, an experience worth building on for the larger AfT effort.

For their part, the prospective beneficiaries of AfT would have to specifically and strongly mainstream trade into national development policies and plans. The prioritization of trade in development is critical to evolving the commitment of stakeholder Governments to trade and to implementing trade-enhancing programmes. Without a counterpart reflection in a national framework, AfT will have limited impact. The WTO Task Force also recommended that developing countries should therefore consider and set up national and regional aid for trade committees to identify their needs. These could be new multi-stakeholder consultative bodies comprising the trade policy community, or they could be existing trade consultative institutions whose functions could be expanded to take on the AfT initiative.

This is a key first step in benefiting from the AfT initiative. The first Global Aid-for-Trade Review conducted by the WTO took place on 19 and 20 November 2007. The took stock of what is happening on Aid for Trade; identified what should happen next; and proposed improvement to WTO monitoring and evaluation. Inputs to the global review came from the outcomes of three regional events on mobilizing AfT for respectively Latin America and the Caribbean , Asia and the Pacific and Africa.

Information and analyses were also provided in a joint WTO/OECD report on Aid for Trade at a Glance 2007: 1Global Review which compiled information provided by Governments and agencies on their perspectives on and involvement in AfT. The report on the review to the WTO General Council by the WTO Deputy Director General Mrs. Valentine Rugwabiza highlighted, *inter alia*, the following consensus: the importance of country leadership, mainstreaming, setting priorities, and improving regional approaches; the direct involvement of the private sector is indispensable; the clear need to scale up the overall ODA envelope – as pledged in Gleneagles and elsewhere – while at the same time acknowledging that recipient countries had a responsibility for making trade a priority and for developing viable projects; and that while Aid for Trade is an important complement to trade opening, especially to a successful Doha Round, it cannot – and should not – be a substitute.

In his report to the WTO General Council also on the periodic work on aid for trade carried out by the WTO Committee on Trade and Development, the Chairman stressed that "there remains a large knowledge or understanding "gap" - between the trade and development communities, between partner and donor countries, and between the various international actors engaged in the delivery of Aid for Trade. Bridging this gap will be key to harnessing trade for development - whether we call it "mainstreaming" or "priority setting" or "national vision". This is one of the main benefits that WTO monitoring through the global review can bring to the AfT initiative and the role that the Committee on Trade and Development is playing as well.

UNCTAD'S ROLE: PROMOTING QUALITATIVE TRADE INTEGRATION

OVERVIEW

A number of emerging trade and development issues have been identified in this report in the context of the new realities and opportunities created by globalization and the persistent challenges of poverty and underdevelopment in the world economy. To help developing countries to benefit from these opportunities, to use trade to meet internationally agreed goals such as the MDGs, as well as to overcome persistent challenges, UNCTAD's contribution to maximizing development gains from the international trading system will be important over the short-to-medium term in the areas of international trade and trade dynamism, commodities, services, fair competition, South-South trade, environmental issues linked to trade, and trade and development aspects of energy, labour mobility and climate change, as well as its contribution to the aid for trade initiative through its trade-related technical assistance.

In this connection for example, UNCTAD member States agreed at the Mid-term Review of the São Paulo Consensus on several areas in which emphasis should be placed. With regards to its research and analysis, UNCTAD monitors trends and systemic developments. It provides strategic perspective and forecasting as well as simultaneously pointing out the practical ways and means of ensuring development gains. UNCTAD's work can bring policy issues into focus through empirical research, and bring best practices to bear on national policies according to the individual characteristics of each developing country.

It can contribute to national/regional trade and development strategy setting, including through multi-stakeholder involvement and consultation, institution building, and human resource development. It could provide useful analytical inputs through policy and sector-specific reviews such as the trade and environment reviews, voluntary competition policy peer reviews, and reviews of new and dynamic sectors. Such reviews can be considered further through, for example, multi-year expert discussions to more systematically identify 'pragmatic solutions' at the national, regional and international levels. This will, in turn, help enhance the enabling environment for development at the national level in terms of public policies and measures as well as corporate policies and practices. Most of all, as the the focal point in the UN System for the integrated treatment of trade and development, UNCTAD can, through its analytical work and consensus-building work, contribute to ideas and norm-setting at the international level in a way that promotes the best possible global governance, coherence, and solidarity for development. Technical cooperation and capacity-building is the practical and concrete manifestation of policy conclusions and options of intergovernmental deliberations, and ahead-of-the-curve thinking and analyses.

UNCTAD's technical assistance on international trade and commodities is being adapted to the new UNCTAD-wide approach of thematic clusters of technical assistance as recommended by UNCTAD member States. This will enable UNCTAD to have a significant impact on development in developing countries, and play a proactive role in the 'one UN' system of operational support at the country level. Inter-agency cooperation, including within the UN System, and partnerships between civil society and the private sector on trade development is being pursued and expanded. These provide practical means through which common development objectives can be achieved by putting together the expertise and resources of partners. UNCTAD's range of trade-related partnerships, including both project-based and research-oriented ones, can be strengthened.

FACILITATING BENEFICIAL INTEGRATION INTO THE INTERNATIONAL TRADING SYSTEM

UNCTAD monitors and assesses the evolution of the international trading system and its development impacts; multilateral, regional and bilateral negotiations and capacity-building; WTO accession; the trade impact of non-tariff measures ; and the Doha Round negotiations and the international trading system generally – all from a development perspective. It endeavours to ensure coherence and interface between regional trade agreements and the multilateral trading system; strengthening the participation of developing countries in the new and dynamic sectors of world trade; and improving trade and development analytical tools such as the Trade and Development Index.

UNCTAD's key contribution lies in rigourously upholding the MDG goal of an open, equitable, rule-based, predictable, and non-discriminatory multilateral trading system. This has been instrumental in monitoring the international trading system, and assessing to what extent the development dimension has been achieved generally and specifically in the WTO, especially in the Doha Round. UNCTAD has provides support to intergovernmental deliberations including the Trade and Development Board and the UN General Assembly.

Its capacity-building assistance at the national, regional and international levels helps promote awareness on the contribution of trade the realization of the MDGs specifically in the area of the Doha negotiations. It also builds up the human, institutional and regulatory capacities of developing countries relevant to engaging in the multilateral trading system; promotes the greater utilization of the Generalized System of Preferences and other trade preferences ; and assesses the implications of preference erosion. UNCTAD helps to enhance the understanding of and active participation in multilateral and regional trade negotiations by developing countries and contributes to clarifying the interface between multilateral and regional trade to ensure coherence and mutual supportiveness.

UNCTAD implements global, regional and country-specific assessments of the development impact of WTO Agreements and the Doha negotiations in developing countries. It strengthens the capacity of countries to understand, manage and participate in the complex and demanding WTO accession process in a sustained manner, helping them in reflecting their national development priorities. UNCTAD's support for all the stages of the WTO accession process – including the postaccession phase – is particularly intensive and wide-ranging. A recent evaluation of its work on the accession process has found its support as being 'very relevant, focused and timely, pro-development and responsive to the changing needs of the beneficiary countries.'

Trade-related technical assistance on trade policy and trade negotiations is a growing need for developing countries in the context of continuing multilateral trade negotiations, the effective management of the WTO Agreements, and their participation in proliferating RTAs. UNCTAD has developed useful and tested products in these areas. These include: advice on WTO Doha negotiations and RTAs; the development of trade in services; regulatory and institutional capacity-building including in African countries, particularly under the JITAP; support in the WTO accession process; help in ACP-EU negotiations of Economic Partnership Agreements ; regional integration in services trade, such as for SADC; and skills training for trade negotiations.

UNCTAD is also provides assistance on the utilization of the dispute settlement system of the WTO and other trade and investment agreements. UNCTAD is working in several countries, *e.g.* in India, over several years to maximize development gains from globalization especially in pro-poor sectors. Such capacity-building activities of UNCTAD can be strengthened and successful experiences replicated. The systematic monitoring, research, and analysis of international trade flows, trends, and patterns by UNCTAD provide updated information, analyses and data for use in trade policy formulation, trade negotiations, and business operations globally. The availability of such information helps in the exploitation of new trading opportunities and in minimizing costs. A tool in this regard is UNCTAD's Trade and Development Index.

It serves as an innovative diagnostic and policymaking tool which incorporates the interactions and interdependence among various factors in the trade and development process that 'enhance the enabling environment' for development. TDI analysis support the argument that there is a symbiosis between developmentrelated structures, policies and processes on the one hand, and trade-related outcomes on the other. Similarly, trade-related processes and outcomes have an impact on development outcomes. A continuous refinement of the TDI will be important. Other key outputs include trade-related analytical, statistical, and information bases and tools and making available – and increasing the transparency of – measures relating to trade such as through the recent joint ITC/WTO/UNCTAD World Tariff Profiles 2006 publication, derived from a common tariffs database.

UNCTAD also provides systematic assessment on the evolving trading system, such as with DESA, through the annual World Economic Situation and Prospects report, and the annual Millennium Development Goals Report. Independent trade policy assessment in different countries could be undertaken to enhance effective trade policy making. Priority areas for analyses can include the performance of dynamically growing and trading countries and the policies they utilize, and global, South-South, and country-level trade activity to assess progress, identify the lessons learnt, and highlight best practices – all to be shared with other countries. These could be discussed at intergovernmental meetings to build consensus on relevant policy options. UNCTAD is promoting the awareness that effective trade liberalisation for the exports of developing countries entails more than addressing the question of tariff barriers.

It also requires addressing the more intractable market entry barriers of non-tariff barriers , product standards, and product quality requirements. UNCTAD is helping to identify, classify, and quantify these NTBs. UNCTAD also promotes stakeholder partnerships in addressing them, especially through the Secretary-General of UNCTAD's Group of Eminent Persons on NTBs and its multi-agency task force. During the process of trade liberalization and reform, developing countries face important implementation, adaptation, and adjustment costs. UNCTAD conducts analyses on such costs and how they need to be factored into the liberalization and reform agendas at the national, regional and international levels. It is also helps developing countries create and strengthen supporting institutional and infrastructural capacities to respond to these costs and take advantage of new trading opportunities.

For example, UNCTAD is assisting developing countries to better assess the possible implications of coping with WTO negotiations on industrial products. Strengthening the participation of developing countries in the dynamic new sectors of world production and trade is needed to positively enhance the integration of developing countries into the international trading system. UNCTAD is contributing through intergovernmental reviews of these sectors,backed by practical, on-the-ground technical assistance and capacity-building initiatives. In this respect, public-private partnerships can be useful vehicles. A trend-setting example is an UNCTAD-Philips initiative on the electronic/electrical sector in Southern Africa. Another example is the recent adoption of an UNCTAD-architectured regional standard for organic agriculture in East Africa: a highly desirable avenue for export promotion in a sector that is not only very dynamic but is also very beneficial developmentally in terms of the economy, ecology, poverty alleviation among small farmers and the social fabric in general. Promoting awareness of the interface between trade and the achievement of MDGs generally and in specific areas such as poverty reduction and gender empowerment remains a priority of UNCTAD.

Such awareness can lead to the identification and implementation of trade policy measures, liberalization practices and capacity-building programmes at international and national level that best promote poverty-sensitive and gender-sensitive trading and help realize propoor trade growth, globalization and development. UNCTAD also develops and implements global, regional and national programmes, with the support of the international donor community, that help developing countries to enhance their preparedness and strategies for pro-poor and gender sensitive trade growth and globalization.

SUSTAINING THE ASCENT OF THE SOUTH AND SOUTH-SOUTH TRADE

South-South trade – be it intra-regional or inter-regional – is taking quantum leaps, and fast accounting for half the world trade of developing countries. The new drivers of the South and their enterprises are at the forefronts of the revival in South-South trade, investment and economic cooperation. This has resulted in a new reality in South-South trade and a stronger and broader economic cooperation among developing countries. UNCTAD can contribute to facilitating and consolidating the ascent of the dynamic South in which many developing countries are gradually moving from the periphery to the centre and from dependence to interdependence. As this can result in a positive sum gain for all countries, this trend is to be encouraged, replicated and deepened within and across countries and continents.

At the same time, as the more successful developing countries climb the ladder, they need to also help pave the way for others to follow. New models and prospects have created opportunities for 'development-transmitting'" trade and investment relationships within the South. With UNCTAD support these can be identified and promoted. UNCTAD identifies ways of harnessing the increased potential for South-South cooperation in trade, investment and knowledge transfers. It can foster new ECDC models including for bilateral, plurilateral and multilateral partnerships; help build new dialogues among the institutions of the South for the South, including through triangular cooperation; and strengthen and set up South-South institutions, networking platforms and partnerships on trade, investment, finance, R&D, enterprise development, technical cooperation, and trade and transport infrastructure. For example, UNCTAD has facilitated the creation and entry into operation of the Global Network of EXIM Banks and Development Finance Institutions to foster South-South trade through financing.

Such efforts can complement North-South trade and development cooperation. Systematic monitoring as well as research and analysis of South-South trade flows is important to identify lessons and best practices that can contribute to the replication of positive development experiences and sustain further development of such trade. The development of a South- South trade information system by UNCTAD is useful in this regard. UNCTAD has also launched an initiative to encourage networking among the RTAs of developing countries through the sharing of experiences on positive development instruments for regional integration.

This initiative can be consolidated to provide a forum for the regular exchange of experiences among RTAs. The continued servicing of the GSTP Agreement and its third round of negotiations by UNCTAD remain central to its work on South-South trade. For sustaining South-South trade, it is important to conclude the third round of GSTP negotiations. The further development of the RTAs of developing countries into effective instruments for trade integration and regional development is important. As UNCTAD's Trade and Development Report 2007 points out, South-South RTAs have a positive impact on trade and development for the countries concerned. They help to improve infrastructure linkages, competitiveness, and value chain participation, as well as spurring FDI. South-South trade in services – especially intraregional trade through regional trade agreements – has to be fully exploited. UNCTAD is conducting pioneering work in this regard – for example with SADC to develop a regional services agreement based on indepth services assessment and negotiations.

Since its creation in 1964, UNCTAD supports ECDC as an essential complement to national development strategies. Over the years, the various facets of ECDC have evolved and now, with the rise of the dynamic South combined with market-driven South-South trade and investment expansion, it is an opportune to examine ways in which ECDC can be strengthened. Given its traditional and longstanding expertise in this field, UNCTAD is well placed to ensure that ECDC becomes a catalytic force for the growth and development of developing countries.

RE-LAUNCHING THE COMMODITY AGENDA

With respect to commodity issues, UNCTAD has traditionally been at the forefront of international efforts to transform the commodity problematic into a commodity boon. With the recent rise in commodity prices and the probability that such trends will be sustained in the medium term, this is a timely opportunity to re-launch the commodity agenda, with UNCTAD playing a catalytic role. A key aspect of this agenda has to include support in managing windfall revenues, for commodity producing and dependent developing countries, especially in Africa and LDCs, that benefit from the boom in the prices of their agriculture, minerals and metals, oil and gas and energy exports.

Addressing the links between international commodity trade and national development, particularly poverty reduction, is being mainstreamed by UNCTAD. UNCTAD monitors developments in commodity markets and assists developing countries – in particular those most dependent on commodities – in formulating strategies and policies that respond to the challenges of commodity markets, including that of over-supply. It can further facilitate the exploitation of growing opportunities for commoditydependent countries. It will also have to contribute to national, regional and international policy efforts to reduce commodity dependence and to diversify into high-value and dynamically growing products. It supports the efforts of commodity-dependent developing countries to diversify their production, address the high volatility of prices of especially agricultural products, develop new generation of commodity financing schemes, and strengthening participation in the global supply value chain.

UNCTAD assists in particular small and poor commodity producers to become competitiveness, meet standards, access commodity information and databases, provide value addition, and reach global markets. It can help mobilize increased flows of development assistance to commodity dependent developing countries, including through the aid for trade initiative. UNCTAD promotes intergovernmental cooperation on commodities, such as assistance to and cooperation with International Commodity Bodies. It can continue to build effective partnerships among stakeholders aiming at sustainable approaches to commodity problems. These should include fostering public-private cooperation in commodity chains with a view to ensuring, *inter alia* through market-based principles, a more equitable distribution of revenues and benefits along the supply chain and supporting diversification. Contributing to the implementation of the Global Initiative on Commodities constitutes one set of activities for re-launching the commodities agenda via a network of cooperation among international agencies.

DEVELOPING SERVICES ECONOMY AND TRADE

Services constitute the new frontier of international trade. UNCTAD conducts national assessments and policy reviews of services; supports multilateral and regional negotiations on services; strengthen services data and statistics; promotes strategies and regulatory frameworks for the development of a competitive service supply capacity ; provides analyses of regional services liberalization, regulatory frameworks and cooperative mechanism on services; and supports South-South negotiations of services agreements and cooperation in services. Comprehensive national assessments and policy reviews of services as well as of trade in services have a central role to play in assisting developing countries, together with support from the international community, to effectively integrate into the services economy. These reviews will enable countries to appropriately pace and sequence the policy reforms which affect the services sectors.

UNCTAD can provide such policy reviews, and facilitate regular intergovernmental deliberations and consensus-building on best practices, lessons learnt, and policy options for the development of services. Follow-up capacity-building support in countries and regional groupings will play an important role in developing and implementing services agreements, putting in place regulatory regimes, and developing competitive services supply capacities. At the same time, the human and social development implications of the service economy have to be addressed in terms of universal access to essential services such as education, energy, health, water, and telecommunications.

UNCTAD has integrated such concerns into its work in the services sector. UNCTAD plays a unique role in raising awareness of the key contribution of services to development, as well as clarifying and improving the understanding of the services paradigm. It has conducted sectoral studies and intergovernmental expert meetings on over 13 services sectors. These include distribution, insurance, audiovisual, logistics, tourism, air transport, environment, energy, professional and construction and financial services, as well as universal access to essential and infrastructural services and Mode 4 of GATS. UNCTAD also assistsdeveloping countries in undertaking the national assessment of their own services sectors. These have enabled them to put in place specific strategies and policies to increase supply capacity and trade. Lack of data and disaggregated statistics are major challenges while undertaking services assessment, devising appropriate policies and regulatory frameworks. UNCTAD is helping in this regard by improving data and statistics in the services sector.

UNLEASHING THE DEVELOPMENT POTENTIAL OF LABOUR MOBILITY

UNCTAD actively promotes the integration of labour flows in national and international development strategies, especially in areas such as domestic regulation, mutual recognition agreements, migration, and gender. It promotes the temporary movement of workers and the trade in skills, while keeping in sight the many related social, economic, cultural and political dimensions. UNCTAD's analysis regarding labour mobility, growth and development focuses on the economic causes and consequences of migration, the imperatives of labour integration and mobility, and the identification of appropriate regulatory frameworks to enhance the benefits and mitigate the downside for both sending and receiving countries. UNCTAD's advocacy and approach is based on the premise that it will be a win-win situation for both the countries of origin and destination when labour movements occur in response economic forces.

Indeed, freer movements of labour will benefit the global economy as a whole if the integration is managed in an enlightened and cooperative manner, in the spirit of pragmatism and realism, and without political or cultural prejudice. UNCTAD's work on the different trade-related facets of labour mobility and integration assists in clarifying issues that lie at the interface of trade, migration and globalization can better equip policymakers everywhere to address these issues. It can also help shape public opinion towards a greater understanding of the balance of benefits accruing from the integration of the labour market. UNCTAD also advances such win-win strategies on labour flows through its active membership of the Global Migration Group.

PROMOTING ENERGY TRADE AND SECURITY

Regarding energy, trade and development, UNCTAD analyses and suggest ways of providing for the growing demand for energy, particularly in the context of how to sustain the development process in developing countries, especially LDCs. It takes into account technologically and economically feasible alternative energy sources ; regional initiatives on energy; possible energy efficiency measures; as well as identification of regulatory and trade issues including capacity-building needs to expand capacity and diversify supply. UNCTAD adopts a holistic approach, helping exporting countries to devise strategies for fostering the development of the energy sector as an engine for growth and development. For some countries, this sector generates over 90 per cent of their total revenues and accounts for over 50 per cent of their GDP.

Key development objectives include channelling oil revenues into capital investments in national and regional infrastructure development and basic services, while avoiding real exchange rate appreciation, and taking due account of each economy's absorption capacity. Oilimporting countries could reap great benefits from cooperation, particularly in the procurement field. Savings can be made from efficient procurement procedures for oil and oil products. Reorganizing the procurement of small volume imports of petroleum products into bulk procurement, and distributing these imports to subregions, will generate economies of scale. Sharing storage infrastructures can also generate savings. However, this requires active cooperation from the governments involved. In Africa, UNCTAD convenes the Africa Oil, Gas, Trade and Finance Conference on an annual basis. The 11Conference held in Kenya in May 2007 brought together Ministers and senior- level executives from the oil, gas and finance sectors.

It provided a meeting place for investors concerned with opportunities and developments in the African energy sector. In this context also, a pre-event to UNCTAD XII, an India-Africa Hydrocarbon Conference & Exhibition, was convened for the first time in New Delhi from 6-7 November 2007. It was jointly organized by the Ministry of Petroleum & Natural Gas of India, the Federation of Indian Chambers of Commerce and Industry, and UNCTAD. Deliberations at the event resulted in the identification of a framework for cooperation and partnership at different levels in the hydrocarbon sector between India and Africa.Among the products emerging from the search of a new economic model based on low-carbon emissions are biofuels – a sector that has experienced considerable development over the past decade.

To ensure that engaging in the production/use of biofuels yields positive environmental and development results, Governments have to take crucial decisions and develop appropriate strategies. These will include deciding whether the production of biofuels is intended for transportation, or for broader energy replacement; what the land requirements are; and which conversion technology is desirable. The economic and environmental impacts, the compatibility of biofuels with existing fuel delivery/use infrastructures, and competing uses for biomass also have to be assessed. UNCTAD assists countries in implementing country-based assessments of the feasibility of engaging in the production of biofuels, and in setting up the required domestic frameworks. UNCTAD's Biofuels Initiative is working in this area.

It has conducted such assessments for several countries. It focuses on sound economic, legal, and trade policy analysis, capacity-building activities, and consensus-building tools. It provides lessons learnt from successful cases, and illustrates the problems encountered by developed and developing countries alike while dealing with the technical, policy, and economic aspects of biofuels development. It is working closely with other intergovernmental organizations, civil society, academia, and the private sector.

Also, UNCTAD and the ECOWAS Bank for Investment and Development have pooled their efforts to promote the financing of the production of biofuels and the development of Jatropha plantations in Africa, drawing upon the Clean Development Mechanism of the Kyoto Protocol. This initiative – the first of its kind – involves creating a fund to finance the agricultural and industrial production of biofuels in Africa. The main objective is to promote investments in the biofuels supply chain, including a window for financing R&D and capacity-building.

ADDRESSING TRADE AND DEVELOPMENT ASPECTS OF TRADE AND ENVIRONMENT

UNCTAD assists developing countries in identifying and addressing issues arising at the interface of trade, environment, and development. UNCTAD has been working in the areas of trade and climate change, particularly in the assessment of the potential for biofuels production in developing countries, as well as in the growing biotrade market opportunities for biodiversity products and services. In this light, the growing national and international commitment towards more stringent policies for addressing climate change enhances UNCTAD potential contribution in this area on trade and development aspects, especially: aspects of trade competitiveness related to climate change policies designed to influence process and production methods, in particular changes in the fossil fuel energy content in tradable goods; trade and investment opportunities from climate change measures; investment promotion in climatefriendly production and trade in developing countries under the Clean Development Mechanism of the Kyoto Protocol; and compatibility issues between climate policy and trade rules. Launched in 1998, UNCTAD's BioTrade initiative is a useful tool to help develop the niche market for biodiversity products and services.

A considerable number of these biodiversity-based products, developed sustainably by SMEs in developing countries, are entering the main export markets. These are increasingly recognizing and demanding respect for species and ecosystems as well as consistency with sustainable production practices. UNCTAD's work towards consolidating the business case for greater market access for sustainably produced biodiversity products is timely. Moreover, greater demand also entails an increasing need to support these typically small businesses in their institutional and entrepreneurial capacity, as well as in their access to good manufacturing and agricultural practices. Many small and large producers lack methodologies and tools that would allow the differentiation of their products in the market.

Likewise, a growing number of cosmetics and pharmaceutical industries seek effective tools to validate their sustainable development claims. The trade of developing countries is increasingly impacted by health, safety and environmental requirements applied by governments or the private sector and NGOs in a mandatory or voluntary way. UNCTAD is helping countries to address such obstacles. It launched several specific initiatives that analyse EHFSRs, and provide capacity-building support to interested developing countries in addressing these daunting challenges. UNCTAD's Consultative Task Force on Environmental Requirements and Market Access for Developing Countries supports the designing of appropriate proactive adjustment strategies to address new EHFSRs.

UNCTAD addresses the difficulties that developing countries have in: monitoring and approaching changes on standards and market access; evaluating their likely impact; and knowing where to go for help in building the capacity to respond in a timely and appropriate fashion. UNCTAD's Consultative Task Force also assists developing countries in their engagement in WTO discussions relating to salient issues of private sector standards and WTO disciplines. The results of such analytical work and stakeholder dialogue have already been presented at various WTO TBT, SPS and CTE meetings. The results should also in the longer term contribute towards more inclusiveness, transparency, and appropriateness in private sector standard-setting and its implementation in developing countries, as well as to sound approaches to adjustment at the national level.

Over several years, the UNCTAD-UNEP Capacity-building Task Force on Trade, Environment and Development conducted a series of activities to promote the production and export of organic agricultural products in several developing regions. In East Africa, this work culminated in the creation of an East African Organic Products Standard. In its third cycle, the CBTF focuses on supporting developing countries in seizing economic, social, and environmental win-win opportunities resulting from the new environmental requirements in export markets. Particular emphasis is placed on 'front-of-pipe' approaches that seize opportunities in new export markets for environmentally preferable goods.

This work includes normative work on creating regional standards that facilitate regional trade and access to overseas export markets. Environmental issues are likely to become more prominent at the WTO and in regional and bilateral trade agreements. This will take place through avenues such as the accelerated liberalization of environmental goods and services, challenges to environmentally-related domestic legislation, and the clarification of the relationship between trade rules and environmental agreements. UNCTAD has a key role to play in ensuring that developing countries are able to identify their interests and effectively pursue them in international policymaking fora. UNCTAD's contribution in providing substantive support to the negotiations on environmental goods and services in these negotiations is important as it brings in the development perspective.

UNCTAD's Trade and Environment Review 2008 is devoted to a detailed examination of the scope for and implications of environmental goods and services liberalization, with particular emphasis on the interface between trade, climate change and development. The Trade and Environment Review series aims to enhance understanding of and promote dialogue on the development dimension of key trade and environment issues. Harnessing knowledge for development has a crucial trade and environment dimension in terms of traditional knowledge, innovations and practices associated with genetic resources. UNCTAD assists developing countries and can help the international community in addressing issues related to promoting, protecting and preserving traditional knowledge.

ENSURING FAIR COMPETITION

A major challenge faced by developing countries is the increased concentration of market power within many sectors of global production and trade, such as some products within agro-industry, electronics, pharmaceuticals, tourism, telecoms, energy or financial services. These put developing country producers, enterprises or consumers at a competitive or bargaining disadvantage.

Developing countries must be enabled to deal with anti-competitive practices or mergers which affect them, whether encountered within their own territories or on international markets. Stronger multilateral and regional cooperation in this area is essential. As mandated by the General Assembly, UNCTAD is playing a unique role in promoting national and regional actions as well as international cooperation in this area through its work on competition law and policy and consumer interest issues. UNCTAD services the quinquennial United Nations Conference for the Review of the Set of Multilaterally Agreed Equitable Principles and Rules for the Control of Restrictive Business Practices.

In between the conferences, the Intergovernmental Group of Experts on Competition Policy and Law, a global forum of competition experts, meets annually to discuss competition issues. Since 2005, UNCTAD has instituted and facilitated a voluntary peer review of competition policies. A key area of work pertains to technical assistance to countries and regional groupings in order to formulate, revise, and implement competition policies as well as build the required institutional enforcement mechanisms. For example, assistance has been provided for Andean countries through the COMPAL programme, UEMOA countries, and SADC countries. Many developing countries and countries with economies in transition have benefited from the unique assistance offered by UNCTAD.

IMPLEMENTING THE AID FOR TRADE INITIATIVE

UNCTAD's analyses, policy-oriented work, and technical assistance have advanced the notion that aid for trade, in addition to aid for development, is a necessary prerequisite to improving the supply capacities and competitiveness of developing countries, as well as enabling them to meet implementation and adjustment costs arising from trade liberalization. This work underpins UNCTAD's efforts to bring the aid for trade initiative into operation and thus contribute the effort by WTO to implement the initiative. UNCTAD's contribution to the aid for trade initiative has been endorsed by the Mid-Term Review of the São Paulo Consensus.

UNCTAD contributes to the Aid for Trade initiative *inter alia* through examining to the best strategies needed to deal with capacity constraints and trade adjustments in developing countries. It has convened brainstorming events on the AfT initiative, held a global conference in March 2006 as a follow-up to the decision taken at the 6WTO Ministerial Conference on the subject, and has actively supported developing countries in responding to the initiative. It has contributed to and participated in first Global Aid for Trade Review conducted by the WTO. It is a member of the WTO Advisory Group on Aid for Trade.

UNCTAD continue to play a role in addressing a number of outstanding issues. These include country eligibility, scope, ownership, delivery mechanism, monitoring and evaluation, national needs assessment and prioritisation, trade mainstreaming both by beneficiaries and donors, the brokering and funding of programmes, additional funding, as well as implementation mechanisms. Such assistance will help to build global public good for the service of all countries. UNCTAD has also gained significant expertise in trade- and development-related technical assistance. Its technical cooperation programmes can help developing countries to achieve development gains from the international trading system and trade negotiations.

CONCLUSION

Globalization is increasing the integration of national markets and the interdependence of countries worldwide for a wide range of goods, services, and commodities. Several factors have engendered such a transition including the liberalization of tariffs and other barriers to trade; foreign direct investment through trade and investment agreements; autonomous unilateral structural reforms; technological innovations in transport and communications; international development cooperation; and the strategic use of policies, experimentation and innovation. Some developing countries are beginning to realize the prospects of a more beneficial integration – both quantitative and qualitative – into the global economy and the international trading system as a result of globalization.

For many others, an increased quantitative integration has not had positive results in terms of poverty reduction, employment or increased welfare. Still others have seen only partial gains. In LDCs especially, the expected gains of trade-driven globalization are still missing or insufficient. There is concern that the costs of trade driven globalization maybe economically, socially, politically, and environmentally unsustainable. A prime concern today for most policymakers everywhere is how to maximize the development benefits of globalization and trade, and to minimize their costs. Assuring development gains from international trade in the context of globalization necessitates improving the *quantitative and qualitative* integration of developing countries into the international trading system and economy.

Accelerated economic growth and increased returns from trade should be channelized into achieving human and social development goals as embodied in internationally agreed development goals, including in the Millennium Development Goals. Reducing inequalities and democratizing the trade and development gains within and across countries should become the essential attributes of the globalizing world. Efforts to create and sustain an enabling environment to benefit from trade driven globalization will have to be pursued in the context of an increasingly differentiated trade and development landscape. The emergence of a dynamic South as an additional motor for world trade and new investment, and an expansion in South-South trade in goods, services and commodities have emerged as key features of the global economy today. It will also be necessary to focus on the specific trade and development concerns of countries in special need, such as LDCs, landlocked countries, and small and vulnerable economies. National, regional, and international trade and development strategies need to take these specificities as well as the baseline scenarios of such countries into account whilst adopting an integrated and holistic approach based on common development denominators. The aid for trade offers a possible mech©yanism to respond to such concerns. The conclusion of the Doha Round of trade negotiations with strong development dimension is a key expectation of countries.

Key trade and development issues to be tackled will include the changing commodity agenda, services trade, fair competition, environmental issues connected with trade, and the trade and development implications of energy, labour mobility and integration, and climate change. The international community including the United Nations can contribute to harnessing globalization for development. In the area of trade, UNCTAD's work through research and analysis, technical assistance, and intergovernmental deliberations and consensus building contributes to making trade and globalization work for successful development.

Index